BELIZE

A Natural Destination

THIRD EDITION

Richard Mahler
Steele Wotkyns
Color Photography by Kevin Schafer

John Muir Publications
Santa Fe, New Mexico

John Muir Publications, P.O. Box 613, Santa Fe, NM 87504

©1991, 1993, 1995 by Richard Mahler, Steele Wotkyns, Kevin Schafer
Cover © 1991, 1993, 1995 by John Muir Publications
Published 1991
Printed in the United States of America

Third edition. First printing November 1995

Library of Congress Cataloging-in-Publication Data
Mahler, Richard.
    Belize : a natural destination / Richard Mahler, Steele Wotkyns ;
color photography by Kevin Schafer. — 3rd ed.
        p. cm.
    Includes bibliographical references (p. 319) and index.
    ISBN 1-56261-221-2 (pbk.)
        1. Belize—Guidebooks. 2. Natural history—Belize—Guidebooks.
3. Outdoor recreation—Belize—Guidebooks.   I. Wotkyns, Steele.
II. Schafer, Kevin. III. Title.
F1443.5.M33   1995
917.28204'5—dc20   95-18902
                                                            CIP

Editor: Elizabeth Wolf, Dianna Delling
Copy Editor: Nancy Gillan
Production: Kathryn Lloyd-Strongin, Janine Lehmann
Cover photo: Green Crested Basilisk, Unicorn Stock Photos/Gerald Lim
Cover art: Susan Surprise
Designer: Susan Surprise
Maps: Jim Wood
Typeface: Plantin
Typesetting: Marilyn Hager
Printer: R.R. Donnelly & Sons

Distributed to the book trade by
Publishers Group West
Emeryville, California

Contents

Acknowledgments

The authors wish to especially thank Rita Cadena for the inspiration to write this guidebook and the warm and wonderful people of Belize for making it possible. We also thank everyone at John Muir Publications for their patience and assistance; and the staff, volunteer pilots, and supporters of LightHawk, the international environmental air force.

Richard Mahler wishes to especially thank Sue Dirksen; Robert Mahler; Lisa Enfield; Al Dugan; Victor Gonzalez; Ricardo Castillo; Rita and Rachel Emmer; Colin and Ellen Howells; J. Christian Headley II; Nasario Coo; Fallet Young; Bob Jones; Neil Rogers; Kate Droney; Mick and Lucy Fleming; Jim and Marguerite Bevis; Bruce and Carolyn Miller; Bart and Suzi Mickler; Lin Sutherland; Klaus Eiberle; Ray Lightburn; Paul and Mary Shave; Charles Colby III; Alvin and Reyna Dawson; Suzanna Mak; Doug and Lou Moore; Therese Rath Bowman; Logan McNatt; Elizabeth Corcoran; Marguerite Wood; Bill MacGowan; Rosita Arvigo; the staff of the Belize Tourist Board; Continental Airlines; and last, but not least, Don and Mary Mahler.

Steele Wotkyns wishes to particularly thank his parents; Charlie Luthin; Betsy Armstrong; Victor Gonzalez; the Belize Audubon Society; the Belize Center for Environmental Studies; Programme for Belize; Dora Weyer; Matthew Miller; Svea Dietrich-Ward; Michael J. Balick; Jerry Hoogerwerf; Bob Martin; Dick Guffey; Tom Grasse;

Karen Johnson at Preferred Adventures; Greg Shropshire; Pio and Ernesto Saqui; Chocolate; Bardy Riverol; Henry Menzies; the Novelo family, Jungle River Tours; Michael Konecny; Nick Brokaw; the Government of Belize; and others whom we have neglected to mention.

Kevin Schafer would like to thank Sharon Matola and other staff members of the Belize Zoo. Thanks also to Meb Cutlack and Katie Stevens, and Rachel and Rita Emmer, all good friends. An especially warm thanks to Ged Caddick, for his help and enormous patience in the field. Finally, an endless debt to my father, who introduced me to Belize and spent his last days there, happily.

Foreword

Media coverage, opinion polls, statements by political leaders, and the sheer number of international projects focusing on conservation activities all indicate that environmental concerns have reached a new peak of public attention globally. This increased attention stems from the concern that wild plants and animals face an increasingly uncertain future—an uncertainty that is a consequence of shrinking habitats brought about by human development.

Added to the pressure of encroachment by humans on wildlife habitat is the potential threat of climate change caused by global warming. It is thought that the increase of a few degrees in temperature and changes in rainfall can affect various species, causing some to migrate and thus disrupting the set pattern of species within a biological community. Considering that tropical moist forests contain more than half the number of species of life forms that inhabit the planet, it is important that efforts be made to conserve the tropical forests and their communities of wild plants and animals.

The tiny country of Belize, Central America, with its peaceful and stable political climate, has embarked on a course to preserve and conserve its natural patrimony. This effort is exemplified by the recent action of the Government of Belize to expand the Cockscomb Basin Wildlife Sanctuary from an area of 3,600 acres to 102,000 acres and by the establishment of the 97,000-acre Bladen Nature Reserve.

Belize, like many Third World countries, is undergoing profound changes as economic development proceeds. This evolution is partly characterized by increased demand for forested areas to be converted into areas of agricultural productivity. While such productivity will bring economic benefits to the people of Belize, it is our *hope* that the conservation efforts of both the private and the public sectors of Belize can also produce economic returns to the people, particularly those who have relied on the forest resources for their livelihood.

One mechanism whereby such economic benefits can be obtained is through "natural history tourism," which is commonly referred to as ecotourism. This type of tourism aims at the marketing of our natural heritage as a tourist attraction. Within the geographic boundaries of Belize, hundreds of species of tropical wild animals and plants can be found. In many instances, the population of some species threatened or overexploited in other parts of Central America can be found in a healthy state here in Belize. As we in Belize ponder our involvement in the fate of tropical forests, we turn our minds to the state of the natural resources that we will bequeath to future Belizeans. Through natural history tourism we may have found a means to be proud of what we bequeath. The great value and significance of *Belize: A Natural Destination* is that it shows the importance of a conservation ethic and promotes a long-term sustainable tourism industry through the marketing of the flora and fauna of Belize, while at the same time preserving them for posterity.

Dr. Victor Gonzalez
Permanent Secretary,
Ministry of Tourism
and the Environment,
Government of Belize

1
History and Culture

The magnificent Sky Palace stands serene in a jungle clearing at Caracol, near Belize's western border with Guatemala. This ancient Mayan city remained completely hidden from outsiders until the 1930s. Today, only a tiny fraction of the sprawling site has been excavated. Standing atop the tallest temple, visitors can see and hear parrots, toucans, monkeys, and other exotic creatures. For hundreds of square miles, all that is visible is lush wilderness. One can almost feel the energy here: of both the vanished Maya and the omnipresent rain forest. The palace's status as Belize's most important architectural structure—long after the disappearance of the highly advanced civilization that built it—is testimony to the unique history and colorful culture of this small, unusual nation. An understanding of these elements helps answer the frequently posed question, "Why would anybody go to Belize?"

Perhaps the most obvious reason is the natural beauty and quiet ambiance of a relatively uncrowded and little-developed subtropical destination. This sliver of Caribbean coastline remains the most sparsely populated nation in Central America, with less than thirty inhabitants per square mile. It is not the smallest, however. With its 8,866 square miles, Belize is slightly larger than El Salvador. But whereas the latter is bursting with more than 8 million people, Belize had an estimated 1995 population of 260,000, about one-third of whom were crowded into a single town: Belize City.

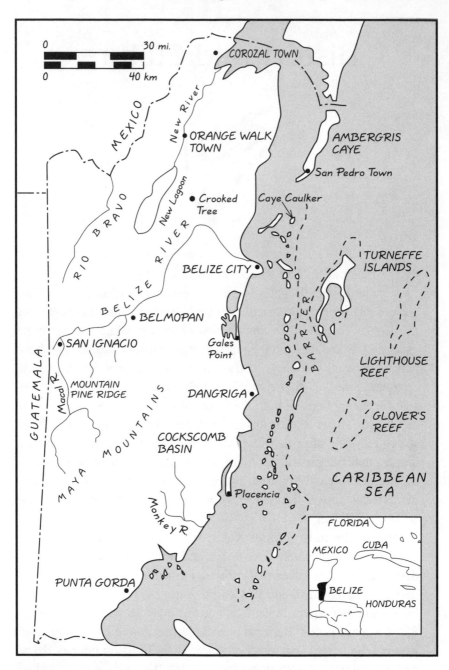

Belize

Remarkably, Belize's modest population may represent only a fraction of what the territory sustained a thousand years ago. At the peak of the vast Mayan empire, archaeologists estimate that up to 1 million Indians may have lived within the borders of Belize, with an equal number dwelling nearby in what is now northeastern Guatemala and southeastern Mexico. Thousands more Maya were scattered across parts of Honduras and El Salvador.

The earliest Maya are believed to have spread into the confines of present-day Belize from Guatemala and Mexico between 2000 B.C. and A.D. 300, after their ancestors had crossed the land bridge from Asia many centuries earlier. There is evidence that archaic tribes roamed the area as early as 7500 B.C., at a time when Central America's climate and habitat was somewhat less tropical, given over to grassy savannas and broadleaf woodlands.

The early, or pre-Classic, Maya period extends from 1000 B.C. to A.D. 300. The Mayan civilization reached its height during the Classic era, from about A.D. 300 to 900. From around A.D. 1000 until the arrival of the Spanish five hundred years later, the Maya were plunged into a precipitous decline (the post-Classic phase), and the underlying structure of their society fell apart.

No one knows for certain why the civilization disintegrated or why many of its members migrated north into the northern Yucatán peninsula and left many—but not all—of their city-states abandoned. Perhaps it was a prolonged war or a loss of faith in the priestly royalty who ruled with absolute authority. It is also possible that a series of droughts, earthquakes, or other natural disasters contributed to the breakdown. Archaeologists are collecting data that may someday help us settle such questions once and for all.

What is now generally agreed upon is that the area currently known as Belize was for many years the very heart of the Mayan empire. From A.D. 300 to 900, this was the center of their complex collection of city-states, linked by trails, rivers, and Caribbean trade routes. Recent excavations have shown that Caracol, the country's largest site, is even bigger than Tikal, long considered the most significant Mayan restoration. Archaeologists now believe that Caracol defeated Tikal militarily as the neighboring cities competed for dominance during the Classic period (see Chapter 6 for a more detailed discussion of Mayan history). Many aspects of the ancient Mayan civilization have disappeared from Belize (about 10 percent of the country's current population are descended from the Maya), but the major archaeological sites at Xunantunich, Caracol, Altun Ha, and Lamanai still reflect its impressive achievements.

What distinguishes the hundreds of Mayan sites of Belize from those of neighboring countries is their relatively pristine character. For various reasons, Belize has left many of its ruins in much the condition they were found. Excavations and restorations are sporadic, undertaken when funds and personnel become available—which isn't often.

In many ways, the ancient Maya were more advanced than their contemporaries in Greece, Italy, France, and England, reaching the zenith of their power during Europe's Dark Ages. These Native Americans were skilled astronomers and mathematicians, and accomplished farmers and engineers. They developed an elaborate religious system that incorporated many complex rituals and commemorated diverse natural phenomena. Their calendar system, for example, is precise within a matter of seconds in tracking phases of the moon, planets, and stars. Over the years, the Maya became expert artists and traders. Excavations in Belize have yielded seashells from the distant Pacific Coast, obsidian and gold from northern Mexico, pottery from the Andes mountains, and jade from the Central American highlands. There is even physical evidence suggesting that Mayan trade routes extended as far as New Mexico, where the Anasazi civilization flourished during the same epoch.

Yet many dimensions of the Mayan way of life are dimly understood and experts can only speculate on what the Maya's daily routine was like. By the time the first Europeans came to the region in the early 1500s, some Maya still lived in some of the ancient cities. Their intricate civilization had largely dissolved by this time and the conquering Spanish tried to destroy much of what remained. Contrary to popular belief, however, the Mayan culture is still very much alive, particularly in rural areas of Belize, Guatemala, and the Mexican state of Chiapas. In Belize's southern Toledo District, Kekchí-speaking

Carved stone face at Mayan ruin of Lamanai (Photo by Kevin Schafer)

Indians still tell folktales that originated during the days of the Mayan empire and perform ritual dances held sacred by their ancestors. In the Cayo District, near Caracol, Mopan- and Yucatec-speaking Maya have revived the ancient art of slate carving, gathering stones from the same riverbeds their ancestors mined centuries ago.

European knowledge of Belize began in 1502, when Christopher Columbus sailed along Central America's coast and named the Bay of Honduras, which begins at the southern end of Belize's barrier reef. Other Spanish navigators followed throughout the 16th century, but few were willing to make the tricky crossing of Belize's reef, and none saw fit to establish a permanent outpost. Other than a successful, plunderous raid on the Mayan trading city of Santa Rita (now Corozal), the initial Spanish presence was limited to a few minor explorations and some missionary work. Catholic churches were established at Lamanai and Tipú in the early 1500s, but the Spanish clerics were ejected before a colony could be firmly established.

Probably the first permanent settlement of foreigners in Belize began in the early 1600s when English-speaking Puritan traders, then based on the swampy Mosquito Coast of eastern Nicaragua, established several outposts on strategic islands, including Tobacco Caye. The colonists ignored the fact that Vicente Yanez Pinzon and Juan Díaz de Solis, among other Spanish explorers, had already claimed the area for Spain. Despite their own lack of interest in starting a Belizean colony, Spanish forces routed the Puritans from their trading posts in 1641.

Seemingly unknown to the Spaniards, a separate group of shipwrecked British sailors had started building their own tiny community on the coast some three years earlier. They were a motley crew, including many buccaneers who had learned of Belize through contact with the Puritan merchants. Gradually, over the next 150 years, more and more English settlers would move into the same area. They were later joined by a contingent of disbanded English sailors and soldiers who fought for the successful British liberation of Jamaica from Spain in 1655. Some of these early settlers were engaged in hardwood logging, others in piracy, and a precious few in farming. All would be forced to defend their primitive villages from sporadic attacks by Mayan Indians and Spaniards.

With few inhabitants, disease-infested backwaters, and a dangerous off-shore reef, Belize was an ideal hideout for these raiders of the Caribbean. By the late 1600s, the most infamous Scottish and English pirates had established permanent bases in Belize, from which they mercilessly attacked Spanish galleons carrying gold, silver, dyes, hardwoods, and other raw materials back to Europe.

The camp set up by Scottish captain Peter Wallace eventually became Belize City. One theory holds that the word "Belize" is a corruption of the Spanish pronunciation of "Wallace." Others insist that it is derived from the Mayan words *belix*, meaning "muddy water," or *belikin*, translated as "land that faces the sea." Yet another theory suggests the name derives from the French *balise*, a reference to the beacons used to guide pirates back to port at night.

Belize's first documented lumbering was undertaken by buccaneer Bart Sharp about 1660. Sharp and his comrades were especially eager to remove logwood (a source of textile dyes) and mahogany (an excellent hardwood used to make fine furniture). Sharp and his cohorts called themselves "Baymen," after the Bay of Honduras to the south.

Unable to eject the Baymen by force, Spain finally signed treaties with Britain, in 1763 and 1786, which secured government cooperation in the suppression of piracy and protection of lumber interests. The British would be allowed to remain as long as they kept to certain areas and left the treasure-laden galleons alone.

As they gradually turned more of their attention toward timber cutting, the white settlers began importing hundreds of African slaves from Jamaica and other British-controlled islands of the Caribbean. They relied on the strength of their charges to accomplish the difficult task of cutting huge logs and hauling them to ships for export. By the 1700s, lumber was a booming industry and the English were going far into the Belizean interior to selectively cut the largest trees they could find.

Still, the British government could not seem to decide what to do with its de facto colony. The crown vacillated between lending aid to the Bay Settlement, as it came to be known, and using the territory as a pawn in its ongoing diplomatic games with Spain. For almost 200 years, the legal status of the region remained vague. At one point, English authorities even ceded control over Belize to Spain, with the understanding that its woodcutting concessions could remain. Other agreements barred the Baymen from erecting fortifications, governing themselves, and establishing plantations. The stouthearted settlers, true to the lawless spirit of their forebears, generally ignored such treaties and set up their own laws. Eventually, with great reluctance, London sent official representatives to the Bay Settlement during the late 1780s.

This action infuriated the Spanish, who felt Britain was overstepping the bounds of its treaties. The showdown came in a 1798 skirmish off St. George's Caye, near Belize City, where a few hundred angry settlers and a British schooner drove off a powerful, battle-hardened wing of the Spanish Armada. Amazingly, even after the battle, England failed to officially seek title to the territory. Predictably, this made little difference to the Baymen, who proclaimed the date of this final victory over Spain as their independence day. September 10 is still celebrated as Belize's "National Day," with a separate holiday on September 21 to mark independence from England in 1981.

Slowly but surely, British influence in Belize grew during the early 1800s. When Spain dismantled its New World empire and granted independence to Mexico and Guatemala in 1821, Britain's Foreign Office loudly rejected those countries' immediate claims to Belize; for separate reasons, each considered the "province" of Belize to be part of its own rightful inheritance from Spain.

By 1826, the Baymen woodcutters had extended their timber harvesting to the Sarstoon River, the present southern boundary of Belize, and had become so prosperous that England could not help but take notice. At the same time, Guatemala remained adamant in its determination to annex the region and periodically waged war against the "trespassing" settlers. In 1859, fearing continued political instability would be bad for its now-sizable business in the region, Britain finally signed a treaty with Guatemala in which the latter confirmed the present-day boundaries of Belize in return for British financing for construction of a road from Guatemala's capital to Belize City. For various reasons, this promise was never honored, thus explaining why Guatemala, which never formally ratified the 1859 agreement, remained hostile. (In 1991, Guatemala's newly elected president, Jorge Serrano, officially recognized Belize's independence in hopes of settling the long-running dispute, but there is still tension between the two countries.)

Similarly, Mexico's claim to Belize was not easily settled. Throughout the 19th century, the Mexican government insisted that the northern half—and perhaps all—of Belize was an extension of its Yucatán holdings. Tensions escalated during the Caste War of 1847–1858, when thousands of Indian and mestizo (mixed-race) slaves in the Yucatán revolted against their masters and fled across the border in search of British protection. Mexican authorities decided not to pursue the renegades; thus several thousand refugees became the nucleus for settlement in the northern districts of Belize, which remain largely Spanish-speaking. Mexico finally renounced any claim to Belize in an 1897 treaty with England.

Throughout much of the 1800s, authorities in London seemed to be sending the colonists a double message. On the one hand, British officials eagerly foiled the attempts by Mexico and Guatemala to take over Belize. On the other hand, they barely inched their way toward granting the Baymen legal status as a colony. Some historians have suggested there is a racial basis for this reluctance. During this period, only about 10 percent of the population was white, while 75 percent consisted of black slaves. Most of the balance were freed slaves, Creoles, or Mayan Indians. The European slave-owners typically lived in the relative comfort of their Belize City homes while work crews of blacks labored in the hot interior. In 1812, these slaves were put to work building St. John's Cathedral, an imposing brick structure still in use along Belize City's Southern Foreshore.

Meanwhile, back in London, fierce debates were raging about the morality of slavery, which probably shoved this Central American backwater further into obscurity. By 1838, slavery was outlawed in the British Empire, including Belize (although former slaves were expressly forbidden from receiving land grants from the Crown).

In 1840, after establishing through various abolition-of-slavery acts that the Central American settlers were indeed its subjects, Great Britain declared Belize to be "the colony of British Honduras." But the declaration was in name only, and administration of the colony did not begin until 1862. It would be another nine years before British Honduras received formal recognition as a Crown colony, and it was not until the 1880s that the territory was administered separately from Jamaica.

With its formal establishment as a colony finally accomplished, development of Belize became more organized. Supervision was badly overdue, since a lack of diversification in industry and over-dependence on imported goods had sent Belize into decline during the Victorian era. The concentration of land-ownership made it difficult for entrepreneurs to start projects that might wean the colony from its motherland. By the late 19th century, a single London-based company (Belize Estate & Produce) owned more than a million acres of land, or one-fifth of the entire territory.

During this period, Belize went through a series of profound cultural changes, yielding a multiethnic society that remains remarkably cohesive. Many of the original English and Scottish settlers intermarried with freed slaves to form the Creole majority that still dominates the population. In the north, Mexican citizens crossed the border and began cultivating small farms. Many of their descendants now grow sugarcane, the country's most lucrative crop. To the south, Kekchí and Mopan Indians sought refuge from forced-labor plantations in Guatemala, and a small contingent of weary Confederate Civil War veterans arrived from the United States to found a plantation colony they called Toledo. From the Bay Islands off Honduras came a large number of Garifuna people. These blacks of mixed African and Carib Indian ancestry had been forcibly expelled from the West Indies in 1797.

Others immigrating to Belize in smaller numbers during the 1800s included Chinese sugarcane workers and Lebanese shopkeepers. Ethnic Sepoys were conscripted to the colony from India after an 1857 rebellion, and many West Indian plantation workers were recruited to do field work by the end of the century. A handful of expatriate Europeans and North Americans also decided to make Belize their home.

Early attempts to diversify the economy met with mixed success. The lack of roads, high transportation costs, and a limited pool of skilled labor stymied developers, and many new crops fell victim to exotic diseases and poor soil conditions. Periodic hurricanes devastated the country, uprooting trees and flattening houses. Then, as today, Belizeans were unable to produce enough food to feed themselves and had to rely heavily on expensive imports. Because their own food was cheap and labor plentiful, neighboring countries such as Honduras and Guatemala easily outproduced Belize in such valuable commodities as bananas, sugar, rubber, and chicle (a natural chewing-gum base). Another problem facing Belize was its large population of freed slaves, who were legally barred from obtaining vacant land that could be used for farming.

By 1900, British Honduras had grown to a population of 37,000. Yet the economy was moribund, wages were low, and discontent was endemic. The situation exploded after World War I, when thousands of returning Creole soldiers rioted in a violent expression of their demand for better social conditions. Joining in the demonstrations were hundreds of men who had helped build the Panama Canal only to join unemployment lines back home. The 1920s saw little improvement, as mechanization of the timber industry increased unemployment and the depression years brought many businesses to a virtual standstill. A destructive 1931 hurricane only compounded the colony's problems. By the late 1930s, Belize's deteriorating economic conditions prompted some residents to begin calling for independence. (Sensing this unrest, Guatemala renewed its claims to sovereignty and to payment from Britain for the promised road to Guatemala City that had never been built. Over the next 20 years, Guatemala became more adamant in its demands, and several forays across the frontier had to be repelled by the British.)

During World War II, many Belizeans again volunteered to fight but returned to a land where living conditions were miserable, work opportunities were limited, and political power was concentrated in

Belizean man and national flag (Photo by Kevin Schafer)

the hands of a wealthy and mostly white elite. Fearful colonial admin-istrators responded to the growing unrest by passing restrictive laws and banning public marches. But in 1950, after a sharp devaluation of the local currency, Belizeans decided they'd had enough. The inde-pendence movement, led by George Price—an American-educated, cautiously liberal Creole divinity student—rapidly increased in size and influence. In 1954 voting rights were extended to all adults, and in 1955 a form of ministerial government was introduced. By 1961, London had agreed to begin the process of setting Belize free.

Full internal, elected self-government was instituted in 1964, mod-eled on the Westminster parliamentary system. Britain remained in charge of foreign relations, defense, and internal security. A bicameral assembly (House and Senate) was established, and its members were popularly elected. (After George Price's People's United Party, the largest political party is the more conservative United Democratic Party, in office from 1985 to 1989, and again beginning in 1993.)

In 1973 the colony's name was officially changed from British Honduras to Belize, as the reins of power were gradually turned over to local authorities. On September 21, 1981, Belizean independence was formally declared. With British troops on full alert and the border sealed, the Guatemalan invasion that some had seriously feared never took place. In fact, the region was subsequently judged secure enough for Britain to withdraw nearly all of its armed forces from Belize during 1994, although the former colony is still a protectorate. Belize is a member of the British Commonwealth and a governor-general continues to represent London's political interests there.

While Belize has successfully thwarted foreign claimants since 1798, it is quietly experiencing a subtle transformation into a Spanish-speaking country. Large numbers of Guatemalans, Salvadorans, and Hondurans have crossed its borders since independence, many of them illegally. In fact, during the early 1990s mestizos reportedly replaced Creoles as Belize's largest single ethnic group. The vast majority of these newcomers are unskilled peasant farmers, attracted by an abundance of available land and relatively high wages, as well as a tradition of peace and political stability. The latter is a truly significant factor for people who have known only military dictatorships, political warfare, and genocidal terrorism.

Compared to other Central American countries, Belize enjoys relative prosperity, adequate health services, improving sanitation, a good public school system, and little of the income disparity that divides its neighbors into feuding factions of rich and poor, Indian and non-Indian. Literacy, estimated at over 80 percent, is higher in Belize than in the vast majority of developing countries. As the economy has slowly diversified and the infrastructure has developed, the standard of living for most Belizeans has noticeably improved.

Still, Belize is heavily dependent on foreign aid—both governmental and private—for its survival. Most oil, food, manufactured goods, and consumer products are of necessity imported and often paid for through loans and grants provided by aid programs from the United States, Britain, and other EEC members. Thousands of Belizeans living in the U.S. and Canada remit millions of dollars to family members every year. Today, one-third as many Belizean citizens live outside the country as inside, with the largest concentrations in Los Angeles, New York, and Chicago.

Hand-cranked ferry at San José Succotz (Photo by Richard Mahler)

While the country's economic base is broadening, progress has been painfully slow. In candid moments, government officials admit that illicit trafficking in marijuana, cocaine, and heroin has been a major contributor to the bottom line. Major drug busts occur regularly in Belize but seem to have little impact on the drug business.

Although timber is still an important Belizean export (most of it pine and cedar now, not hardwood), the major agricultural crops are sugarcane and citrus fruit, cultivated in the north and south, respectively. Bananas and fish products (mainly shrimp, conch, and lobster) are also important exports, along with honey, maize, pineapples, beans, mangos, papayas, cocoa, and rice. Poultry and cattle are raised domestically, and light manufacturing (mostly clothing and furniture) now accounts for about 15 percent of the gross domestic product.

Observers consider the Belizean economy "fragile," since the country imports much more than it exports and remains vulnerable both to fluctuations in the price of plantation products and to trade preferences imposed by other countries. In an attempt to improve the situation, during the early 1990s Belize added powerful new incentives for investors, including duty-free export zones near the Guatemalan and Mexican borders. Many Belizeans hope that their country can soon become self-sufficient at least in food, a top priority of each successive government. In 1995, simple foodstuffs still accounted for more than 25 percent of all imports.

Tourism is closing in on agriculture as the biggest contributor to Belize's bottom line, thanks to a steady increase in the number of foreign visitors to nearly 250,000 per year. Indeed, tourism is now Belize's fastest-growing industry, and the government actively supports this trend through a cabinet-level department of tourism, established in 1989.

2
Conservation and Responsible Tourism in Belize

At one time or another, most of us entertain a tropical island fantasy. We dream about getting away from it all on an idyllic vacation in a remote, sunny paradise. We picture ourselves sprawled on a sandy beach under the shady fronds of a swaying coconut palm, sipping a rum punch and staring hypnotically at a shimmering horizon. Or perhaps we see ourselves gliding through warm, turquoise water, sharing a dazzling marine environment with multicolored coral, jaunty sea horses, and four-eyed butterfly fish.

Maybe you've even been lucky enough to take such a trip—only to return with the unsettled feeling that something vital was missing. Like eating a rich dessert full of empty calories, the experience was pleasing but not quite satisfying. Next time, we recommend an adventure in what we call "natural history tourism," which is exactly the sort of unique vacation Belize has to offer. In the pages that follow, we'll take you to our favorite destinations in this plucky little country.

In many ways, Belize is far ahead of other less-developed nations in redefining tourism as one economic strategy that can preserve, rather than destroy, its priceless resources. Belize has won praise from international conservationists for the so-called "sustainable development" strategies it has implemented to protect its impressive treasures of nature and artifacts of Mayan history, while at the same time making sure that its people benefit from the public lands set aside for environmental purposes. It has managed to succeed in this campaign despite

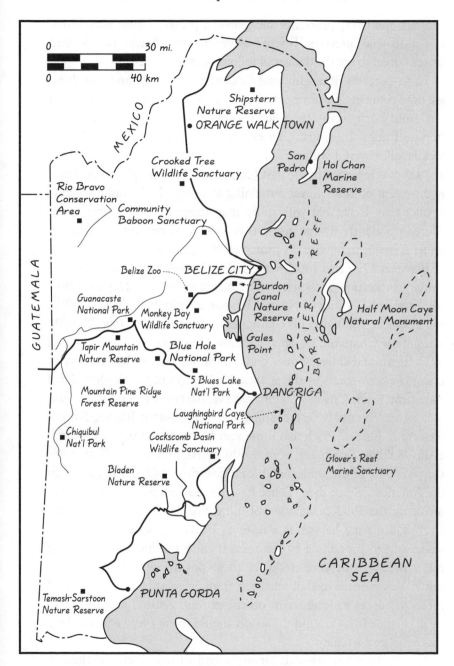

Belize's Parks, Reserves, and Monuments

constant monetary problems and growing pressure from agricultural and industrial interests. Belize's government officials have looked around them to see the danger of following another path.

Large portions of neighboring Guatemala, Mexico, and Honduras are now completely deforested, with plantations, timber interests, and slash-and-burn subsistence farms quickly replacing the remaining tropical forests. In contrast, an estimated 70 percent of Belize's land area is still covered with forest, only some of which has been thinly and selectively logged in the past (compared, for example, to the barely 2 percent of intact forest remaining in nearby El Salvador, slightly smaller than Belize but with more than thirty times its population). More importantly, a large proportion—about 35 percent—of Belize is under some form of officially protected designation.

Between 1990 and 1992, some 535,235 acres were put under permanent protection by Belize, with leadership by then Deputy Prime Minister and Minister of Natural Resources, Florencio Marin. While still in office, Marin and his colleagues designated more than 200,000 acres of the Chiquibul region as a national park. Then they responded to Belizean and international concern about the worldwide loss of mangrove ecosystems by designating 6,000 acres of the Burdon Canal zone near Belize City as a nature reserve. Marin began these remarkable achievements by establishing the 97,000-acre Bladen Nature Reserve in June of 1990; that same year he expanded the Cockscomb Basin Wildlife Sanctuary from 3,600 to 102,000 acres. Both areas contain some of the wildest and least disturbed subtropical habitat in the Americas. Since then, Belize has added more parks and reserves, including the 1993 designation of the entire 75-square-mile Glover's Reef atoll marine habitat as a reserve. Belize has shown remarkable leadership in protecting tropical forests and marine resources, and many Belizeans deserve credit for these positive actions. Now, as a result, Belize needs to shift attention from establishment of parks and protected areas to long-term, on-the-ground natural area management. People from around the world should make every effort to help make this goal a reality.

Nature-based tourism is strongly and officially encouraged in Belize, partly as a justification for this determined conservation

Conservation class for Belizean schoolchildren (Photo by Kevin Schafer)

approach, which has come under some criticism. "We need the fuel, in terms of firewood, and we need the income from logging," concedes Dr. Victor Gonzalez, Belize's Permanent Secretary for the Ministry of Tourism and Environment. "Even though the industrial nations are crying out about the alarming rate of forest destruction, we in the Third World often lack the finances to stop it. It is very difficult for us to conserve." However, Henry Young, Minister of Tourism and Environment since 1993, told the *Belize Review*, "I would prefer for us to struggle with the problems of tourism as opposed to struggling with the problems of heavy industry." Young is particularly eager to see increased local ownership in tourism. He and other politicians are hopeful that Belize can learn from the mistakes of others, weighing the advantages of badly needed foreign income against the irreversible damage that unbounded tourism and agriculture might inflict.

Environmentalists are well aware of what can—and too often does—occur when tropical travel is promoted with little regard for natural resources: protective mangrove trees are stripped by builders from sandy shorelines; fragile coral reefs are damaged by inquisitive but uninformed divers and snorkelers; commercial marine species, such as conch and lobster, are depleted to meet restaurant demands; and indiscriminate poaching may decimate wildlife populations, so that exotic species such as gibnut, brocket deer, and sea turtle might needlessly grace a restaurant menu. Despite its own best efforts, Belize has not escaped this long list of injuries.

Perhaps the parts of the country facing the most intense development pressure are the coral reef formations immediately surrounding the most-visited cayes, Ambergris and Caulker. Coral reefs are the marine equivalents of tropical rain forests. "In most coral species, each individual polyp lays down a skeletal container of calcium carbonate that surrounds and protects its soft body," writes Edward O. Wilson. "Coral colonies grow by the budding of individual polyps, with the skeletal cups being added one on another in a set geometric pattern particular to each species. The result is a lovely, bewildering array of skeletal forms that mass together to make the whole reef—a tangled field of horn corals, brain corals, staghorn corals, organ pipes, sea fans, and sea whips." Some formations are thousands of years old.

Belize's barrier reef suffers injury every time a boat anchor is randomly cast and hauled in or a diver bumps against a piece of living coral. When these centuries-old marine architects are touched, they begin to turn black and die. Unfortunately, many collectors cannot seem to resist the urge to (illegally) collect sea fans, black coral, and other fragile underwater treasures. Commercial fishing throws the food chain out of balance when desired species are removed en masse. Important breeding and feeding grounds for lobster, conch, turtles, fish, and waterfowl are destroyed when mangrove and sea grass beds are removed by developers. Over the long run, no one knows what the cumulative effect of all these changes will be.

Meanwhile, in Belize's interior, habitat destruction in the form of deforestation and selective woodcutting continues to cause serious damage to pristine ecosystems. "Today the refugees and their *milpa* [slash-and-burn farming of staple crops] are causing great problems for Belize," the former chief forest officer, Oscar Rosado, told a reporter in 1990. "We must be aware of what could happen if immigration went unchecked and the situation got out of hand."

According to the government, as many as 10,000 refugees a year are entering Belize from other Central American countries, mostly Guatemala, El Salvador, and Honduras. They are drawn by Belize's relaxed attitude toward homesteading, and they bring with them a strong tradition of slash-and-burn agriculture. Unfortunately, these methods quickly drain nutrients from the shallow jungle soil, and new trees must be cleared every few years to secure fresh farmland. Many refugees also hunt wild game in the forests near their homes, supplementing their meager diets.

Just as significant, owners of large citrus, banana, pineapple, and sugarcane plantations are lobbying government ministries to change the status of several forest reserves to allow more large-scale agriculture. The citrus industry has charged ahead in recent years, clearing vast tracts of pristine tropical forests. Yet export prices for oranges, sugar, and several other tropical farm products are in decline, thanks to oversupply on the world market.

Belizeans pay the price for this kind of development in the fouling of their potable water by acidic, pesticide-laden runoff from citrus fields. The removal of natural vegetation is also a factor in local and regional climate changes, upsetting the cycles of rain and drought. In many areas, Mennonites are rapidly clearing forests to plant corn and other food crops. Other parts of Belize are being stripped by subsistence farmers who have no other way to feed their families.

In a nation that still cannot feed itself, it is very tempting to give in to pressures for more agricultural exploitation. In many instances, however, the government of Belize is operating under the premise that there are more long-term gains to be realized through nature-based tourism than through non-sustainable farming. Visitors won't pay to see citrus orchards and cane fields, but they'll keep coming back to jungles and coral reefs.

Yet, with the opportunities of tourism come fresh challenges. Such growth forces decisions about establishment of a better infrastructure of roads, communications, hotels, police protection, and food distribution. Deterioration of cultural institutions and ancient Mayan ruins must also be checked. And last—but by no means least—promotion of tourism must be carried out in a way that benefits Belizeans and is

Immigrant homesteading along the Hummingbird Highway (Photo by
Richard Mahler)

not detrimental to the very destinations that foreigners are being
lured to visit.

As one of the world's most environmentally aware countries, Belize
has already set a standard of behavior that speaks for itself. Later on in
this book you will read about the Community Baboon Sanctuary, the
Cockscomb Basin Wildlife Sanctuary, and the Río Bravo Conservation Area, three among many innovative examples of how the
demands of conservation can be successfully balanced with the fundamental economic needs of local people.

Another "appropriate scale" project in the southern part of the
country demonstrates such sensitivity in action. In the largely undeveloped Toledo District, Mayan villagers have opened simple thatch-roof
guesthouses for travelers. Others have opened their own simple homes
to visitors who want a firsthand look at a subsistence farming culture
that has persisted for centuries. (See Chapter 5 for more information.)

Similar innovative, community-level approaches are proving to be
key models for long-term protection of Belize's tropical forests. The
Friends of Five Blues was formed to manage the spectacular Five
Blues Lake National Park, with its 200-foot-deep inland lake sur-

rounded by some 4,200 acres of pristine tropical forest, interwoven with an otherworldly labyrinth of limestone caves. The Friends of Five Blues' complementary goal is to ensure that the local community directs and benefits from natural history tourism and that the people of nearby St. Margaret's Village realize financial rewards from tourism-related enterprises. "Only a long-term commitment from the world's conservation community can keep grassroots efforts like Friends of Five Blues alive and kicking into maturity," reminded its director, Leon Wengrzyn, in an interview with *Americas* magazine. (See Chapter 5 for details and visitor information.)

The Monkey Bay Nature Reserve and National Park, near the Western Highway between Belize City and Belmopan, is another fine Belizean model for community-based conservation. In addition to Monkey Bay's existing 3,300-acre protected wildlands corridor in the Sibun River watershed, efforts are underway to coordinate expansion of this protected corridor through linkages with Five Blues Lake National Park and the Manatee Special Development Area. (See Chapter 5 for a closer look at conservation, tourism, and natural history education at Monkey Bay.)

While Belize's record of conservation achievements is admirable—especially for such a young and impoverished nation—there is a clear need for financial support from around the world to perpetuate the country's successes and implement new strategies.

On-the-ground local management of protected areas is a top priority. The list of areas that need more patrols and boundary enforcement includes the Bladen Nature Reserve, Community Baboon (Howler Monkey) Sanctuary, Cockscomb Basin Wildlife Sanctuary, Crooked Tree Wildlife Sanctuary, Laughing Bird Caye National Park, Tapir Mountain Nature Reserve, Chiquibul National Park and Caracol Archaeology Reserve, Guanacaste National Park, Glover's Reef Marine Reserve, and Half Moon Caye National Monument, all described in this book.

There is also a clear demand for more tourism facilities in Belize, particularly small guesthouses and restaurants owned and operated by locals rather than foreigners. As of mid-1995, foreign interests controlled about two-thirds of the tourism industry. Again, decisions need to be made in view of their potential impact not only on the natural environment, but also on the livelihood of the Belizean people.

Support to ensure the success of Belize's protected areas and small communities near them could readily be generated through contributions from the many international tour companies and conservation organizations that host "adventure" trips to Belize. These companies realize enormous financial benefits through subtle exploitation of the country's rich natural resources. Such organizations often provide few direct economic benefits to Belizeans. We suggest that it is time these groups began putting as much into Belize as they're taking out. Taken together, relatively small individual contributions from each enterprise could have a very powerful and positive impact.

In order to better promote and protect Belize's treasures, a permanent fund or endowment might be established to which foreign-based nature-oriented tourism companies would be "strongly encouraged" to contribute. Those funds could be matched by contributions from a standardized visitor fee system that includes a discount or waiver for Belizeans, so that citizens will not be denied access to protected areas. A uniform visitor fee has been hotly debated within Belize for some time. If administered fairly—with funds going back to the communities in or near the place of collection—such an entrance fee system might become the lifeblood of protected areas management. Some money could then be directed in the form of grants or loans to Belizean enterprises that help manage protected areas or operate conservation-oriented businesses.

Here's a single practical accomplishment that could be supported through this kind of income. One of Belize's most important freshwater ecosystems is the Mussel Creek wetlands in central Belize, about 20 miles west of Belize City. Conservation leader Dora Weyer, the Belize Audubon Society, the Belize Center for Environmental Studies and other individuals and organizations have for many years had an active interest in protecting this rich habitat. In 1994, Weyer wrote a proposal to designate the area as a wildlife sanctuary, a proposal that has allies within the Government of Belize.

The Mussel Creek drainage literally teems with life: water lilies cover the rippling surface of its slow-moving stream, roseate spoon-

Tapping chicle from a sapodilla tree (Photo by Kevin Schafer)

bills create pink mosaics along the water's edge as they methodically dredge up microorganisms from the rich lagoon bottoms, cattle egrets and wood storks soar in tight formation up the winding channel at dusk every evening, endangered hickatee river turtles and Morelet's crocodiles bob to the surface in search of their swimming prey, and belted kingfishers plunge from tall kapok trees to snag tiny minnows from the waterway. In all, 12 officially threatened or endangered species have been recorded in the Mussel Creek drainage, including the fun-loving but endangered Central American river otter. Weyer reports that some 31 mammal species, 44 reptiles, and 314 bird species are known to the area. As much as any natural wonder in Belize, the Mussel Creek wetlands call out for protection.

If our proposed funding sources were implemented, land along Mussel Creek and all other areas identified in Dora Weyer's proposal for a wildlife sanctuary could be protected before further human encroachment occurs. Local people are eager to act as guides for visitors and to patrol the area as reserve managers. "The people of Flowers Bank village are already interested in developing a tourist business in connection with boat trips on Mussel Creek," according to Weyer. She cautions, however, that tourism must be regulated and that too many boats, too much noise, and the hunting of crocodiles would be detrimental. With support from Belizeans and a commitment of management funds, it is possible that the fragile Mussel Creek ecosystem could be protected—and soon.

If you are interested in lending your support to ongoing conservation projects, there are many practical things you can do to help the environmental movement in Belize. One simple thing is to visit, learn more about, and support the innovative but struggling community conservation efforts described in this book. You might also contact the established conservation groups in Belize City and contribute to the work they are doing. The Programme for Belize can be reached at 2-75616, the Belize Audubon Society's number is 2-34987, and the Belize Center for Environmental Studies can be reached at 2-45545. See the Appendix for a more complete description of conservation groups working in Belize.

Even if you make no direct contact with any environmental groups, it is important to know that simply visiting the destinations described in this book makes you a part of ongoing efforts to save a precious part of our planet. By financially supporting and/or volunteering with the groups of your choice, you empower them to carry out their vital missions.

If you use the services of a so-called ecotourism hotel, guide service, or travel operator, we urge you to take a careful look at their practices. Do they hire local guides and book guests into locally owned hotels? Are they actively involved in training, conservation, or supporting local communities or field research in the country they send travelers to? Are they a member of the Belize Ecotourism Society and do they subscribe to its code of ethics (which, for example, requires that its members eliminate their use of plastic disposables in serving tourists)? Do they display the toucan emblem of Belize's environmentally responsible tourism operators? We suggest you ask such questions before booking your trip.

In the meantime, while you are in Belize, we hope you'll keep in mind a list of "dos and don'ts" put together by one of the first truly "green" travel agents in the United States, our friend Karen Johnson at Preferred Adventures in St. Paul, Minnesota.

1. Respect the earth and understand how fragile and complex is the web of life that we are all a part of. Conservation is not just a matter of aesthetics. It is a matter of survival.

2. Leave only footprints—no graffiti and no litter! Never take "souvenirs" from historic or natural sites.

3. To make your travels more meaningful, do your homework. Learn in advance about the geography, natural history, and culture of countries you plan to visit.

4. Respect the privacy and dignity of others; try to understand how you would feel if you were in their place.

5. Do not buy products made from endangered plants or animals, such as ivory, tortoise shell, animal skins, and feathers. Read "Know Before You Go," the U.S. Customs Service list of wildlife products that cannot be imported.

6. Always follow designated trails. Do not disturb plants, animals, or their habitats.

7. Learn about and support conservation programs and organizations working in the countries you will visit.

8. Never harass animals or disturb plant life for the sake of a photograph; ask permission before taking pictures of local people.

9. Patronize travel agents, tour operators, airlines, hotels and resorts, and cruise lines that respect the environment and support conservation programs.

Here is one more item we would like to add to the Preferred Adventures roster:

10. Become a positive contributor to Belize's experiment in developing a new, responsible tourism ethic. You help such a country's conservation projects succeed by joining, by visiting, or by volunteering to participate in them. Your presence is itself a vote of confidence in the difficult decisions government and business leaders must make.

3

Practical Travel Information

If you have already spent time in Mexico or Central America, you're in for some surprises when you first visit Belize. First of all, just about everybody speaks English. A linguistic island in a sea of Spanish and Indian dialects, Belize looks and feels more like the relaxed, post-colonial British Caribbean than Latin America. And for travelers accustomed to the extremes of poverty, overcrowding, inefficiency, corruption, and militarism that arc typical of some Latin destinations, the comparative tranquillity and prosperity of Belize will come as a welcome change. Its singular status as the only non-Spanish-speaking nation between Mexico's Rio Grande and South America's Guyana explains some of Belize's eccentricities, the most notable of which are discussed below and in the Inside Belize section.

As a subtropical country that is close enough to North America to be subject to its seasonal air currents, Belize has warm and wet summer/fall periods (June through November) followed by relatively cool and dry winter/springs (December through April). There is often also a brief dry spell in August. The driest months are February and March, although rain can (and does) fall at any time of the year. It's hottest in April and May. Humidity is fairly high no matter what the season. Trade winds tend to keep things less sticky along the coast, although this area is subject to sudden storms. Winds are generally calm in midsummer, except near thunderstorms. For details, contact the Belize Weather Bureau at 25-2480.

Most visitors prefer to travel to Belize during the Northern

Street scene at San Pedro, Ambergris Caye (Photo by Kevin Schafer)

Hemisphere's winter months. Daytime coastal temperatures during this period are in the 70s and 80s. Even during the hottest summer months, shade temperatures seldom rise above 90 degrees F (38°C) near the coast. During the "cold" spells of December and January, the thermometer sometimes falls below 55 degrees F (13°C). Temperature extremes are greater inland, where mountain nights are generally cool, even plunging into the low 40s in the highlands. The average temperature throughout the year is 79 degrees F. Water temperatures along the barrier reef range from the high 70s to mid-80s.

Hurricanes are rare but can threaten Belize at any time between June and November. After Belize City was twice destroyed by severe storms earlier this century, an efficient warning system was set up and hurricane shelters were established throughout the country. You will be warned well in advance if a potentially destructive storm is expected in Belize, which seems to happen once every 15 years or so. The last big hurricane struck in 1979.

Rainfall in Belize increases from north to south. About 50 inches a year falls near the Mexican border in Corozal, 65 inches in Belize City and the Cayo District, 95 inches in Dangriga, and 170 inches around Punta Gorda, across the Bay of Honduras from Guatemala.

English is the mode of instruction in all Belizean schools and is the official language of government and commerce. Outside Belize City and environs, Spanish is widely spoken (many of the nation's newest immigrants, in fact, speak little or no English). About one-third of the people speak a kind of "Creole" English not unlike the heavily accented patois of Jamaica and other former British island colonies of the Caribbean.

Spanish is most common in the far south, north, and west, near the borders. An estimated 60 percent of the population is bilingual (mostly Spanish/English), and at least 40 percent regard Spanish as their mother tongue. The 9 percent of Belizeans identified as Garifuna or Black Carib speak their own language, as do the 8 percent who are Indian (mostly Mopan, Kekchí, or Yucatec). Most of the country's 6,000 Mennonites converse in an archaic Low German dialect, although most of the men (and a smaller percentage of the women) also speak English, and many speak Spanish.

Entry and Exit Requirements

To enter Belize, all nationalities must have valid passports, plus "sufficient funds" (currently a $50 per day minimum) and an onward ticket out of the country. In recent years, the last two requirements have not been strictly enforced, although there are occasional reports of border authorities turning away individuals whose appearance was deemed unsavory and/or who carried less than $30 per day for the duration of their intended visit. Don't be surprised if an immigration or customs official asks exactly where you will be staying and precisely how much cash you have, especially if you are a long-haired backpacker. For stays longer than 30 days, an extension must be obtained (for a $12.50 fee) from the Immigration office at 115 Barracks Road in Belize City.

Visas are not required from citizens of the United States, Canada, Mexico, Germany, France, the United Kingdom, British Commonwealth countries and most members of the European Economic

Community. Visa requirements vary, so check with a travel agent or Belizean authorities if in doubt.

Visas may not be purchased at the border, although they can be obtained for $10 from the Belizean consulate in Chetumal, Mexico, just north of the international crossing. These documents can also be arranged at Belizean embassies in Mexico City, Washington, D.C., and other capitals, and, in some instances, through British consulates. Free transit visas are available at the border for periods of 24 or 48 hours, and visas are sometimes not needed if the visitor has an onward ticket in hand. If visiting other countries after leaving Belize, travelers should obtain visas before arriving in Belize. Guatemala now has both an embassy and a consulate in Belize, for visitors needing a visa or tourist card (see Chapter 6 for further details).

Tourists are initially granted 14- or 30-day permits to visit Belize, which can be renewed for up to six months. (After six months, travelers must exit the country for at least 24 hours.) As tourists, visitors may not do any kind of work (paid or unpaid) without first obtaining a permit from the Department of Labor. With domestic unemployment hovering around 20 percent, permission is not easily granted.

Drivers should carry valid licenses and vehicle registration documents if driving their own cars. International Driver's Licenses may be used in Belize, but domestic equivalents are acceptable. If your vehicle is not going to be sold in Belize, you must obtain a temporary permit at Customs Control waiving the otherwise hefty import duty. Third-party insurance is compulsory and can be purchased at border crossings or in major towns for about $70 a month. There is an exit fee of $2.50 per car. Visitors are permitted to use a Canadian or U.S. driver's license for 90 days, after which they must obtain a Belizean license ($20, plus photos and a medical examination report).

For those leaving Belize by land or sea, there is no longer any departure tax. An $11.25 tax must be paid for all international air departures (either in U.S. or Belizean dollars); if the individual has spent less than 24 hours in the country, there is no fee.

Immunization and Staying Healthy

No immunizations are required for entry, and public health standards in Belize are generally good. Public water supplies in most large communities are chlorinated, although there have been some reports of tap water contamination. Many travelers take the added precaution of drinking only bottled water and/or other beverages. A drop of iodine or bleach can be added to each liter of local water for purification, although stronger chemical solutions such as Bactrim and Metronidazole may be needed to kill some parasites and especially virulent bacteria. Be advised that giardia is a waterborne parasite that neither chlorine nor boiling is sure to kill.

Since Belizean pharmacies are somewhat limited and occasionally hard to find, bring along your regular medications and items such as contact lens solutions or prescription eyeglasses.

Mosquitoes and biting flies are common, especially during the rainy season, and it is advisable to carry repellent at all times: Cutter's, Jungle Juice, Repel, and other preparations with a high DEET content. Some travelers report excellent results from Avon Skin-So-Soft lotion, citronella oil, and the consumption of garlic. Rubbing alcohol will soothe itching. Since most insects cannot fly well in a breeze, a fan is also useful.

Tropical diseases are reasonably well-controlled in Belize, but mosquito-borne malaria and dengue fever are still reported. Yellow fever, cholera, and tuberculosis are rare but do occur. The cautious traveler who plans to spend extended time in the interior may want to take antimalarial drugs and obtain gamma globulin (for hepatitis), as well as oral typhoid immunization and tetanus inoculation. It's a good idea to get a tetanus booster (usually combined with diphtheria) at least once every ten years, in any event. As of mid-1995, there were no reports of chloroquine-resistant strains of malaria in Belize, as there are in parts of South America and other continents. Outpatient medical attention in Belize is free at government clinics and hospitals, and there are a number of private physicians' offices throughout the country. A brand-new hospital opened in 1994 in Belize City, replacing an older facility that provided medical care of highly variable quality.

Snakes are found in much of Belize, so be careful when hiking or walking off the road. Only nine of the country's 54 snake species have enough venom to seriously threaten a human, but the roster includes the deadly tommygoff (also called fer-de-lance, among other names), as well as several varieties of coral snakes and rattlers. Scorpions, spiders, ticks, biting flies, and carnivorous ants are found in much of the interior.

On the reef and cayes, the most common problems are overexposure to the sun, scratches from sharp coral or sea urchins, and the annoying bites of such otherwise harmless flying insects as no-see-ums and sand fleas. Stepping on stingrays can cause extremely painful wounds that are potentially deadly if not treated. The scorpion fish and jellyfish are an infrequent hazard. Barracuda, eels, and sharks are common in these waters (especially the non-aggressive lemon and nurse sharks) but almost never attack humans unless provoked or drawn by bleeding wounds, including those of speared fish. Do not touch these animals—it may trigger an aggressive response.

Fair-skinned visitors should wear shirts when snorkeling (to protect their backs from sunburn) and water-resistant sunscreen. Bring along a hat, a long-sleeved cotton shirt, cotton trousers, and sunglasses to wear outdoors during midday hours.

Food is generally safe in established hotels and restaurants. As in any underdeveloped country, some risk is involved in eating at roadside stands and sidewalk vendors, particularly where unrefrigerated meat, uncooked fish, and unwashed fruits or vegetables are concerned. Cholera and hepatitis, easily transferred through such foods, are a continuing problem in Belize. Bottled drinks are safe. Remember that cooking seafood does not destroy ciguatera toxin, which has been occasionally found in barracuda in Belize. Symptoms range from nausea and numbness to diarrhea and heart arrhythmia. Check locally about any reports of ciguatera poisoning, which also may occur in large red snapper, hogfish, and grouper.

"No to Drugs" billboard on the outskirts of Orange Walk Town (Photo by Richard Mahler)

Safety

Several urban centers, notably Belize City, Caye Caulker, and Orange Walk Town, have acquired reputations as being "unsafe" and even downright inhospitable to tourists. In each of these communities, there are persistent reports of street crime in certain neighborhoods and some degree of drug trafficking. Production of marijuana and transshipment of cocaine are big businesses in Belize, despite aggressive attempts by the United States, British, and Belize governments to squelch such illicit activity. Visitors should inquire before setting out on foot into areas that seem questionable, particularly at night. In Belize City, we recommend you go with a friend and take taxis. As you would at home, be aware of your surroundings and avoid carrying large amounts of cash or expensive jewelry. The most common harassment is strictly verbal, and the perpetrators will usually leave you alone if you ignore them, politely turn down their solicitation, or banter good-naturedly. Anything beyond this should be reported to the authorities immediately.

As in many other countries, it is a good idea to keep your expensive jewelry, flashy watches, and other signs of wealth at home. Tote your camera only when you plan to use it. Carry money and important documents in a money belt hidden under your clothes. Keep only as much cash in your wallet or purse as you expect to spend that particular day. Make sure you have a duplicate of valuable papers (including front pages of your passport) and keep a list of traveler's check identification numbers separate from the originals. It's also prudent to leave a copy of these items with a friend or relative back home. Always leave valuables in your hotel safe, if available, but always obtain an accurate receipt for such items. Immediately report any theft to local police and get a written report from them. To reach the police, dial 911. For the fire department or ambulance service in Belize, dial 90. The U.S. State Department is a good source of up-to-date information about safety conditions in Belize and other foreign countries; contact the Office of Overseas Services at (202) 647-5225. In 1991 and 1992, State Department advisories warned Belize visitors about street crime and urged group rather than individual travel to remote inland sites.

An altogether different sort of hazard is posed by powerboats. Several tourists have been badly injured and even killed in recent years while swimming in areas where fast-moving boats regularly travel. The most dangerous areas are off Ambergris Caye near San Pedro and in or near the "cut" at Caye Caulker. Before you swim, dive, or snorkel, ask about powerboat hazards and stick to designated areas.

Airlines, Buses, Boats, Autos, and Railroads

Belize is currently served from the United States by two U.S. and one Central American airline via the Phillip Goldson International Airport near Belize City. Belize can be reached most directly from Miami (American, Taca), New Orleans (Taca), and Houston (Taca, Continental).

Taca also flies to Belize from San Pedro Sula and Tegucigalpa, connecting to San José, Guatemala City, San Salvador, and Panama City. The Guatemalan airlines, Aviateca and Aerovías, have biweekly schedules from Flores and Guatemala City to Belize City. A domestic carrier, Tropic, flies twice a week between Flores and Belize City, as well as between Belize City and Puerto Barrios, Guatemala. Bonanza Airlines flies between Belize City and Chetumal, Mexico, with connections from there to Mérida, Cancún, and Mexico City. Jamaica Air has regular service between Belize City and both Jamaica and the Cayman Islands.

There is currently no direct service to Europe, although this could change at any time. Now, most European visitors transfer at one of the American gateway cities, in Cancún, or in Guatemala City.

From Belize City, frequent flights to smaller towns are offered by Tropic Air, Maya Airways, Sky Bird, Su-Bec, Javier's, and Island Air. Tropic, Maya, and others will also arrange charters to Mexico, Guatemala, and Honduras, as well as to destinations within Belize (see Inside Belize).

There is minimal sea-passenger service directly to Belize, most of it through the southern village of Punta Gorda. A twice-weekly (Tuesday and Friday mornings) ferry shuttles between here and Puerto Barrios in Guatemala, with onward connections to Honduras. A weekly open-boat ferry operates between Dangriga and Puerto Barrios. Private yachts, live-aboard dive boats, fishing vessels, and the odd cruise ship ply Belizean waters, but passage must be arranged on a case-by-case basis. See Chapter 4 and Inside Belize for information about boats to the cayes and offshore islands, or about entering Belize by your own private craft.

Belize no longer has railroads. The few railways established during colonial days for logging and citrus have been dismantled, and today the nearest railheads are in Mérida, Mexico, and Puerto Barrios, Guatemala.

While the Belizean road infrastructure is improving, only one (the Western Highway) is currently smooth and well maintained. All others vary in quality, ranging from rough dirt track to potholed pavement. Foreign aid money was obtained in 1995, however, to upgrade and pave many miles of road, including the notoriously rough Southern Highway.

Overland entry to Belize by foreigners is permitted only from eastern Guatemala (at the Western Highway crossing between Melchor de Mencos and Benque Viejo) or Mexico's Yucatán peninsula (where the Northern Highway crosses the Río Hondo at Santa Elena and Chetumal). A small Mexican crossing is sometimes open (for foot traffic only) at La Unión, a village northwest of Orange Walk. The 1,300-mile drive from south Texas to Belize takes from two to seven days, depending on the number of hours spent driving and the road conditions. Belizean buses—many purchased secondhand from American and Canadian public schools—run regularly between Chetumal, Mexico, and Belize City. Seats can be reserved in advance, and ticket prices are reasonable. Passengers may pay on board. Batty Brothers and Venus are the two main companies, both charging about $8 for the four-hour trip. From Chetumal it is a 220-mile bus ride to Cancún, where there are many inexpensive flights each day to the U.S. and Europe.

Crossing into Belize from Guatemala is bit more problematic than from Mexico (see Chapter 6 for specific details on crossing the frontier). Few public buses cross the border; therefore, it is sometimes necessary to walk about 50 yards from one side to the other to buy an onward ticket and change vehicles. The crossing is open from 6:00 a.m. to midnight and sometimes closed for the midday siesta (noon to 2:00 p.m.). Guatemala charges a $5 fee for entering and leaving the country by land. There is no charge to land travelers as they exit Belize. Guatemalan and Belizean tourist cards are issued at the border, but visas usually are not. There is a Guatemalan consulate in Belize City, however, and a Belizean consulate in Guatemala City.

While it is possible to rent a private car in Belize, many travelers are put off by the high cost (typically $70 or more per day) and limited selection (mostly Suzuki Samurais). If you're traveling to remote areas, a four-wheel-drive with spare tire and jack is advisable. Some tourists have complained about unscrupulous rental companies that have allegedly overcharged them for insurance and unnecessary repairs. Only one or two rental agencies will allow Belizean vehicles to travel into Guatemala and vice versa. It is possible to rent a car in Mexico and drive it into Belize, but agents will charge more if informed that this is your destination. If your Mexican car breaks

Fort Street Guest House, Belize City (Photo by Kevin Schafer)

down in Belize, you may have to pay for it to be towed back to Mexico for repairs and spare parts, both hard to find in Belize. Gas is also much more expensive in oil-poor Belize (about $2.75 U.S. per gallon in 1995) and is sometimes difficult to find because of spot shortages.

Set your watch in Belize to Central Standard Time, the equivalent of the American Midwest. Daylight savings time is not observed. Electrical current is the same as the United States and Canada: 110 volts A.C.

What to Bring

Visitors to Belize are allowed to bring virtually anything they might reasonably be expected to need during their stay, including fishing gear and diving equipment. Light, informal clothing is recommended. Firearms are prohibited without prior clearance. Pets are allowed into the country only with proof of rabies vaccination and a certificate of good health signed by a veterinarian. Up to 200 cigarettes, 20 ounces of liquor, and one bottle of perfume may be brought in duty-free.

In contrast to most other Central American countries, Belize is a relatively expensive country to visit. Almost everything, including food, is imported and subject to substantial duty taxes. Therefore, it's best to bring along all the clothing, equipment, film, books, maps, diapers, and toiletries you think you'll need. If not, you can expect to pay much more than you would at home for such items, provided they are available. If you wish to make friends among the locals, bring along fishhooks and small tackle items for men, cosmetics for women, books and small toys (e.g., balloons and magnifying glasses) for children.

Photography

Belize is a subtropical country posing special considerations for the photographer. Moisture, for example, can be a serious problem. High humidity may cause condensation on (or in) lenses, promote fungus growth on equipment, and speed corrosion of camera parts. Rain can splatter on lenses and work its way inside a camera. Perspiration may make handling slippery. Precautions include a tight-fitting camera case, lens-cleaning materials, and an absorbent cloth for your own sweaty hands and brow.

Light is also important in tropical photography. Midday sunlight is very intense and yields sharp contrasts; shoot in morning and late afternoon light for softer, richer effects. When taking pictures under the forest canopy, beware of shadows and streaks.

A high-powered lens and/or sighting scope will help capture fast-moving and faraway fauna. Remember that most animals can see, hear, or smell you long before you see them. The jaguar, for instance, has eyesight six times as powerful as a human's.

If you are going to be in Belize for some length of time, consider storing your film and other gear in airtight plastic bags, preferably with moisture absorbents. In offshore areas, try to keep sand away from your gear.

Reservations

Reservations for airline tickets and hotel rooms are often needed and recommended during the "high season" in Belize, which begins just before Christmas and continues through April. A growing number of travel agents specialize in Belize (see Inside Belize), and most of the country's larger tourism businesses can easily be reached by telephone or fax. Direct-dial calls to and from Belize are not difficult—remember to always dial 011 from the U.S. to get an overseas circuit. Belize's international country code is 501, followed by a one- or two-digit region code that varies with each district. When calling direct from the United States or Canada, dial 011-501, drop the first zero from the local number, then dial the remaining numbers. Within the country, it is sometimes necessary to dial a zero before the local number. Remember, 800 numbers in the U.S. cannot be accessed from overseas telephones.

At the Airport

Phillip Goldson International Airport is located in Ladyville, about 20 minutes northwest of Belize City. Immigration and customs procedures are straightforward. Taxi rates are regulated by the government. The cost is $15 to $20 for the 9-mile ride into town. (Taxis are identified by their green license plates.) Some hotels and resorts will arrange private pickup by van or cab, but there are no shuttle buses. Cars can be rented at the airport terminal building,

Tourist information is available at the airport, travel agencies, and the lobbies of most hotels. In the U.S., call the government-sponsored Belize Tourist Board at (800) 624-0686, or fax (212) 563-6033.

When leaving the country, bear in mind that Belize bans the export of marine curios, turtles, and turtle products, as well as such national treasures as Mayan artifacts and endangered plants or animals. A maximum of 20 pounds of fish may be taken out of the country, but visitors are urged to either release their catches or consume them while in Belize. See the Appendix for a complete list of prohibitions.

Anyone tempted to fly out of Belize with cocaine or other illegal drugs should be aware that baggage inspections are quite thorough, and even a small amount of marijuana can yield a stiff fine and/or jail term.

Camping

Camping throughout Belize is restricted by government regulation. Unless otherwise posted or granted, prior permission must be obtained from private owners before camping on deeded land or, on government land, by writing the Ministry of Natural Resources, Attention: Permanent Secretary, Belmopan, Belize, C.A. (tel. 8-22630). Camping is still something of a novelty in Belize, although a growing number of tourism operators cater to campers, and camping is now permitted at many national parks and archaeological sites, with prior permission. Personal items on any camping trip in Belize should include a flashlight, insect repellent, rain gear, sun protection, first-aid kit, and waterproof shoes or boots. A set of warm clothes is a good idea, too, since it can get chilly at night.

Currency, Banks, and Credit Cards

Although the U.S. dollar is widely accepted—particularly on Ambergris Caye—the preferred currency is the Belize dollar, stabilized at a fixed exchange rate of $2 Belizean to $1 American. Coinages from 1 to 25 cents are in use, with the latter referred to as either a "quarter" or a "shilling."

The best rates of exchange for foreign currencies are at the borders, with Mexican pesos sometimes obtaining an especially good rate. Belizean banks charge 3 percent for the exchange of foreign currency or traveler's checks, so it may be preferable to make such transactions with merchants, hotels, or individuals, who will almost always make a straight two-for-one swap for U.S. dollars.

The Belize Bank and Barclays, among others, will draft cash on

VISA and MasterCard accounts, also for a fee. A maximum of $200 may be withdrawn in cash, with any higher amounts in traveler's checks (you may be asked for your onward ticket). Money can be telexed to the larger banks in Belize. There is no black market, as financial rates are generally uniform from one institution to another.

All banks are open Mondays through Thursdays from 8:00 a.m. to 1:00 p.m. and reopen from 3:00 p.m. to 6:00 p.m. on Fridays. After closing time, moneychangers can often be found in the vicinity of major banks. They offer fair exchange rates for most major currencies. Credit cards have long been welcome in the larger hotels and are becoming increasingly acceptable among tour operators and other businesses that cater to foreigners, although a surtax of 5 percent or more is usually added automatically.

In mid-1995 there was talk that the Belize dollar might be devalued for the first time since independence. If this occurs, the two-for-one exchange with the U.S. dollar will be altered. We suggest you inquire locally about the currency's status before you spend money in Belize.

Tourist Information

Employees of the government-sponsored Belize Tourist Board, located at 83 North Front Street in Belize City (or P.O. Box 325), are friendly and helpful. The local telephone number is 2-77213 (10 North Park Street). The office is open from 8:00 a.m. to noon and 1:00 to 5:00 p.m. The board maintains an overseas office in New York City (421 Seventh Avenue, Suite 701, New York, N.Y. 10001, tel. 800-624-0686 or 800-4-BELISE) which can answer questions and send informational brochures. Embassies and consulates in Belize also provide basic travel materials.

The Belize Tourism Industry Association, a private trade organization, is another a good source of information; their Belize City telephone number is 2-75717. They can provide local contacts for information throughout Belize. Most travel agencies, hotels, and gifts shops also have plenty of maps, brochures, and domestic airline information.

Communications

There are few public telephones in Belize, but most hotels will allow visitors to make calls at fixed rates. The larger of these will also make their telex and fax facilities available. Direct-access long distance service is available at some hotels and the international airport. In most large towns there is a Belize Telephone Long-distance (BTL) office where operator-assisted calls can be made. Some of the island and jungle lodges can be reached only by shortwave radio or radio-telephone, which can be problematic. Keep trying—and remember that your conversation is often being overhead by others who belong to this "party line" system.

Mail service is inexpensive and reliable. Cards or letters sent from Belize usually reach overseas destinations within a week (U.S. and Canada) or two (Europe, Asia, Australia). Stamps are available at many large hotels. Belize is known among collectors for its beautiful postage stamps, many of which depict the country's flora and fauna. A special department for collectors is located at the main post office in Belize City.

Taxes and Tipping

In larger hotels and restaurants, a service charge is sometimes added to the bill. If not, tips are based on the quality of service, usually ranging from 5 to 10 percent, although many Belizeans do not tip at all in restaurants, and only Americans seem to tip 15 percent. Taxi drivers and boatmen are tipped at the discretion of the individual, but the practice is less common than in the United States, since taxi fares are fixed. A 6 percent government room tax is automatically added to any bill for overnight accommodations and is usually not included in the quoted rate.

Business Hours, Holidays, and Festivals

Normal business hours are 8:00 a.m. to noon and 1:00 p.m. to 5:00 p.m. Some stores are open during the morning only on Wednesday and Saturday, or evenings from 7:00 to 9:00. Few establishments open on Sundays, and regular bus and airline schedules may be canceled or curtailed. Banks, shops, and government offices may be closed on the following holidays:

> New Year's Day–*January 1*
> Baron Bliss Day–*March 9*
> Good Friday–*date varies*
> Holy Saturday–*date varies*
> Easter–*date varies*
> Easter Monday–*date varies*
> Labor Day–*May 1*
> Commonwealth Day–*May 24*
> National (St. George's Caye) Day–*September 10*
> Independence Day–*September 21*
> Pan American (Columbus) Day–*October 12*
> Garifuna (Settlement) Day–*November 19*
> Christmas Day–*December 25*
> Boxing Day–*December 26*

An increasing number of special events and annual festivals take place in Belize. Among the more interesting are the Baron Bliss Regatta (March 8), Crooked Tree Cashew Festival (early May), Caye Caulker Coconut Festival (late May), San Pedro Sea & Air Festival (mid-August), Belize City Festival Grand Market (mid-September), and Hike & Bike for the Rainforest (a countrywide athletic competition in late October that benefits environmental conservation).

4

The Offshore

The main—and often the only—attraction of interest to many first-time visitors to Belize is the country's barrier reef, a spectacular coral-based formation that runs almost the entire 185-mile length of the coast and swings from within 10 to 40 miles of the mainland. In sheer size this magnificent natural wonder is surpassed only by Australia's Great Barrier Reef and a few others in the South Pacific. One of the richest ecosystems on the planet, Belize's reef is punctuated by scores of beautiful tiny islands (spelled "cayes" but pronounced "keys"), sand bores, patch reefs, and various underwater structures that are home to hundreds of animal and plant species, including 220 types of fish and untold hundreds of invertebrates. So exquisite is this habitat that the United Nations has proposed preservation of the reef as a World Heritage Site, arguing that its deterioration or disappearance would result in "a harmful impoverishment of the heritage of all nations of the world."

Belize finds itself engaged in a delicate balancing act: it is vigorously promoting tourism, diving, snorkeling, and fishing on its barrier reef, while at the same time trying to protect this exceedingly fragile environment from man's harmful influence. Certain species, such as lobster, conch and shrimp, are already being severely depleted, and some irreversible damage has been done to the reef by careless fishermen and visitors.

Belize responded to the growing need to protect marine resources

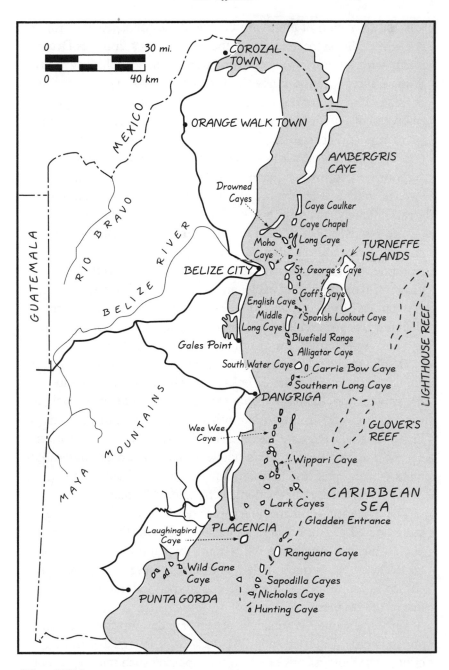

The Offshore

with the formation of the Belize Coastal Zone Management Project, or CZM. CZM is spearheaded by the government's Fisheries Department, with support from conservation groups, including World Wildlife Fund and the Belize Audubon Society. Project leaders are working on many activities through the CZM, including fisheries law enforcement, public education, suggestions for improved legislation for marine and coastal resources, and comprehensive recommendations for an expanded marine and coastal protected areas system.

Another promising marine resources conservation approach involves shifting at least some foreign visitors away from high-impact areas—namely, the Ambergris-Caulker-Chapel Caye corridor—toward lesser-known destinations that can more easily absorb the impact of newcomers. Rampant development on Ambergris Caye prompted the government to declare the northern two-thirds of the island off-limits to further exploitation—but not before one last major development broke ground. There has been talk of reactivating an abandoned airstrip on the north tip of Ambergris and founding a second town several miles away from fast-growing San Pedro.

Despite this trend, there are still dozens of islands along the southern half of the reef that are completely uninhabited and have much to offer visitors, including first-rate skin diving, snorkeling, kayaking, windsurfing, and fishing. Also overlooked in most discussions of Belize's coastal waters are the several atolls, banks, and reefs that exist beyond the barrier strip. As a whole, Belize has an estimated 350 miles of coral reef line and 280 square miles of island land mass. Much of this territory has seldom been explored by outsiders.

The atolls and southernmost cayes are not as accessible and offer more limited accommodations than the more northern barrier reef islands, but the extra effort yields some very unusual and rewarding experiences. For serious anglers and divers, these sites provide the chance to fish and dive in almost undisturbed natural environments that teem with marine life.

Since many outer destinations are an easy day trip from the hotels on Ambergris, Caulker, and Chapel Cayes, it is arguably more efficient to use those islands as a base for exploring such remote offshore locations as Lighthouse Reef and the Turneffe Islands (see Inside

Belize for accommodations and outfitters). Although there are places to stay and eat on the farthest cayes, cost and access may be a problem for travelers with tight budgets or time constraints. Those fortunate enough to have their own kayaks and boats will be pleased to know that the barrier reef provides innumerable safe anchorages and some of the finest paddling and sailing conditions anywhere.

The Barrier Reef and Cayes

Most of the 200-odd cayes of Belize lie in relatively shallow water along the barrier reef itself. The long, narrow stretch of water between the reef and the mainland—known as the Inner Channel—is also dotted with dozens of small islands, as are some of the country's inland lagoons.

The word "caye" is testimony to the varied history of the various islands. It is a corruption of the Spanish *cayo*, translated in English as "small island." Early Spanish explorers were the first Europeans to set foot on the barrier chain, and they apparently stopped regularly to obtain fresh water and repair their ships. The Spaniards no doubt encountered Mayan Indians, who established many fishing and trading outposts here over a period of centuries.

English, French, and Scottish pirates, along with Puritan traders, were next to arrive. They found the cayes ideally suited for their respective sea-based livelihoods, and old coins, bottles, and tools are sometimes still found on the sandy beaches, along with ancient Mayan pottery and artifacts. Europeans also settled here as fishermen, whalers, and plantation owners. They were to be joined in the late 1800s by a wave of Mexican immigrants eager to escape the brutal Yucatán Caste Wars.

Ambergris Caye
The largest and best known of the cayes, Ambergris is part of a wide limestone peninsula dangling south from the Yucatán coast of the Mexican state of Quintana Roo. Most Ambergris residents are of Mexican ancestry and speak Spanish among themselves. Early in

Belize's history, its northern neighbor even laid claim to the island. Ambergris Caye has about the same land area as Barbados, although much of it is uninhabitable mangrove swamp.

To reach Ambergris (the name is a holdover from colonial whaling days and refers to a waxy substance, believed to originate in sperm whale intestines, that was once used in making perfume), most visitors take a boat or airplane across lower Chetumal Bay from Belize City, 35 miles to the southwest. Locals refer to passenger boats as "skiffs" and their smaller canoe-like vessels as "dories." The crossing takes about 1¼ hours by skiff and less than 20 minutes by plane.

Fishing was once the caye's principal industry, but within the last twenty years tourism has taken over. Many fishermen now use their boats exclusively to cater to visitors' needs. San Pedro, the island's only town, offers a wide choice of hotels, restaurants, bars, gift shops, and travel agencies to suit every recreational interest and pocketbook.

While San Pedro in some ways seems to be suffering under the strain of rapid growth, Ambergris Caye, on the whole, has much to recommend it. People are friendly, accommodations are comfortable, and there's plenty to do. Resorts on the outskirts of San Pedro are more expensive, but tend to be more tranquil and luxurious than hotels in town. Hikers and bicyclists will find that much of the island is covered with a high broadleaf forest interspersed with freshwater sinks that attract lots of wildlife, including an abundance of birds. Visitors can spot flamingos, egrets, herons, pelicans, and frigate birds. Bird Caye, located on the bay (leeward) side of Ambergris, shelters rookeries for 30 species, including the reddish egret, greater egret, and cormorant. Spoonbills, avocets, and ducks also congregate here. Turtles nest on certain yet-undeveloped beaches, and even ocelots have been seen prowling through the mangroves. Thousands of shells litter the beaches. (The coral reef is less than a mile offshore.)

Ambergris has the largest single concentration of tourist services in Belize, yet it still manages to retain a laid-back atmosphere. The streets are sandy and belong to barefoot, slow-paced strollers, since vehicles (mostly electric golf carts) are few and far between. The water is turquoise blue and immediately accessible. A cooling breeze sweeps

Relaxing Belize-style in a hammock on a tropical beach (Photo by Norm Shrewsbury/Slickrock Adventures)

in from the Caribbean much of the time, keeping insect pests at bay. The vast majority of San Pedro's 1,700 residents are good-humored and tolerant, their lifestyle casual and simple. The tin-roofed, colorfully painted wooden houses are cheerfully dilapidated, giving the distinct impression that it's okay to simply relax all day if that's your choice. A wide variety of food and drink is also available, and some of the country's best cooks are happy to prepare fresh seafood exactly the way you like it.

For all these reasons, Ambergris Caye makes a fine base for excursions to nearby attractions and the more distant islands or atolls. Experienced guides are easy to find and some of the best outfitters for fishing, snorkeling, wind surfing, kayaking, and diving are also based here, along with plenty of charter boats. There are massive coral canyons full of caves and tunnels near San Pedro, and snorkelers report aquarium-like conditions. Within the confines of the reef itself, the Mexican Rocks area on the windward side is highly recommended. Conditions are also ideal here and among the island's 13 lagoons for sailing, wind surfing, and sea kayaking.

A few words of caution are in order, however. Some of the more than 700 hotel rooms on Ambergris Caye are very basic by American or European standards. Furnishings and other physical amenities are usually minimal, so what you are paying for is location and service, not luxury. For most visitors this is no problem, because they spend so much time outdoors. The more luxurious resorts are located outside the village.

San Pedro has only five streets, and staying in town puts you close to the action—or noise, depending on your point of view. Keep in mind that some rooms are less than 100 yards from the airport, and takeoffs go right over the town. San Pedro's beach is narrow and there is virtually no chance of sunbathing within the town itself, what with boats, passengers, and cargo being constantly hauled on and off. You pay higher prices to stay in a hotel farther away because the beach is wider and the ambiance decidedly less frenetic. If you stay outside the town, transportation to and from San Pedro is usually provided by your hotel. Bicycles and motor scooters also are available for rent.

In general, the more sociable visitors will be happier in San Pedro, while those in search of a more rustic setting would do well to investigate outlying accommodations on Caye Caulker and other more southerly islands.

Quiet, upscale hotels on Ambergris include the recommended Ramon's Village, a large family-oriented lodge with guided sportfishing and diving; Victoria House, with a good restaurant and full service dive shop, including instruction; Paradise Villas, with kitchens and separate rental units; the Spindrift Resort Hotel, with furnished apartments and boats for hire; and Caribbean Villas, condo-style accommodations with kitchens and two outdoor hot tubs. For those seeking more moderate or budget rates, we recommend Changes in Latitudes (a Canadian-owned bed-and-breakfast), San Pedro Holiday Hotel (owned by San Pedro native Celi McCorkle), SunBreeze Beach Hotel (with its own 100-foot pier), Lily's, Barrier Reef Hotel, Sands Hotel, San Pedrano Hotel, Martha's Hotel, the Green Parrot (6 miles north), Cruz Apartments, Pirate's Lantern Guest House, Milo's, and Rubie's. Some accommodations can be rented by the week or month. One of the most luxurious resorts is Captain Morgan's Retreat (co-owned by Pep Simek, founder of the Tombstone Pizza chain), located 3½ miles north of San Pedro, with giant freshwater swimming pool, restaurant, bar, 21 beachfront casitas, and a wide variety of excursion options. In the same price range is the Belize Yacht Club, south of San Pedro, which features a pool, health club, and spacious rooms with kitchens.

There are many restaurants to choose from. Those with good reputations include Little Italy's, the Jade Garden, Elvi's Kitchen, Holiday Hotel, and Ramon's Village. Other San Pedro services include a bank, a pharmacy, a post office, and a library. One source of general information is Victoria Collins (26-2070) at the weekly newspaper, the *San Pedro Sun*. Recent visitors also recommend Travel & Tour Belize in San Pedro (tel. 26-2031) for arranging travel throughout Belize and for information on Ambergris Caye. See Inside Belize and the Appendix for further details.

San Pedro has many fishing guides and you should inquire locally for recommendations. We've heard good comments about Billy Leslie, Roberto Bradley Jr., Melanie Paz, Romel Gomez, and Luz Guerrero.

Besides the usual water sports, volleyball, and bird-watching, activities on Ambergris include tours of the country's first-ever conch hatchery, a turtle-nesting beach on the northeast corner of the island, and several unrestored but difficult-to-reach ancient Mayan sites. San Juan, near the island's northern tip, has recently been excavated by Texas archaeologists. At least one local entrepreneur, Island Equestrian Trails, offers horseback riding, and sailing can be arranged through Islands & Reef Cruise at the Paradise Hotel pier. Annual events include the San Pedro Carnival (February 10-12) and Festival of St. Peter (June 29), which includes the blessing of the fishing fleet.

If You Go: Tropic, Maya, and Island airlines have as many as nine daily flights each to Ambergris from Belize City's municipal and international airports. Connecting flights are easily arranged to Corozal, Dangriga, and other Belizean cities. (If you are nervous about single-engine flying, the Tropic Air twin-engine aircraft are considered more stable.)

The island can also be reached by private or chartered aircraft, and San Pedro's airport is within walking distance of town. The flight from Belize City lasts about 20 minutes.

Boats regularly ply the channel between Ambergris and the mainland, departing from several locations in Belize City. The *Andrea*, one of the best-known vessels, makes one roundtrip each day, departing Belize City in late afternoon (from the Bellevue Hotel pier on Baron Bliss Promenade) and returning from Ambergris at 8:00 a.m. The trip takes a little over an hour each way and cost about $15 in 1995. Private boats can also be chartered, or you can hop a ride with a supply or fishing vessel (check the customs wharf near the Fort George lighthouse). Other departure points include the North Front Street Texaco Service Station and Swing Bridge.

Once on Ambergris, there are regular boats to Caye Caulker and Caye Chapel, plus charters to virtually any scrap of reef or atoll you care to visit. Caye Chapel also has an airport where pilots of domestic airlines are usually happy to touch down if requested. Private pilots are also welcome to use the paved Chapel strip.

Hol Chan Marine Reserve

About 4 miles southeast of San Pedro, off the southern end of Ambergris, is a natural break in the barrier reef called Hol Chan, Mayan for "little channel." The channel is around 30 feet deep, has been protected since 1987 as a national marine reserve, and has become a major spawning ground that is strengthening underwater animal populations.

Hol Chan is unusually rich in marine life, including hundreds of fish species and a variety of living corals, fans, sponges, crabs, and eels. (Be careful about getting too close to the nearsighted moray eel, which can chomp off a finger in an eye-blink.) The sides of the channel, lined with both living and dead coral, are interrupted from time to time by small limestone caves and sinkholes, such as the spectacular Boca Ciega, a collapsed cave with an underwater freshwater spring that teems with tropical fish. (The latter should be explored only by experienced divers.) Humans share the clear waters here with everything from nervous squirrelfish to curious grey angels, to parading parrot fish. Large schools of yellowtail snapper, horse-eye jacks, and blue-striped grunts cruise by, along with spotted eagle rays and purple cleaner shrimp.

Divers can take advantage of Hol Chan's relatively shallow depth and stay down for an hour or more, drifting among the lovely spotted drum, hatfish, damsel, and butterfly fish. If a diver remains stationary, the shy hermit crab may make an appearance. Night diving can also be very rewarding, providing a rare chance to glimpse flaming scallops, octopus, spider crabs, lobsters, and other nocturnal species. Eerie bioluminescent ostracods (tiny shrimplike creatures) shimmer like tiny fireflies atop the water's surface, becoming especially noticeable in the wake of passing boats.

The 5-square-mile reserve is divided into three distinct ecological zones, marked on the water's surface by anchored buoys. Zone A is the channel itself, where swimmers should be mindful of strong tidal currents while diving or snorkeling. Zone B encompasses broad beds of sea grasses as well as the Boca Ciega. The sea and turtle grass serve as an important feeding and breeding ground; visitors will see hundreds of tiny fish here. Zone C encompasses several mangrove cayes, a source of important nutrients and a critical habitat for the youngest sea creatures, who subsequently migrate into the sea grass beds and finally the outer waters. Above the surface, the mangrove islands provide a nesting area for several large bird species, such as herons, egrets, pelicans, rails, frigate birds, and ospreys. The mangrove ecosystem is also home to sponges, anemones, sea urchins, crabs, jellyfish, mollusks, sea squirts, and sea horses.

As you explore Hol Chan, remember that all flora and fauna are protected. Feeding the fish is discouraged, since it upsets the balance of nature and can lead to some potentially dangerous encounters with certain sharp-toothed animals. Sharks and barracuda, for example, are quickly attracted by free meals.

Radio-equipped patrol boats regularly visit the area, on the lookout for anyone in trouble—or at odds with the law. The rangers also monitor anchoring activities, making sure private boats use mooring buoys whenever possible. (Throughout Belize, mooring buoys should always be used if and when available.)

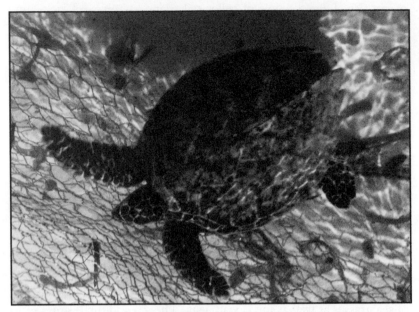

Loggerhead turtle captured for an aquarium off the coast of Belize (Photo by Richard Mahler)

The Belize Audubon Society advises visitors to any coral habitat in the country that collecting these tiny organisms is prohibited and that overturning or disturbing any live coral will eventually kill them. Always be very careful when stepping or dropping anchor on the ocean floor and try to avoid touching live coral at all costs, as this can kill the polyps. Even a vigorous kick by a swimmer can stir up enough sand to clog their orifices. Contact with fire (also called red) coral can be especially painful. Here, as in other areas with busy marine traffic, be careful of speeding powerboats that may be unable to see you bobbing in the water—an encounter can be deadly.

Beyond the border of the reserve, at the swampy southern extremity of Ambergris Caye, is the Marco Gonzalez archaeological site. This small Mayan ruin, named after the young boy who found it, was once part of a large trade network linking inland Indians with settlements up and down the Mexican and Central American coast. Occupied between 200 B.C. and A.D. 1500, Marco Gonzalez has been excavated since 1986 by Canadian archaeologists, who have confirmed that some structures are built entirely from conch shells. The location is not well marked and is best approached with the help of a knowledgeable guide. Bring mosquito repellent!

Hol Chan Marine Reserve is jointly sponsored by the Belizean government, the World Wildlife Fund, and the U.S. Agency for International Development. The U.S. Peace Corps, the Belize Audubon Society, and the Wildlife Conservation Society have also provided assistance. The reserve is the first park of its kind in Central America, and donations are welcome. Your contribution will encourage Belize and neighboring countries to expand such worthy experiments. A resident manager can be contacted for any necessary permits or further information at the Hol Chan visitors center in San Pedro on Caribena Street (tel. 26-2420). This headquarters is well stocked with brochures and information about the underwater flora and fauna encountered in Belizean waters. It's a good idea to stop in before heading out to Hol Chan so you will better understand what you will be seeing later on.

If You Go: Because of its close proximity to San Pedro, Hol Chan can easily be visited for a half-day (or even an hour) by booking a boat through a hotel, or simply showing up on any of the piers in San Pedro. Dive boats usually head out about 9:00 a.m. and 2:00 p.m. each day, returning in midday or later afternoon. Expect to pay at least $15 for a round trip. Several glass-bottom touring craft follow a similar schedule. Snorkelers and swimmers are welcome on board either type of vessel, and prices are reasonable. If you have small children who wish to snorkel, it's good to hire an experienced guide who can help keep an eye on them in the water. They—and their parents—should wear water-repelling sunscreen and consider wearing T-shirts to avoid burning.

Caye Caulker

Lying directly south of Ambergris, about 14 miles away, Caye Caulker (sometimes spelled Corker) is a popular destination among many visitors who want an experience more akin to the laid-back San Pedro Town of the 1970s, before the latter was "discovered."

Caulker is "less" of many things San Pedro has become: less

expensive, less crowded, and less noisy. However, the village of about 800 people also has fewer hotels, restaurants, dive shops, fishing guides, and services than its northern neighbor. Therefore, some visitors make it a point to visit both islands, content to absorb the "action" of Ambergris for a while and then slow the pace down on Caulker.

The island was dubbed *Hicaco* by the Spanish, their name for the coco plum palms found here. Over the years, the English pirates who settled here apparently began pronouncing it "Corker," and, with their British accents, the word finally evolved into "Caulker."

The caye is fairly small, and the inhabited portion covers a few sandy blocks. There are only two streets: Front (east) and Back (west). Like Ambergris, a good portion of Caulker is bug-infested mangrove swamp. Visitors walk everywhere, since nothing is far away, and vehicles are almost nonexistent. About 800 people live here year-round, and within a few days' time, it seems a traveler has waved to or chatted with them all. This friendliness, coupled with comparatively modest prices and a nice beach, has enticed many first-timers to extend their stay on Caulker. A few foreigners—many of them budget-minded regulars on the "gringo trail"—have stayed for years and intermarried with the locals. An airport opened in 1991, and the island's tempo has speeded up somewhat, but by keeping control of Caulker's pace of progress, residents have been able to remain owners and operators of the rustic guesthouses, home-style restaurants, and simple shops that cater to visitors.

The island offers many of the same attractions as Ambergris, including snorkeling, diving, sailing, windsurfing, kayaking, sunbathing and fishing. Anglers can catch one exotic game fish after another off the caye's main pier. Caulker natives have long been known as expert fishermen (lobster, conch, snapper) and boatmen, so you are sure to find skilled guides here for virtually any water-related activity. Particularly recommended is Leonel Heredia, known simply as "Chocolate" (P.O. Box 986, Belize City, telephone 22-2151). He and his boat, *Soledad*, specialize in taking visitors to see manatees or to set up campsites on more remote cayes. Chocolate can also recommend other boatmen for excursions as far away as Glover's Reef.

Two fishing guides with good reputations are Melvin Bandillo Jr. and Sylvano Canto. Frenchie's Services, Ricardo's Adventure Tours, and Pegasus Boat Service also provide fish-finding expertise.

A special attraction for divers is an underground cave system—said to be the largest of its kind anywhere—that lies between Caulker and Ambergris. For information on the area's natural history and ecology, look up James Beveridge. He is also an excellent underwater photographer who occasionally does slide presentations.

Camping on Caulker is available from Vega's Far Inn, which also rents private rooms and arranges snorkeling or fishing trips. The Vega family rents snorkeling gear and small (Sunfish) sailboats. Other recommended moderate to low-cost accommodations include the Rainbow Hotel, Tom's Hotel, the Hideway (cheap—but next to a Pentecostal church), Castaways (with restaurant and bar), Jimenez's Cabañas, and Sea Beezzz (closed in the summer). Located a bit out of town, where things are quieter, are the moderately-priced Anchorage (half-price in summer) and Shirley's Guest House. Off the beaten path in the other (northerly) direction is the Island Sun Guest House. At the top of the scale is the Tropical Paradise, offering hot water, fans, and a spa, plus a choice of ten main building rooms or five beachfront cabañas. Rooms and houses can be rented for stays of two days or more through Heredia's House Rental (22-2132).

Local restaurants of note include the I and I, Sobre de Olas, Fisherman's Wharf, Marin's, Martinez Caribbean Inn, Tropical Paradise, and Sea Beezzz. Some of Caulker's eateries are simply open-air kitchens operated by local women outside their homes. Nightlife on the island consists of dancing and drinking at the Reef Bar or watching television. (Yes, even Caye Caulker has satellite dishes and cable.) See Inside Belize for a complete list of services and amenities.

The best swimming (the offshore water is otherwise very shallow) is in a channel known as The Cut, which bisects the island just north of the village. It was formed in 1961 by powerful Hurricane Hattie, the same storm that virtually leveled Belize City. The water here is clear and fairly shallow, but beware of the currents (and avoid brushing up against the coral reef). This expanding channel is a good illustration of what can happen when protective mangroves are removed from an

Walking path on Caye Caulker (Photo by Steele Wotkyns)

island's outer boundaries. In 1994, land on the village side of The Cut was bought by some Americans, who now rent cabins at the site.

Its idyllic surroundings, dominated by coconut trees, make Caulker a nice place to walk. A sandy path to the southeast part of the island brings visitors to a quieter, less developed side of Caulker (although the breezy silence is now punctuated by the periodic roar of an aircraft taking off or landing at Caulker's airstrip). On this path you are treated to fine views of the Caribbean Sea through the mangrove, and you may glimpse iguanas or osprey.

Among the few persistent annoyances on Caye Caulker are sand flies and mosquitoes, which can make hikes and beach excursions very uncomfortable in calm or rainy weather. Since most of the houses are built on tall stilts, these biting insects are less of a nuisance indoors. Another problem is a pack of seemingly unemployed young men who panhandle, sell drugs, and engage in petty theft. The local authorities have been unable (or unwilling) to deal with these aggravating vagrants, who love to pester newly arrived tourists, particularly fair-skinned women. Our best advice is to ignore and avoid these fellows, reporting any trouble to the police and/or your hotel owner.

If You Go: Boats making the 20-mile (45-minute) trip to Caye Caulker leave Belize City each morning from the Haulover Creek moorings behind the Texaco Service Station on North Front Street, about 100 yards inland from the Swing Bridge. Keep in mind that the passage may be bouncy (but faster) on smaller, high-powered craft, which tend to zigzag through the mangrove cayes en route.

Chocolate (who also operates a guest house on Caulker) is still the best boatman for hire, but nowadays he makes the journey only a few times a week. Other members of the Caye Caulker Water Taxi Association are equally happy, once enough passengers are loaded, to whisk you between Belize City, Caye Caulker and Ambergris Caye. Expect to pay about $7.50 for the one-way trip to Caulker.

Belize's domestic airlines make a total of 15 or more daily trips to Caye Caulker. Some travelers fly to airstrips on one of the two neighboring islands (Ambergris and Chapel) and later make the remaining short hop to Caulker by water or air. From either island you can easily arrange for a boat to pick you up on Caulker.

Caye Chapel and Long Caye
Heading south from Caye Caulker, the next island in the barrier reef chain is Chapel, distinguished by large groves of coconut palms. Easily visible across the horizon from Caulker, it's about 15 miles northeast of Belize City.

Only 1 mile by 3 miles in size and privately owned, Caye Chapel is blessed with some of Belize's best beaches and the nation's second-longest airstrip. The latter is a paved runway serving the Pyramid Island Resort, which owns all of Chapel and provides upscale services that include fishing, sailing, snorkeling, diving, tennis, volleyball, basketball, and even golf. There is a gift shop, a restaurant, a bar, and a full-service marina, all open to casual visitors. Rooms here are nothing special, but the setting is marvelous.

Warships of the Spanish Armada came here to nurse their wounds after the decisive 1798 battle that effectively ended Spain's claim on Belize. Some of the fleet's soldiers were buried here and there are also graves of English colonials, who fished and cultivated coconuts. Mayan artifacts have been found, most recently at the site of a large vegetable garden planted by the owners of the Pyramid Island Resort.

A small resort has operated in past years on nearby mangrove-studded Long Caye (also called Northern Long Caye) but was closed as this book went to press in mid-1995. Inquire locally about its current status. Both Long and Chapel Cayes provide good diving, snorkeling, and fishing in their offshore waters.

If You Go: Maya, Tropic, and Island airlines will land on Caye Chapel en route to or from Ambergris and Caulker at the request of passengers. A pier and full-service marina handle all boat traffic to and from the island, and the resort's helpful staff will arrange onward transportation for travelers dropped off here. Nearby Long Caye is accessible only by private boat.

St. George's Caye

During Belize's early years as a haven for British pirates and traders, its largest settlement was on St. George's Caye, located 9 miles northeast of Belize City. It served as the Bay Settlement's informal capital for nearly two centuries, starting in the mid-1600s. Manatees and turtles were slaughtered here by the thousands, their smoked meat later sold to the crews of oceangoing vessels.

This small island is best known as the focal point of a great sea battle between a ragged band of Baymen, a single British schooner, and seasoned Spanish naval forces. Despite the overwhelming odds against them, the Belizeans prevailed. Thus, the day Spain was defeated, September 10, 1798, is a national holiday (St. George's Caye Day). On the island's southern tip is a small cemetery where some of the early settlers were buried. Tropical storms have washed away most of the grave markers (along with dozens of houses), but old coins, bottles, and other artifacts are still found occasionally on the caye.

Today, there's not a great deal here to interest the casual or budget-minded traveler. Accommodations are available at only two locations. The expensive, highly regarded St. George's Lodge caters almost exclusively to scuba divers (certification available), although fishing enthusiasts and snorkelers are welcome. This resort is solidly built of tropical hardwood and has elegantly handcrafted furniture in its public areas. Power is supplied by windmills and solar collectors. Some of the ten cabañas are built on stilts right over the waters of the Caribbean; others are on the island's sandy soil. The food served here (family style) is first-rate. Bring your own liquor if you wish to drink. Unlike many diving lodges, the atmosphere is very relaxed. You may be tempted to curl up in a hammock all day and do nothing but watch pelicans.

The Bellevue Hotel also manages Cottage Colony, a cluster of five charming bungalows. Transportation is provided to and from the hotel's wharf in Belize City. Prices are upmarket and can include meals and fishing or diving packages.

There are a number of piers (called "bridges") on St. George's where day-trippers can tie up for an hour or so. A footpath encircles the island, and the snorkeling offshore is rated excellent. St. George's Caye is home to a few fishermen and has several cottages belonging to wealthy Belizeans.

If You Go: There is no regular public transportation to St. George's Caye, but private boats can be hired to make the 20-minute crossing from Belize City. En route, visitors will pass a number of uninhabited mangrove cayes that have little or no dry land, including Mapp's, Swallow, and Riders Cayes. Keep the binoculars handy, since this dense foliage harbors plenty of bird life. This trip provides a good chance to observe the wooden, sail-driven fishing ships, known locally as "lighters," which fill the waters from Mexico to Honduras.

Moho and Drowned Cayes

Only a half-mile off the coast, opposite St. John's College on the north side of Belize City, Moho Caye is a very small island with a big past. It is the site of an ancient Mayan fishing settlement, where thousands of pounds of old manatee bones have been found. The large mammals were apparently butchered in great numbers here, and the meat then prepared for transportation to other Mayan communities. Fortunately, the Caribbean (also called West Indian) manatee can still be found in these waters. Their whiskered noses can be seen popping into breathing holes near the Belize Municipal Airport, where the Belize River enters the sea. The docile creatures have become very rare in much of their range, which extends as far as south Florida, but are holding their own in Belize, thanks to government protection.

During colonial times, Moho was used as a quarantine area for sufferers of smallpox and other contagious diseases. A small graveyard marks the final resting place of many victims. The privately owned caye is the site of a sportfishing and diving resort, the Belize River Lodge, and access to the island comes with their permission only.

East of Moho, in the shallow Inner Channel waters, is a dense maze of mangrove islands known as the Drowned Cayes. While they hold almost no dry land, these lush cayes provide excellent anchorage during storms and are an important manatee habitat. Several local tour companies provide trips to breathing holes where a glimpse of this unusual marine mammal is almost guaranteed.

English, Gallows Point, Goff's, Rendezvous, Sergeant's, and Spanish Lookout Cayes

Each of these tiny cayes retains the kind of charm visitors typically associate with exotic tropical islands. They are only a few acres in size, consisting of little more than a mound of sandy beach and a dozen or so coconut palms. Even native Belizeans like to visit them for an afternoon or weekend of snorkeling, fishing, and picnicking. No regularly scheduled transportation serves these cayes, but day trips can easily be arranged through the larger Belize City hotels and travel agencies.

As you approach the islands from Belize City or points farther north, you will pass sugar barges taking their loads out to oceangoing cargo ships that cannot anchor any closer because of the shallow water. Within the Inner Channel, depths range up to 150 feet; they quickly plunge to 2,000 feet or more beyond the barrier reef.

Gallows Caye, located about 7 miles southeast of Belize City, derives its name from the hangman's gallows used here many years ago for the execution of convicted criminals. Today the island is home to The Wave: Gallows Point Resort, a six-room fishing and diving facility (in a large house) that offers a variety of services, including yacht anchorages. Meals are provided on the premises and transportation is arranged from Belize City. The resort also lines up day trips or weekend excursions from the mainland.

Sergeant's Caye has only three coconut trees surrounded by a long expanse of gorgeous beach. The island used to be much larger, but almost disappeared as a result of Hurricane Hattie. Situated directly on the reef, it is ideally suited for snorkeling and diving both "in" and "out" of the reef ecosystem.

English Caye, located south of the swampy Gallows Point Reef, has been an important navigational aid for hundreds of years. It marks the entrance of the deep English Caye Channel that large commercial ships follow into the Belize City harbor. The island is dominated by a brick lighthouse, where oceangoing ships stop to pick up one of the two pilots who navigate them through the Inner Channel, and the lighthouse keeper's small home. Visitors are welcome, and overnight stays can be arranged with special permission.

Goff's and Rendezvous Cayes are mere specks of palm-shaded sand off the major shipping lanes which make excellent stopping points for snorkeling, fishing, swimming, and diving. Both are perched right on the edge of the reef, which allows visitors to swim in either deep or shallow water. Overnight camping and anchorage is allowed. Local fishermen frequently visit Goff's and Rendezvous Cayes in their shallow-draft dories, mostly to find lobster and conch that will be sold to restaurants in Belize City and San Pedro.

Spanish Lookout Caye is 10 miles southeast of Belize City and 2 miles west of the main barrier reef. Once used by British pirates to spy on Spanish galleons, it now holds a small bungalow-style lodge,

Goff's Caye (Photo by Kevin Schafer)

Spanish Bay Resort, with five over-the-water units and an accompanying restaurant, bar, dive shop, and complement of experienced fishing guides. We recommend this Belizean-owned facility, which caters to nature lovers, fishing enthusiasts, divers, and snorkelers. It is well positioned for those who wish to patrol the outer reef and Turneffe Islands. A powerful dive barge—complete with compressors and other necessary paraphernalia—can take visitors to uncharted waters. The atmosphere is casual and friendly. Many visitors have praised Spanish Bay personnel for their environmentally sensitive approach to tourism.

Bluefield Range, Alligator Caye, and Middle Long Caye

Along Belize's barrier reef, the word "range" refers to the marshy clusters of mangroves that seem to be half land and half water. At least part (and in many cases, all) of every caye seems to fit this description; therefore, we do not mention here the scores of islands on which it is virtually impossible to set foot. The Belize government has imposed a ban on purchase of these and other unoccupied islands in the hope that many, if not most, can someday be included in a national park system.

Bluefield Range is unusual in that it supports several habitats. A couple of the mangrove cayes are permanently soggy, while the largest has a thin strip of high ground that accommodates Ricardo Castillo's Beach Huts. Ricardo and his family have built guest cabañas and a restaurant on stilts right over the water. Several tent sites on a pleasant stretch of sand are also available at $3 per person per day. This beach is a favorite stopping point for southbound sea kayakers. Cabañas are $75 a night, including meals.

Staying with Castillo offers visitors the unusual opportunity of observing traditional Belizean lobster fishing firsthand. Ricardo is a lifelong fisherman and free diver, originally from the boat-building village of Sarteneja, on the Shipstern Peninsula. He will take you along as he checks traps over a meandering route above nearby sea grass beds. Lobsters are still plentiful enough in these waters that they can be enticed into bait-free traps—such as wooden cages equipped with trapdoors and anchored with stones—that rely entirely on the animal's natural inclination to seek refuge during the day in dark places. Ricardo is a by-the-book member of Belize's large fishing cooperative and immediately throws back any undersized lobster, along with the occasional crab or fish that wanders into his traps. Later, you will dine on fresh lobster cooked to perfection. Boats hail Castillo via marine-band radio from as far away as Guatemala to make dinner reservations in the tiny restaurant.

Bluefield Range is a good base for excursions to other nearby cayes and reefs, plus the many pristine diving and fishing sites hereabouts. Ricardo serves as an experienced guide to little-known underwater limestone caves, coral canyons, and cayes. Snorkelers and nature buffs can easily arrange trips to uninhabited islands where exotic birds and other creatures make their homes.

Recommended nearby destinations include Columbus Caye, which has an underwater sinkhole more than 140 feet deep where large jewfish and sharks have been sighted. Caye Glory, a submerged coral formation off Southern Long Caye, is an important breeding

Rudolfo Avila outside his Moonlight Shadow Lodge on Middle Long Caye (Photo by Richard Mahler)

ground for grouper and other fish. Snorkelers and divers in this area will see black coral and, occasionally, sea turtles.

Saltwater crocodiles and waterfowl are plentiful on Middle Long Caye (also called Alligator Caye), a few miles north of Bluefield Range. This large, swampy island is the site of Moonlight Shadow Lodge, a rustic, bungalow-style resort with a small restaurant, operated by native Belizean fisherman Rudolfo Avila. For years, local fishermen have used Middle Long Caye's tiny beaches as campgrounds, and this is a good place to get to know native Belizeans firsthand. The manager of Moonlight Shadow will be happy to arrange tours throughout the area.

Tobacco Range, Twin Cayes, South Water Caye, and Carrie Bow Caye

Farther south from Belize City, lying 10 to 20 miles off the town of Dangriga, several little-known cayes offer attractions and services to visitors eager to explore the reef in relative solitude.

The islands of Tobacco Range have been used over the centuries for fishing camps and trading centers. In fact, Puritans set up a post here more than 300 years ago from which goods (including tobacco) were exchanged with visiting mariners. On Tobacco Caye, the largest island in the complex, travelers have several choices of modest accommodations, including Elwood Fairweather & Friends, Gaviota Coral Reef Resort, and Rosie's Guest House & Store. Local fishermen and their spouses operate most of the friendly rustic resorts here as a supplement to their income during months when sea creatures are breeding or when the weather is too foul to venture out on boats. You'll either cook your own meals on Tobacco or arrange to eat with your host or a neighbor. Excellent, well-informed fishing and diving guides are available here at good prices, and camping can be arranged (try Mark Bradley or Elwood Fairweather). Excellent snorkeling begins as soon as you enter the water. Boats to Tobacco Caye can be arranged easily in Dangriga (10 miles west) for a one-way fare of about $15 per person, assuming there are other paying passengers. Expect to pay much more for a boat transfer from Belize City, 36 miles to the northwest.

Mark Bradley's Island Camps is recommended for those seeking a quiet, peaceful visit. There are a couple of cabins with shared bath and one with private facilities. Bradley's moderate rates include all meals. Snorkeling and fishing trips can be arranged for an extra fee. Reef's End, in the same price range, rents rooms and cabañas, each with private bath. At the restaurant and bar, you can eat and drink right over the water.

Perhaps the most upscale Tobacco Caye resort is Ocean's Edge Lodge, operated by Evan and Margaret Evans. They cater especially to fishing enthusiasts, snorkelers, and divers. Visitors should bring all their own equipment, although Ocean's Edge provides weights, tanks, and air for scuba. As is the case at most Belize resorts, you must be certified (and bring your card) to participate in scuba activities. The lodge arranges airport pickup on request, and Caribbean-style meals are included in accommodation prices.

More luxurious services are available on South Water Caye, a picturesque 12-acre, palm-covered island a few miles south of Tobacco Range. The marine life around the caye is so rich that the Belize

69

government is seriously considering a proposal to make it a protected nature reserve. At the north end of South Water, the Blue Marlin Lodge has 14 double rooms and six bungalows, plus a restaurant, a bar, a volleyball pit, a billiard table, and complete dive and fish shops. Fishing boats, guides, and a divemaster are also available for the eager anglers and scuba enthusiasts drawn to this picturesque, flat island. Game fish found near South Water Caye include tarpon, snook, grouper, bonefish, permit, marlin, sailfish, tuna, and wahoo. Blue Marlin is a PADI dive-training facility praised for the quality of its instruction. The island is clean and quiet, home to ospreys, royal terns, green herons, kingfishers, and crocodiles.

At the south end of South Water Caye, Dangriga's Pelican Beach Resort maintains a modest hideaway—on the grounds of a renovated Catholic nunnery—which caters particularly to snorkelers and nature lovers. A cabin and dormitory are available for rental, and the hotel will send over a resident cook on request. Pelican University is a facility made available for large groups, such as those studying local flora and fauna.

On the island, marine ecology workshops are offered to the general public by International Zoological Expeditions (IZE) at its recently constructed biological research station. With more than 25 years experience in Belize, this Massachusetts-based outfitter is respected for the quality of its instruction and accommodations. Guests stay in either dormitories or waterfront cottages, with all meals included. Day trips are made to nearby cayes and reef formations to study birds and marine life. A full-service dive operation is also available, with all necessary dive and snorkeling gear available for rent. IZE maintains separate research stations on Long Caye at Glover's Reef and at Blue Creek in the Toledo District rain forest.

Yet another overnight option on South Water is Leslie Cottages, a five-bungalow complex on the south end of the island that is operated by members of an extended Belizean family and sometimes accommodates IZE guests. Diving, snorkeling, and fishing trips can easily be arranged here.

Like the Tobacco Range cluster, South Water Caye sits on the outer edge of the barrier reef. Because the island is also next to a relatively deep cut through the reef, marine life is particularly abundant—so abundant that the Washington, D.C.-based Smithsonian Institution operates a major research station directly across the South Water Cut on tiny Carrie Bow Caye. On South Water itself, the England-based Coral Caye Conservation Association has conducted underwater studies since 1986, working with Belizean students interested in pursuing careers in environmental studies.

Carrie Bow Caye is only about an acre in size—it was twice as big before the mangroves were chopped down and several devastating storms struck. The Smithsonian leases it from the Bowman family, which also owns part of South Water Caye and operates the Pelican Beach Resort in Dangriga. Scientists from all over the world come to Carrie Bow to study the hundreds of species of underwater plants and animals, including mangrove and other important flora and fauna. As many as five scientists at a time are working on the island, whose waters provide some of the Caribbean's best snorkeling. Over the years, these experts have set up a baseline of valuable data that are being used to track the impact of agriculture, fishing, storm systems, pollution, and other influences on the fragile coral reef ecosystem.

Visitors are welcome at the research center by prior appointment, which can be arranged (along with transportation) through Tony Rath or Therese Bowman Rath at their Pelican Beach Resort in Dangriga. Overnight accommodations in the house and dormitory are limited to Smithsonian personnel. The underwater marine area surrounding Carrie Bow teems with many varieties of multicolored fish, sponges, and coral and is easily accessible from the island's concrete pier. Again, beware of strong currents through the reef cut.

The Smithsonian, active in the area since 1977, also conducts research on Twin Cayes, several miles northwest of Carrie Bow. Studies in this area, which is not permanently occupied, concentrate on the mangrove ecosystem flora and fauna. In one curious (and unsuccessful) experiment, scientists attempted to rebuild nearby Curlew Caye by planting mangrove at the site of the island, which became submerged some years ago by a series of hurricanes. Man-O'-War Caye, not far away, is an important rookery for several species of large water birds, including the magnificent frigate bird (also called the man-o'-war bird). If you pass by during mating season, you'll see the male puffing out his immense red throat balloon. Man-O'-War Caye is federally protected, and you should not attempt to land here.

A small, privately operated marine research station is based on Wee Wee Caye, about 8 miles farther south, run by Paul and Mary Shave of the nearby Possum Point Biological Research Station on the Sittee River. Overnight accommodations at Wee Wee Caye are limited and should be arranged well in advance of your visit. The name, by the way, derives from the local name for leaf-cutter ants: wee wees.

The Southernmost Cayes

As visitors head farther south in Belizean waters, the barrier reef gradually swings away from the mainland. These cayes are remote and, for the most part, uninhabited. Aside from fishing shanties, rustic cabins, and sandy campgrounds, there are only a few overnight accommodations. This situation is changing, however, and you may wish to inquire locally about any new lodges that have opened since this book's publication.

In large measure because they are so inaccessible, these islands and the marine life surrounding them are almost exactly as they were centuries ago, when the Maya paddled among them in dugout canoes. Bird-watchers can expect to log dozens of species here, including many varieties of tern, gull, pelican, booby, heron, and egret. Grackles, vireos, hummingbirds, cuckoos, and pigeons also breed on the cayes. During the winter, many migratory birds visit these cayes on their way to and from North and Central America.

Some of the cayes also shelter a surprising number of land-based animals, such as lizards, iguanas, frogs, crabs, snakes, and even large mammals like opossums, raccoons, pacas, and armadillos.

Several of the southern cayes, including Laughingbird, Bugle, Colson, and Lark, are popular destinations for day trips out of Placencia, where the services of boats and guides are easily arranged. Other than group excursions out of Placencia, Punta Gorda, and Dangriga, the best way to visit these pristine areas is by private boat.

Divers, snorkelers, and fishing enthusiasts eager for a taste of

Creole life in a seldom-visited part of the reef are encouraged to visit Wippari Caye (sometimes spelled Whiprey), where friendly George and Hortense Cabral operate a six-cabin resort that provides excellent meals and first-class guide service. George is a former Placencia store-keeper who moved his family to Wippari—the local word for eagle ray—about 15 years ago. They've planted trees, established an extensive garden, and discovered one of the country's best bonefish flats on the perimeter of their tiny island, located about 9 miles east of Placencia. Two of the couple's sons—Pow and Breeze—are among the best fishing guides in Belize. Contact the Cabrals by VHF radio, or through either the Rum Point Inn or Kitty's Place in Placencia.

The Little Water Caye Resort, a small, exclusive lodge reopened in 1995 under new ownership, offers full scuba services, snorkeling, fishing, sailing, and a full-service restaurant. Little Water Caye is about 12 miles southeast of Placencia.

Rustic but comfortable bungalow accommodations are available on Ranguana Caye, about 20 miles southeast of Placencia, at Eddie Leslie's Ranguana Reef Resort. Visitors are reminded to bring their own food and that bathrooms are shared. Fishing and diving trips are a specialty here, but you'll need to bring your own equipment. Ranguana is one of the few places in Belize where sea kayaks can be rented. Paddling conditions are excellent. Camping is also available.

On Nicholas Caye, about 10 miles farther south among the Sapodilla Cayes, an upscale 20-cottage resort with bar and restaurant was also scheduled to open in 1995. A lodge on nearby Lime Caye was also in development as this book went to press. Check locally on the status of these facilities, which are expected to cater primarily to visitors from Guatemala.

Be careful about stopping on inhabited islands in southern Belize, since Mosquito Caye, Pompion Caye, and several of the others are privately owned.

Island-hoppers heading south will find a campground on Rendezvous Caye, directly east of Placencia (not to be confused with the island of the same name near Bluefield Range), and nearby Colson Caye. Overnight visits are now discouraged at Laughingbird Caye, a national park, in order to encourage the return of nesting gulls. Another recommended campsite is on Ranguana Caye, farther to the south.

By the time you reach the Toledo District, the barrier reef is out of sight across the northeastern horizon. Because the archipelago is a considerable distance from the mainland, travelers should expect to stay overnight and pay a hefty price for the trip. A campground, a picnic area, and sparsely furnished cabins are available for general use on Hunting Caye; a diving/fishing lodge there is under development. The caye also hosts a small outpost of the Belize Defense Forces, charged with interdicting smugglers and other lawbreakers.

The waters of the Sapodilla complex remain almost completely unexplored by anyone except local fishermen and Guatemalan vacationers. The coral walls that plunge steeply into the ocean's depths offer spectacular viewing opportunities for experienced divers. The islands have secluded, shaded beaches that make idyllic camping and picnicking spots. British scientists began a long-term ecological study of the Sapodilla Cayes in 1992.

From Punta Gorda, excursions can also be arranged to the Snake Cayes, small islands hugging the coastline a few miles northeast of town. Many of these are swampy mangrove ranges, but a few have enough high ground to support significant numbers of coconut palms, wild figs, buttonwoods, and other native trees. These cayes are not a part of the barrier reef system, but instead lie on their own coral reefs emerging from a limestone ledge that extends several miles into the Caribbean Sea. One small island, Wild Cane Caye, is the site of an important ancient Mayan ceremonial center that is now being excavated. The area's sportfishing is rated excellent (especially around river mouths), and several hotels and guest houses in Punta Gorda make a good base of operations. The town is also a jumping-off point for trips to Guatemala and, from there, Honduras and the Bay Islands. In recent years, several resorts specializing in sportfishing and diving have operated north and south of Punta Gorda town, around Punta Negra and Punta Ycacos. Contact Kingfisher Belize Adventures in Placencia or Nature's Way Guest House in Punta Gorda for details.

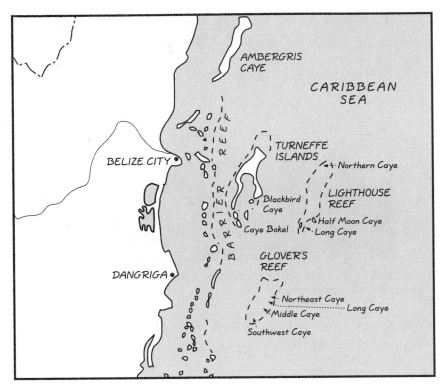

The Atolls

The Atolls

An atoll is a ring-shaped coral island and associated reef formations that fringe an enclosed, relatively shallow lagoon. While such formations are common in the South Pacific and other tropical oceans of the world, only four of any size exist in the Caribbean. Three of the four are located off the barrier reef of Belize. Because of their isolation from the mainland, atolls are often home to many species of flora and fauna rarely seen anywhere else. Their waters tend to be exceptionally clear, calm, and unpolluted, which makes them ideal for diving, fishing, snorkeling, windsurfing, sailing, and kayaking. The islands themselves are frequently used as breeding grounds by birds and other animals that prefer undisturbed habitats for raising their young. Belize has moved swiftly to preserve the pristine quality of its offshore

Snorkelers explore the pristine waters of Glover's Reef (Photo by Norm Shrewsbury/Slickrock Adventures)

atolls. A trip to one or more of these destinations takes extra effort (and money), but the rewards are unmatched.

Turneffe Islands

Like its companion atolls, Glover's Reef and Lighthouse Reef, Turneffe has also been given a deceptive name. Instead of "islands," the archipelago is actually a cluster of about 35 tiny coral islets and mangrove ranges (also known as "wet cayes") that encircles a shallow lagoon punctuated by seaward channels. The Turneffe Islands comprise the largest of the country's three atolls, measuring a maximum of 30 miles long, 10 miles wide, and covering a surface area of 205 square miles. It is also the nearest atoll, separated from the barrier reef by a 6-to-10-mile channel that plunges to a depth of 1,000 feet or more. During the Classic and Late Classic periods, Mayan fishermen and traders established small outposts here as well as at Glover's Reef. Later, pirates set up camps on the Turneffe Islands (complete with enslaved Indian women) and preyed on Spanish trade ships. In the early 20th century, the Turneffes were well known for their sponges and coconuts, largely wiped out by diseases and hurricanes in recent decades. Only a few fishermen, coconut collectors, and resort operators now make these islands their home.

The water is more crystalline here than on reefs closer to the mainland, where some turbidity is caused by the muddy runoff from mountain-draining rivers. Visibility in the warm (74- to 84-degree) water is often more than 100 feet in any direction.

At Turneffe, most of the cayes are covered with thick forests of red and black mangrove that form a rich and vital breeding ground for conch, lobster, and fish, as well as waterbirds. Close inspection reveals many of the islands on the west (or leeward) side to be little more than dense masses of mangrove trees clutching at the shallow sandbeds. On the eastern (or windward) side, a few acres of land rise high enough above the tide line to support human habitation and several of these sites (easily identified by coconut palm clusters) are occupied by either sportfishing/diving lodges or "fish camps" operated by individual Belizeans. Openings between the mangrove thickets are called "bogues," and they connect the shallow interior lagoons with the outer waters of the Caribbean.

The most unusual resort complex, occupying a stretch of east-facing beach on 4,000-acre Blackbird Caye, is described by its American backer, Houston-based oil and real estate entrepreneur Al W. Dugan, as both a living marine/land resource management community and an environmentally sensitive resort. Blackbird Caye Resort (named for the great-tailed grackles found in abundance) provides a little-disturbed setting for visits to the nearby coral reef, turtle nesting sites, saltwater crocodile habitat, manatee breathing holes, and breeding areas for several bird species. Nearby Soldier's Caye is a sanctuary for nesting roseate terns and white crowned pigeons, both rare in Belize. Animals native to the Turneffe archipelago include boa constrictors, raccoons, lizards, and land crabs.

A Texas A&M University research station at Blackbird Caye studies the behavior of bottlenose dolphins, which frequent nearby lagoons. This is the first such research undertaken in a diverse environment where mangrove islands, coral reefs, and sea grass beds form a delicately balanced ecosystem. San Francisco-based Oceanic Society Expeditions conducts excursions here that allow visitors to participate in surface and underwater studies of bottlenose behavior and distribution. Visitors swim with the dolphins or observe them from boats, plotting locations and collecting other data. The Oceanic Society offers some of these options in cooperation with the Elderhostel program, catering specifically to older travelers.

A cabaña-style lodge is used by nature-oriented tour groups and scientific research teams that arrive by boat from the mainland. Besides marine ecology studies, activities include diving, snorkeling, fishing, hiking, and beachcombing. Blackbird Caye Resort accommodates as many as 16 visitors with a full-service kitchen, electricity, hot water, fishing guides, and a certified dive instructor.

Blackbird Caye has become a mecca for international marine science and for Belizean students of reef ecology. A large marine research vessel, the *Heraclitus*, has been anchored nearby since 1992 and will help coordinate scientific work and diver training at least through 1995. The ship is the home of NAUI instructor Klaus Eiberle's highly recommended Blue Planet Divers Diving School, catering to casual visitors as well as those visiting Blackbird with tour groups. Special rates are extended to guests of Blackbird Caye Resort.

Although Blackbird Caye Resort is the largest lodge in the Turneffe Islands, it is not the first. The earliest tourist accommodations were built to house sportfishermen on Caye Bokel, at the southernmost tip of the atoll. Turneffe Island Lodge has nine rooms (six doubles and two quads), plus a dining hall and bar. Several boats are outfitted for diving and fishing. The lodge caters primarily to experienced divers, who are attracted to such popular nearby underwater destinations as the Elbow and the shipwreck *Sayonara*. Wall-diving off the reef is a favorite pastime among visitors. The resort's 38-foot dive boat can take visitors to remote locations for up to three dives a day. Bonefish and permit are found in large numbers on the periphery of the 12-acre island.

Turneffe Flats, midway up the atoll's east side on the northeast tip of Blackbird Caye, is built on the site of an old fishing camp that dates back to the Mayan era. The piles of weathered conch shells here are several feet high in places. The American-owned lodge can accommodate 12 guests among several bungalows. Beach camping is allowed by advance reservation. The facility specializes in fly-fishing, although divers, bird-watchers, and snorkelers are also welcome. Bonefish, permit, and tarpon are the most sought-after species here, and all are found in abundance. Guides, boats, equipment, transportation, and meals are provided.

On Calabash Caye, immediately south of Blackbird, the Planetary Coral Reef Foundation (PCRF) has a research station where coral reef ecology is being studied. Visitors must have permission from PCRF to visit. Calabash and the other islands south to the tip of Turneffe have been declared a national marine reserve by the Belize government. An important part of the scientific analysis is comparing reef response to Blackbird's ecotourism and Calabash's restricted visitation.

The least expensive diving/fishing resort on the Turneffe Islands is the Golden Bonefish Lodge on Cockney Point Caye, at the southeast corner of the archipelago near fine bonefishing flats. Fishing/diving packages, including transfer by 22-foot skiff from Belize City, run from Saturday to Saturday. (A similar week-long schedule is followed by most offshore diving and fishing resorts.) Sightseeing tours on the reef and mainland can also be arranged by the Golden Bonefish's Belize City representative, Doug Moore of One Moore Tours. For nonfishing guests, six-day rates begin at $550 (half the fishing package cost). Accommodations are bungalow style, with meals included.

The waters around the Turneffe atoll, especially the shallow coral-debris "flats," are teeming with permit, barracuda, and bonefish. Tarpon are plentiful from March through June around Turneffe's channels and inlets, and larger, deeper-water species include mackerel, bonito, marlin, blackfin tuna, grouper, sailfish, and wahoo.

Divers are especially fond of the atoll's steep dropoffs and tall coral heads adorned with colorful tube sponges, fan coral, sea fans and gorgonians among the natural crags and occasional shipwrecks. Black coral and sponges are especially evident in the inland waters of Vincent's Lagoon. Mauger Caye, at the atoll's north end, is a popular location for divers, who find a wide variety of sharks there. The island is identified by its lighthouse, in place since 1821.

Two areas in the Turneffe Islands group have been recommended by the Belize Center for Environmental Studies for establishment as government reserves. Vincent's (also known as Northern) Lagoon is a breeding ground for the Morelet's crocodile and Caribbean manatee, both endangered. Soldier Caye, east of Blackbird Caye and mentioned above, is the nesting site of several species of birds. There is also a small rookery on Blackbird itself. Increased human activity could have a negative effect on all these areas.

If You Go: There is no regular public transportation to the Turneffe Islands. The vast majority of visitors arrive as part of sportfishing or diving packages offered by the handful of resorts based on the islands (transportation from Belize City is prearranged by private vessel). Because it is close to the mainland in comparison to the other two atolls, Turneffe can be reached fairly easily through arrangements with local charter or live-aboard boat operators, either as a final destination or a stopping point en route to the Lighthouse Reef and/or Glover's Reef atolls. Expect to pay at least $75 per person for the 90-minute trip from Belize City. See Inside Belize for further details.

Lighthouse Reef

A largely uninhabited offshore atoll (about 50 miles east of Belize City), Lighthouse Reef is 28 miles long and 2 miles to 6 miles wide. The center lagoon is almost completely surrounded by coral formations. Its six islands are widely separated and form a nearly perfect semicircle.

The atoll is best known to most visitors as the site of Half Moon Caye Natural Monument, established in 1982 as Belize's first area protected under the 1981 National Parks System and Wildlife Protection Acts. The monument—comprised of 10,000 acres of the atoll and more than 15 square miles of surrounding waters—protects a large nesting colony of red-footed boobies, an estimated 77 migratory bird species, and the magnificent frigate bird (an arch-enemy of the booby). The 4,000-member booby colony is one of only two in the Caribbean (the other is on Tobago Island off Venezuela), and the nesting area can be observed from a special viewing platform. The slow-witted boobies are so named because they showed no fear of early sailors, who killed them easily and indiscriminately for food. Red-footed boobies are usually dull brown, but most of the Half Moon Caye birds have white feathers accentuated by pale gold heads and long blue-gray beaks.

Red-footed booby at Half Moon Caye (Photo by Kevin Schafer)

The Belize Audubon Society, caretaker of the sanctuary, has counted 98 bird species on Half Moon, among them the black-chinned hummingbird, white-crowned pigeon, and mangrove warbler. Several species of reptiles also live here, and both hawksbill and loggerhead turtles lay their eggs on the caye's beaches, where you may also see the largest species of land crab in Belize.

Camping and hiking are allowed on Half Moon Caye with consent of the resident warden, who can provide maps, information on sanitation facilities, and camping assignments. Permission from Belize

Audubon is no longer necessary before visiting the island. An unstaffed lighthouse, first built in 1820 and now solar powered, provides good views of the atoll and bird colonies. German U-boats refueled here during World War II, but no physical evidence of their visits remains.

The underwater area immediately surrounding Half Moon Caye is also protected and is full of marine life: more than 220 species of reef fish have been identified. Conch, which has almost disappeared from local waters, is gradually being reintroduced. The marine park surrounding Half Moon is easily accessible from a broad sandy beach or the leeward pier. Swimmers, divers, snorkelers, and kayakers are all welcome, provided they stay in designated areas and observe marine conservation rules.

Some distance north of Half Moon is Sandbore Caye, which also has an old lighthouse. Despite the presence of such stations, many ships have gone down in these waters. The Spanish trade ship Juan Batista sank about a mile offshore in 1822 and is said to have carried a cargo of still-unrecovered gold and silver bullion.

Located 8 miles north of Half Moon Caye is the popular Blue Hole, an almost perfectly circular limestone sinkhole that is more than 300 feet across and 412 feet deep. Created by the collapse of an underwater cavern some 12,000 years ago, the Blue Hole was the subject of a 1984 documentary by underwater explorer Jacques Cousteau, who concluded that a network of caves and crevices extends beneath the entire reef. Sport divers (limited to a depth of 130 feet) can admire its outstanding stalagmite and stalactite formations, while swimming in crystal-clear water that appears to be a peculiar shade of deep blue when seen from the surface. The hole is a habitat for shrimp and jewfish, but you should not expect to see much besides an occasional shark or tuna if you dive here. Surrounding waters are only about 20 feet deep, and big fish have trouble finding their way in.

At other popular dive sites in the area, depths plunge dramatically from 30 to several thousand feet within a short distance. The range of marine life includes some deep-water species that seldom enter Belize's shallower reef areas. Also look for enormous sponges, grouper, hogfish, and snapper.

Vegetation on the cayes is rich and varied, thanks in part to the natural fertilizer provided by thousands of birds and reptiles. Ficus (fig) trees, ziricote, gumbo-limbo, sea grape, spider lily, and coconut palm are all abundant here.

The only developed facility on the atoll is the exclusive and expensive Lighthouse Reef Resort, a 20-unit full-service diving facility on Northern Two Caye, which has its own private paved airstrip for shuttling guests from Belize International and plans to open a second lodge on the same island. The lodge specializes in week-long diving and fishing packages, with all meals, guides, and other services included in a single price. The resort grounds encompass 16 acres (not counting the airport runway). Contact a local travel agency for its current status. All other visitors to the atoll must bring their own food, drink, and fuel. Advance permission is required to land on the airstrip.

Ecosummer Expeditions, of Vancouver, B.C., has been offering week-long sea kayaking expeditions to Lighthouse Reef, including the Blue Hole, since 1982. Participants camp on Half Moon Caye and spend their days exploring the area. Instruction, equipment, meals, and transportation from Belize City are provided. Ecosummer also arranges one-week sailing trips to Lighthouse Reef from San Pedro aboard the 48-foot traditional Belizean lighter *Excellence*. Guests are taken to the best snorkeling and fishing spots, including the Turneffe and Glover's atolls. Meals and accommodations are provided, and trip extensions to the Belize interior can be arranged.

If You Go: Day trips to Half Moon Caye and the Blue Hole start at about $75 per person for groups of several individuals (the trip takes roughly 6 hours from Belize City or San Pedro). Other vessels charge $150 and up for more extensive trips. It is possible to be dropped off for a few days of camping and then picked up at whatever time you choose. Some live-aboard dive boats based in Belize City (and elsewhere) make trips to Lighthouse, as well as the two other atolls. Try Out Island Divers and Indigo Belize, both in San Pedro, for information on their dive trips to Lighthouse.

Because of its remote location, trips to the atoll by individuals or couples are fairly costly; it is wise to make the trip with others to reduce the per-person expenses. Boats are allowed to dock only at the pier on the leeward side of Half Moon Caye, and deep-draught vessels may anchor only in designated areas. Charter flights can be made to the Northern Caye strip with permission of the Lighthouse Reef Resort.

Glover's Reef Atoll

Glover's is a splendid offshore atoll, the most remote island group in the country, located about 20 miles east of the barrier reef, 40 miles from the mainland, and 70 miles southeast of Belize City. Rising from a depth of over 2,000 feet, Glover's Atoll consists of a well-defined, oval-shaped coral formation (15 miles long and 5 miles wide) that surrounds a deep lagoon. More than 700 patch reefs are found inside its 75-square-mile crystalline lagoon. The many coral pinnacles arising from within are an important breeding ground for grouper and snapper. Surrounding walls begin at about 30 feet and drop suddenly to well over 2,000 feet. The atoll is named after 17th-century pirate John Glover, who used the remote island cluster as the base for his raids against Spanish galleons heading in and out of the Bay of Honduras. During the early 1970s, a visiting team of international scientists pronounced this the biologically richest atoll in the Caribbean Basin; most of the ecosystem was declared a marine reserve by the Belize government in 1993. All six of the atoll's islands except Northeast Caye are zoned as conservation areas and one, Middle Caye, is a designated wilderness. Seasonal closures of the surrounding fisheries allow species to recuperate.

In 1991, Middle Caye was purchased from its private owner by the Wildlife Conservation Society, part of the New York Zoological Society. This 15-acre island has been called the keystone to the long-term preservation of Glover's Reef, in that Belize Audubon and the Belize government can now use Middle Caye as their base for monitoring activities around the atoll. Marine ecologists and enforcement officers can study the atoll's rich fauna and simultaneously protect the remote area from such human disturbances as overfishing and unregulated diving. The University of New England and Belize Fisheries Department have proposed a long-term, large-scale ecological study of the area, in which commercial fishing will be strictly managed. Middle Caye may eventually become the headquarters for a national marine park and include environmental education as well as field research facilities. There is increasing concern that fishing and diving in this fragile ecosystem may quickly degrade what remains one of the world's most pristine marine environments. A study of groupers, an important commercial species common around Glover's Reef, is now underway here. Access to Middle Caye is by permit only.

Two lodges operate on the atoll and for part of each year a sea kayaking outfitter operates on Northeast Caye. Privately owned Southwest Caye, on the archipelago's southernmost tip, is home to the exclusive Manta Reef Resort, a haven for anglers and divers from all over the world. Like its counterparts on Turneffe and Lighthouse, this complex caters to serious fishers eager to hook bonefish, permit, and barracuda, which are abundant on the atoll's coral flats. Conditions are also excellent for tarpon, snapper, grouper, marlin, jack, tuna, bonito, wahoo, sailfish, and other billfish (plus the huge manta rays that give the resort its name). Open since 1989, Manta provides lodging on the 12-acre island in comfortable thatched-roof cabañas and transportation for divers in small V-hull boats. Forested with coconut palms, like all of this atoll's other islands, Southwest Caye is bisected by a hurricane-induced cut and dominated at its southernmost end by a government-operated lighthouse. Transportation to Manta Reef Resort is by boat (included in the package price) from Belize City. Contrary to published reports, the island has no airstrip.

The rustic and remarkably inexpensive ($100 per week) Glover's Reef Resort and Marine Biology Field Station, located on 12-acre Long Caye, also specializes in extended diving, snorkeling, and fishing trips for individuals and small groups. Members of the

French-American Lomont family, who manage the eight cabañas, campground, dive shop/school, and informal restaurant, live on a tiny portion of Long Caye (labeled Lomont Caye on some maps), separated from the main island by erosion-created channels. The Lomonts guarantee visitors access to underwater locations where no one has ever dived, snorkeled, or fished before. Given their location amid the 700 patch reefs of Glover's Atoll, the boast is probably accurate. Canoes, powerboats, guides, compressors and water recreation gear are available, but remember that there is no electricity or indoor plumbing. Meals can be purchased at the resort's open-air headquarters, but visitors are encouraged to bring their own food (cooking gear and water are provided). Campers (bring your own tent and sleeping bag) are charged $60 per week. Rates for guests who stay a second week are sharply reduced. Guests are picked up by Gil Lomont every Sunday morning at the Sittee River Guest House, south of Dangriga, for the five-hour voyage to Long Caye. The boat returns the following Saturday afternoon. The resort is closed from September through November, although the Lomonts invite visits from educational groups at any time of the year (there is a classroom and meals can be provided). The resort prefers reservations, and visitors should arrive in Sittee River Village for pickup the day before departure. Excursions can be arranged to the jaguar sanctuary and historic sugar mill.

Although members of the Lomont family have lived and worked on the island for many years, International Zoological Expeditions now claims ownership of Long Caye. In 1995, the dispute between the two parties was winding its way through Belizean courts. In the meantime, the southern half of the tiny island is off-limits to Glover's Reef Resort guests and is being used by IZE as an annex for participants in its marine ecology seminars, based on South Water Caye.

Meanwhile, Northeast Caye is leased from the Lomonts from early December through April by Slickrock Adventures of Moab, Utah, which offers week-long package trips featuring kayaking, windsurfing, snorkeling, fishing, and diving (through neighboring Glover's Reef Resort). Guests spend part of each day paddling among the islands, observing underwater flora and fauna in remote parts of the atoll. Instruction, most equipment, meals, and rustic cabaña accommoda-

Beached sea kayaks on Northeast Caye, Glover's Reef (Photo by Norm Shrewsbury/Slickrock Adventures)

tions are provided, along with transportation by boat to and from Belize City. Bring your own snorkeling mask, fishing gear, and sleeping bag. During months when Slickrock and other companies are not operating on Northeast Caye, it is available to patrons of Glover's Reef Resort, who otherwise can visit the island only with permission. Slickrock offers trip extensions to Mayan ruins and other attractions in the interior.

A NAUI scuba certification course is offered on Northeast Caye every July by instructor Lynda Sierra. Her package trip to Glover's includes all meals and equipment for diving and snorkeling. Fishing excursions can also be arranged. Telephone (408) 479-4969 for details.

Attractions on 12-acre Northeast Caye include an amazingly old and massive gumbo-limbo tree, which shelters the graves of several pirates whose descendants lived here well into the 20th century. Turtles nest on some of the island's beaches, and ospreys are common.

Except for resort folks, a few visiting fishermen (from as far away as Guatemala and Honduras), and a lighthouse-keeper on Southwest Caye, the reef itself is usually deserted. Conditions for snorkeling and diving are excellent, and several interesting underwater shipwrecks lie at the atoll's north and south ends. In many areas the coral walls drop abruptly to a depth of over 2,600 feet a short distance from the shoreline. Marine life is especially abundant here.

If You Go: Lomont's Reef Resort, Manta Reef Resort, and Slickrock Adventures provide transportation to and from the atoll as part of their diving and sportfishing packages, which usually last from one to two weeks. Because of the distance from the mainland, expect to pay a minimum of $150 for a charter boat to Glover's Reef, probably departing from Placencia or Big Creek. An alternative is to sign onto one of the several live-aboard dive boats that regularly anchor off the atoll. For further information, see Inside Belize.

5

The Coast

For the purposes of this guidebook, the coastal destinations of Belize are generally defined as those located within 30 miles of the mainland's Caribbean coast. Noteworthy exceptions to our rule are all but one of the coastal Mayan ruins. We have included a detailed description of this ruin, Altun Ha, in this chapter (descriptions of all other Mayan sites are in Chapter 6) because it is the only major ruin we consider to be an easy day trip for those staying in Belize City. For the same reason, the Belize Zoo, the Monkey Bay Wildlife Sanctuary, and the Community Baboon (Howler Monkey) Sanctuary are discussed here, even though they are located some distance from the coast.

Coastal Belize has a distinctive cultural personality, since it was the first part of the country settled by Europeans. The vast majority of the nation's people live along this narrow strip, including most of the Creole and European-descended population. The climate is warm and humid; the terrain is swampy and crisscrossed by waterways. Nature-lovers can find plenty of wading birds here, and anglers can hook a wide variety of fish in the jungle rivers.

For most travelers, however, the Belize coast has limited appeal. This area is the most cultivated in the country, particularly in the north, and lacks the dramatic scenery and abundant wildlife of the offshore islands and interior mountains. Yet we highly recommend some attractions, including the Placencia Peninsula, Shipstern Nature

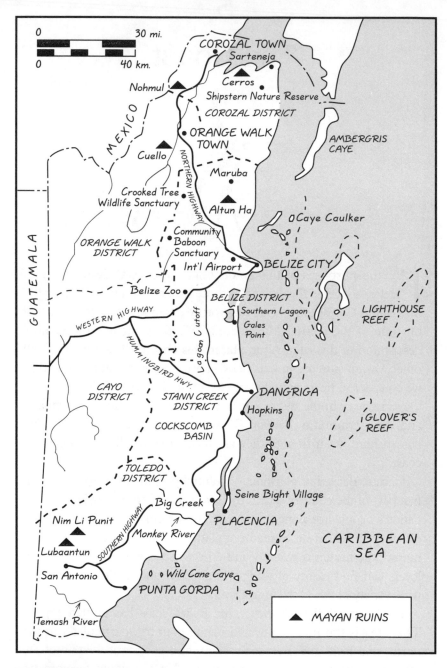

The Coast

Reserve, Gales Point Manatee Community Sanctuary, and the Community Baboon Sanctuary. For these reasons, we hope you will spend at least part of your tour of Belize in its coastal zone.

Corozal District

The serene northern coast of Belize, particularly the Corozal District (which borders the Mexican state of Quintana Roo), masks a turbulent past. A series of massacres of mestizos and whites by enslaved Indians throughout the Yucatán peninsula led to a long, bloody retaliation in the mid-19th century known as The Caste Wars. Thousands of people, Indians and mestizos alike, fled to safety across the Río Hondo into British Honduras; today their Spanish-speaking descendants make up the majority of the population in this, Belize's northernmost district. Their farming expertise was welcomed by colonial authorities and, as a direct result, Corozal is today one of the country's most extensively cultivated areas (primarily sugarcane). The main city, Corozal Town, and surrounding areas are a good escape from the sometimes hectic pace of travel in other parts of Belize. Except for the sticky summer season, there are almost constant trade winds off the water, and extremes of precipitation and temperature are unusual here.

The Corozal District was originally settled in 1849 by refugees from an Indian massacre in Bacalar, Mexico. For a good visual description of this history, see the fine mural by Manuel Villamor Reyes in Corozal Town's municipal building. (If the town hall is closed, the Reyes mural can be seen though windows on the ground floor.) In 1986, the painting was restored and updated to show the economic exploitation of immigrant workers in the district during the 1850s and 1860s.

The word *Corozal* is modified from the Spanish name for the cohune palm tree, which ancient Mayans considered to be a symbol of fertility. This area—along with most of northern Belize—has always been relatively prosperous because of its fertile soil and benign climate. Corozal Town, located about 85 miles from Belize City and less than 10 miles from the Mexican border, consists of a mixture of clapboard wooden houses and concrete block buildings. All are built on foundations of the Mayan ceremonial center of Santa Rita (see Chapter 6).

In 1955, Hurricane Janet destroyed much of the town, which until then featured mostly adobe (mud-and-straw brick) buildings. Its mid-1995 population was estimated to be about 12,000. Surrounding Corozal Town's Central Park are a modern Catholic church, a library, the city hall, an Adventist church, and government offices. There are also several old brick "pillboxes," used as defensive fortifications by the British during the last century. Although Corozal Town is built along the shoreline of Chetumal Bay, there is no beach here and the water immediately adjacent to the city is polluted. Corozal Town comes alive at Lent, Columbus Day, and Christmas, turning each of these holidays into boisterous, Mexican-style fiestas. The economy of the entire Corozal District centers on the sugar industry. The old Aventura Sugar Mill, about 5 miles south of Corozal Town, started operation in the 1800s. Although the processing plant is no longer in use, its chimney stands as a symbol of an industry that generates an estimated 80 cents out of every dollar earned here. The foundation of an old Spanish colonial church is also on the site. Raw sugarcane is now processed at two other area mills: La Libertad and Tower Hill. Tours of the mills now operating are available by prior arrangement; the facilities usually shut down from July until December.

The Santa Cruz Lodge, a resort opened in the sugar mill area in 1994, offers tours of the Petrojam Sugar Factory, as well as guided excursions to local ruins and nature destinations. Santa Cruz is located on 35 acres a few miles south of Corozal, in what once served as homes for sugar industry executives. Besides 18 air-conditioned rooms, the lodge has two restaurants, a bar, swimming pool, and tennis court. Expansion plans call for a jogging track, golf course, and health spa.

About 7 miles to the north of Corozal Town and less than 2 miles from the Mexican border (off the right side of the main road to Chetumal) is picturesque Four Mile Lagoon. Locals use this as a favorite picnicking, swimming, fishing, and weekend hangout. It is recommended for foreign visitors, too, especially those interested in sailing, windsurfing, and kayaking, all well-suited to these calm waters. Camping and full-hookup RV parking is available at Lagoon Campground, operated by Americans Rosalie and William Dixon. They maintain a boat launch and rent both canoes and sailboats. The Dixons have lived in Belize for several years and can answer questions about what to see and do in the area.

Besides the small ruin of Santa Rita, now surrounded by the modern roads and buildings of Corozal Town, an interesting coastal Maya site known as Cerros (and sometimes Cerro Maya) is an quick boat ride across Corozal Bay. More fully described in Chapter 6, Cerros is a late Pre-Classic trading center boasting tombs, ball courts, and a magnificent temple with a fine view back across the bay to Corozal Town. Manuel Hoare is recommended as an excellent area guide to Mayan ruins and as a skilled boatman (office, 4-22744; fax, 4-23375).

About 8 miles northeast of Corozal Town, near the tip of the Corozal Peninsula, is the pleasant coastal village of Consejo Shores. Several holiday homes in the area are available for rent or purchase.

Accommodations in Corozal Town itself are rather limited, and the restaurants are generally undistinguished. One exception is the Caribbean Village Resort, opposite Corozal Bay at the southern entrance to the city. This inexpensive facility, which includes a good restaurant (Hailey's), was recently purchased by Henry Menzies, a Corozal local who also runs the area's best travel service, offers expert advice, and answers any and all questions about northern Belize. Tony's Inn, located a short distance away, is also recommended for its more upscale rooms, restaurant, and services. Nestor's Hotel, at 123 Fifth Avenue, and the moderately priced Maya Hotel (great view of the bay) on the Corozal-Orange Walk Road are popular among experienced budget travelers. Also recommended is the moderately priced Hotel Posada Mama at 77 G Street South. Crises Restaurant serves above average Belizean cuisine and is recommended for its home-style atmosphere and excellent beans-and-rice dishes. Nightlife in Corozal is limited to a few bars, some of which occasionally have live music on weekends.

If You Go: For the best experience while in Corozal, we recommend

San Pablo post office and store, typical of area's mestizo-owned businesses
(Photo by Richard Mahler)

Henry Menzies of the Caribbean Village Resort and Menzies Travel
and Tours, at the south end of Corozal Town (office, 4-22725; fax,
4-23414). Since Menzies lives next to the airport, it is very convenient
to have him meet your party there. A native of the area, he is particularly helpful for tours of local Mayan sites or quick, efficient access
across the border to Chetumal and farther destinations in Mexico.
As of early 1995, Menzies planned to add a boat to his repertoire.
Commercial airfares from the United States to Cancún can be half
the cost of airfares from the United States to Belize International.
Menzies can meet you or your group in Cancún. Good service is also
reported by travelers using Jal's Travel Agency in south Corozal
Town, where tours and airplane tickets are available.

The Venus and Batty bus lines have frequent service to Corozal
from Chetumal, Orange Walk Town, Belize City, and smaller communities. Local buses, which stop wherever passengers desire, run
about once each hour during the daytime and evening. Express buses
operate about four times each day. The express trip from Corozal to

Chetumal takes about 20 minutes and to Belize City, around 3 hours. That time can double for all destinations on local runs. Tropic Air offers twice daily flights to San Pedro (on Ambergris Caye) from the Corozal Airport. Island Air also serves Corozal twice daily. Other airlines occasionally offer service here, too.

Orange Walk District

Slightly inland from Corozal but still influenced by the coastal climate, Orange Walk District is one of the least-visited areas in Belize. This is because most accessible parts of Orange Walk are highly cultivated in the form of sugarcane and citrus plantations, as well as Mennonite farms of corn, sorghum, rice, and vegetables. In addition, there is no seacoast, and most of the pristine wildlife habitat is either privately owned or inaccessible. An exception is the Río Bravo Conservation Area, described in Chapter 6. Orange Walk District is also home to the spectacular ruins of Lamanai (also described in Chapter 6) and Belize's largest lake, the New River Lagoon.

A good base of operations for visitors is Orange Walk Town, a bustling mercantile center of about 14,000 residents, located roughly 60 miles north of Belize City on the banks of the New River. Major roads from here lead in four directions and link the more than twenty villages of the Orange Walk District, consisting mostly of Spanish-speaking mestizo, English-speaking Creole, and German-speaking Mennonite farmers.

Settled largely by refugees from the Caste War, Orange Walk Town has the badly eroded ruins of two forts, Mundy and Cairns, that recall the scene of bloody conflicts between Belizean settlers and the district's earlier occupants, the Icaiche Maya. The latter bitterly fought the settlers in an unsuccessful attempt to rid the area of intruders. The final battle took place on September 1, 1872. One of the last remnants of this standoff is the old flagpole in front of the Orange Walk City Hall.

Before settlement by mestizos occurred in the late 1880s, the Orange Walk District was dominated by loggers for more than a century. During that time, all the timber taken from the region was floated down the New River into Corozal Bay. From there, it was transferred through the Inner Channel to Belize City and finally shipped to the outside world.

Now agriculture is king. Sugar has been the most important crop for many decades (surpassing chicle and corn earlier this century), and Belizean rum (distilled at the Cuello processing plant under the "Caribbean" label) is one lucrative market for the cane that is grown and harvested here. Other cane is rendered into molasses and, of course, sugar. The region is also an important producer of citrus, papaya, and beef cattle.

For the natural history tourist, Orange Walk Town does not offer much as yet. However, if you are interested in seeing some of Belize's more than 110 native species of orchids, Carlos Godoy offers a tour that will bring you face to face with Belize's national flower: the black orchid. Godoy greets visitors at his home (4 Trial Farm Road, tel. 3-22969) and guides them down the New River to see some of the many exotic species that thrive in Belize. Operating under a government permit, he gathers and propagates orchids and bromeliads that would otherwise be destroyed by logging and farming. For the serious orchid enthusiast, Godoy can also facilitate the customs and legal procedures involved in exporting these delicately beautiful flowers. He also runs nature/archaeology tours and boat trips up the New River to Lamanai and other destinations.

If You Go: Buses from Belize City to Orange Walk run daily at about one-hour intervals. Check the Venus or Batty Brothers bus service for fares and schedules. A private car or express bus can make the trip in roughly an hour; local buses take slightly longer. There is frequent service from Chetumal and Corozal Town, and connections can be made in Orange Walk Town for Sarteneja and villages en route to the Shipstern Peninsula. All through-buses stop for about 20 minutes in Orange Walk Town, where passengers can buy food and change money.

Accommodations in Orange Walk Town are nothing special and the best of the lot is D'Victoria, which has 31 rooms, a bar, swimming pool, and other amenities. More moderately priced options include the Chula Vista Hotel, Jane's Guest House, and Mi Amor Hotel. Some hotel locations are very noisy, and be advised that there are at least a dozen rowdy brothels in Orange Walk, fronting as hotels and/or restaurants. Cocaine and marijuana are sometimes sold openly here, despite severe government penalties. Unless you want to risk spending time in a Belize jail, resist the temptation to buy illegal drugs.

There are several restaurants in Orange Walk, and some hotels also serve food. HL's Burgers are a favorite among locals for American-style fast food. The Diner, on Clark Street, serves Belizean and international food at all three daily meals. Orange Walk has many Chinese restaurants; get a recommendation from a local before picking one, since Chinese food in Belize is of variable quality. The best gift shop is KU's (26 Liberty Ave.), which sells ceramics, wind chimes, and cotton boxes.

Several hotels arrange tours to Mayan sites and boat trips along the district's various inland waterways, which are home to a wide variety of birds and other animals (see Inside Belize for further information). Some of the more reliable tour operators are the aforementioned Carlos Godoy and Mayaworld Safaris (2-32285 or 2-31063). For a recommended trip down the New River to the Mayan ruin of Lamanai, contact Jungle River Tours (Antonio, Herminio, and Wilfredo Novelo, tel. 3-22293). Wilfredo is one of the best Belizean guides for archaeology. The widely-acclaimed, conservation-minded Novelo family at Jungle River Tours provides a superb day trip of birding on the New River and sightseeing at the Mayan ruins. The Novelos can also drop you off after the tour at the splendid Lamanai Outpost Lodge; see below and the Inside Belize section for more details.

Indian Church

A recommended destination near the Lamanai ruins (a 20-minute walk or 10-minute canoe ride) is the Lamanai Outpost Lodge (voice/fax 2-33578), which overlooks the 28-mile-long New River Lagoon near the Spanish-speaking village of Indian Church. Opened in 1992 by expatriates Colin and Ellen Howells, this impressively

Lamanai sugar mill (Photo by Richard Mahler)

landscaped, cabaña-style retreat offers canoeing, swimming, wind-surfing, fishing, nature treks, and even therapeutic massage. As you would expect in this remote location, prices are upmarket. Tours to the nearby Lamanai ruins, Río Bravo Conservation Area, Mennonite farms, and Mexican border village of La Unión are available. The lodge is a bird-watchers' paradise, with a sweeping view of the nearby lake, forest, and Mayan ruins. The facility was constructed using largely local materials and labor, in a manner that minimizes any neg-ative environmental impact. Septic systems, for example, are set up to percolate "gray water" back into the soil, and mulch is used to retard erosion and discourage weed growth. Among the many amenities are a pontoon boat for nighttime "safaris" on New River Lagoon. Spot-lights are used to illuminate caymans and other exotic animals.

The Outpost's excellent restaurant and bar are open to casual visi-tors. Fresh food is grown on the premises or in the nearby village. Most employees are Guatemalan refugees who settled here in the early 1980s. The lodge may be reached in about 2½ hours, by either auto or auto/boat combination, from Belize City. From Orange Walk Town, take the Yo Creek road to San Felipe and turn left for the final 12 miles to Indian Creek. For more on the Lamanai ruins, see Chapter 6.

The Shipstern Peninsula

Sticking out like a hitchhiker's thumb into the northern end of Chetumal Bay, the Shipstern Peninsula is one of the least developed areas in all of Belize. Until relatively recently, it could only be reached by private boat. A few thousand mostly Spanish-speaking people live in this vast expanse of waterlogged jungle, savanna, and mangrove swamp, most of them concentrated in the isolated fishing village of Sarteneja, which perches on a small patch of dry ground near the peninsula's northeastern tip.

Before 1988, the few roads that had been cut through this moist Corozal District forest were impassable much of the year due to muddy conditions and high water. The main road has since been improved and closures are uncommon, however a four-wheel-drive vehicle is still advisable during the wet season.

Progresso, Chunox, Little Belize, and a few other small settlements punctuate the picturesque landscape en route to Sarteneja, but the peninsula's main attraction is the Shipstern Nature Reserve. This 32-square-mile nature sanctuary is not far from the government's large Freshwater Creek Forest Reserve. A newly-renovated wardens' quarters and education center of the Shipstern Nature Reserve is located about 10 miles south of Sarteneja.

Founded by the Switzerland-based International Tropical Conservation Foundation (ITCF), Shipstern Nature Reserve's 22,000 acres include northern hardwood forests, saline lagoon systems, and mangrove shorelines almost totally undisturbed by humans. In 1994, the ITCF signed a contract with the Belize Audubon Society for transfer of Shipstern's management to the latter organization, with important management funds granted by ITCF. Management of the reserve was transferred from long-time conservationist Jan Meerman to former Crooked Tree Wildlife Sanctuary manager Donald Tillett and three Sarteneja-resident wardens.

The nature reserve is named after the abandoned village of Shipstern, located in the southern part of the reserve, and is considered an exceptional example of a heterogeneous forest regenerating from devastating tropical storm damage. (Most of the mature trees were destroyed by Hurricane Janet in 1955.)

The flora and fauna have made a remarkable recovery during the past four decades, and hundreds of plant and animal species have been recorded here, including scores of migratory birds from North America that winter in Shipstern. The moist forest of the Shipstern Peninsula, still largely untouched, is the only protected area in the country that includes the more seasonal hardwood trees, as well as vast saltwater estuaries that are an especially important habitat for many wading and fish-eating birds. Bird-watchers can expect to see several species of flycatcher, toucan, warbler, aracari, and parrots. Among the colorful birds recorded here are the Yucatán jay, reddish egret, wood stork, and black catbird (previously assumed to be restricted to the offshore cayes). All five species of Belize's native cats, along with tapir, paca, coatimundi, deer, peccary, and armadillo, roam the Shipstern forests and savanna. Five different jaguars have been sighted within a 5-mile radius of the Shipstern Nature Reserve's headquarters.

Facilities for scientists and trails for casual visitors are slowly being developed within the reserve, as funds allow. In 1994, a new nature trail was added within the reserve around the banks of Xo-pol Pond. Another recommended hike is along the Chiclero Botanical Trail, located in thick forest near the headquarters building. A self-guiding brochure explains the traditional medicinal and ceremonial uses of dozens of trees identified along the path. One of Shipstern's main goals is to show how countries like Belize can make conservation areas self-supporting through low-impact tourism.

The reserve's butterfly breeding program was discontinued in 1994 and a nearby commercial breeder has also ceased operations. (In 1995, the only butterfly breeding in Belize was believed to be a small facility at Chaa Creek Cottages, near San Ignacio.)

The village of Sarteneja, northeast of the Shipstern reserve, was almost completely washed away by Hurricane Janet. One resident was killed, and only three brick structures—the school, clinic, and old sugar mill—survived the flood. The tin-roofed clapboard settlement has been rebuilt several times in its history, always around a well located in a massive piece of seemingly solid stone. Legend has it that this particular well, once used by seafaring Maya, has never gone dry. *Sarteneja* is a Spanish word meaning "water between the rocks."

The Maya apparently abandoned the original village about A.D. 1700. During the mid-1800s, Yucatán settlers fleeing the Caste Wars reestablished Sarteneja, which became widely known for its skilled boatbuilders. To this day, Sarteneja's fishermen sail as far south as Guatemala and Honduras in the beautiful handcrafted sailing vessels they call "lighters." The fishermen sell their catch in Belize City, San Pedro, or Chetumal on the way home, then turn around and start another fishing expedition a few days later. They often pick up sand and coconuts on the cayes they visit, which they sell on the mainland. Every Easter, a huge sailing regatta is held in the small Sarteneja harbor and prizes are awarded for the fastest and most elegant boats.

Although more than 400 Mayan sites have been pinpointed on the Shipstern peninsula, only one ancient structure has been excavated. While the world's archaeologists organize themselves, local residents continue to dismantle many of the old buildings block by block to make modern houses of their own. Farmers sometimes drag the Mayan limestone bricks out of their fields and grind them up as ingredients for plaster and cement. Jade, gold, copper, and shell artifacts periodically turn up here but are usually sold to traders or kept in private collections.

A growing number of foreign sportfishermen are now plying the waters off Shipstern in search of barracuda, grouper, snook, yellowtail, and tarpon, which are all plentiful. The native shrimp, lobster, and conch, once very common, have been severely depleted by commercial fishermen.

A couple of cayes and reefs offer snorkeling possibilities here, but they are difficult to reach without a chartered boat. The area's murky lagoons are important feeding grounds for such rare waterbirds as the flamingo and spoonbill, as well as manatees and crocodiles. Tour arrangements can be made with local travel agents and guides based in Orange Walk Town and Corozal Town (see Inside Belize chapter for suggestions).

You might also want to make a side trip to Chacan Chac Mol, a small lake southwest of Sarteneja. Finally, the Shipstern ruins are an infrequently explored Mayan ceremonial center. Access is through the Shipstern Nature Reserve, but advance arrangements must be made with reserve management.

If You Go: All-weather gravel roads to Sarteneja branch off the Northern Highway from several points in and around Orange Walk Town. The trip by car takes about 1 hour from Orange Walk Town and 2 hours from Belize City, in good weather. The daily direct bus from Belize City leaves from the Texaco Gas Station on North Front Street at about noon, returning around 3:00 a.m. Venus Bus Lines also has daily service to Sarteneja from Belize City, with a stop in Orange Walk Town en route.

From Orange Walk Town, take the northeast road toward Progresso and turn right just before that village, toward the Mennonite settlement of Little Belize. From there, head to Chunox and on to

Sarteneja. The Shipstern Nature Reserve headquarters is 3 miles before the village of Sarteneja.

Domestic airlines ferry passengers to Sarteneja via Corozal, and boat transportation can be easily arranged from Corozal Town or Ambergris Caye.

Lodgings have come and gone in the village over the years. At last report, the only accommodation was at Diana's Hotel and Bar, not visited by the authors but described as simple and budget-priced.

Tours to nearby areas, including night trips into the jungle to observe some of the forest's unusual nocturnal wildlife, can be arranged in Sarteneja by simply asking around town for a knowledgeable guide. If the tour will include outlying parts of the Shipstern Nature Reserve, permission should be obtained from the Belize Audubon Society reserve management in advance (P.O. Box 1001, Belize City, tel. 2-35004 or 2-34987).

Belize City

Characterizing Belize City as the nation's hub is an understatement. Indeed, people commonly refer to this community of about 70,000 residents simply as "Belize." For many, Belize City *is* Belize. Located at the mouth of the Belize River on the Caribbean Sea, midway between the Mexican and Guatemalan borders, this seaport town is the country's largest urban center. Belize City supports and manages a growing tourism infrastructure, as well as many other services, industries, and retail businesses. It also provides a base for some important Belizean conservation groups.

Sadly, the reputation of Belize City has gone from bad to worse in recent years, fueled by well-publicized accounts of street crime, drug trafficking, and panhandling. There seems to be no end to the number of horror stories visitors tell about their unfortunate adventures in this ramshackle, slightly seedy community. It's our opinion that Belize City is not nearly as dangerous as many people make it out to be, although reasonable precautions should be taken when going from one place to another, especially on foot.

Walking alone in certain areas—ask at your hotel or travel agency

Clapboard house, Belize City (Photo by Sue Dirksen)

for a detailed description of trouble spots—is not recommended because a small but aggressive contingent of Belizeans is persistent in demanding money or selling drugs. At night, a single person on foot may encounter even more significant trouble; the dangers of being attacked and robbed are very real here, as they are in large urban centers throughout the world. Taxis within Belize City's limits are inexpensive and readily available. We advise you to use them, and to not carry unnecessary valuables on your person. Although Belize City does have a municipal bus system, we hesitate to recommend it because routes are confusing and not well posted.

The authors have found that here, as elsewhere in the country, 99 percent of Belizeans are helpful, courteous, and genuinely happy to welcome tourists. In our view, Belize City's smiling residents and relaxed pace are among its greatest attractions. From hotel employees to restaurant workers, taxi drivers to conservation leaders, travel agents to bank tellers—almost everyone is eager to share information and exchange pleasantries with visitors. This laid-back, tolerant attitude is perhaps a tribute to Belize City's colorful history and multicultural traditions.

The first full-time residents of what is now Belize City are believed to have been Mayan Indians, who maintained a busy fishing camp on nearby Moho Caye for several centuries. Bones and other artifacts excavated at this site suggest there was abundant marine life, including large numbers of turtles and manatees. In the late 1600s, after the area had been mostly abandoned by the Maya, pirates from Scotland, England, and France began to spend time during the annual rainy season at the mouth of the Belize River. Over the years, these buccaneers and their African slaves harvested tropical hardwoods in the interior and used the broad, slow-moving waterway to float the precious timber to oceangoing vessels anchored offshore. By the 18th century, the settlement of Belize Town had been solidly established by members of what the British referred to as their Bay Settlement (named after the nearby Bay of Honduras). Historians say the city is built on a foundation of loose coral, logwood chips, and rum bottles. Whatever its exact composition, this pile of debris seems to be sinking, as much of the urban area is now barely above sea level.

To make matters worse, several violent hurricanes and accompanying surges have battered Belize City over the years. These storms occur primarily in autumn, as evidenced by Hurricane Hattie's destructive visit on October 31, 1961, which took hundreds of lives and nearly leveled the town. This was the prime motivation for Belizeans to move their capital some 50 miles inland to Belmopan, even though most residents have chosen to take their chances by staying in Belize City. (Only about 6,500 people reside permanently in Belmopan, and a large percentage of government workers commute every day.) In spite of Mother Nature's unpredictable and destructive forces, Belize City remains home to about one-third of the country's population.

Several impressive landmarks have withstood the various storms and can be seen during even a brief taxi tour of Belize City. At the gateway to Belize Harbor is Fort George Lighthouse, dominating a finger of land that was originally the easternmost point on Fort George Island. The channel separating the island and mainland was filled in during the 1920s, long after Fort George had fulfilled its function as an army base. Views of nearby cayes covered in mangroves now await visitors to the site, and brown pelicans often fish in small groups near the shore.

Next to the lighthouse is a small park and the Baron Bliss Memorial, a tribute to the "Fourth Baron Bliss of the former Kingdom of Portugal," Henry Edward Ernest Victor Bliss. An Englishman by birth, this eccentric adventurer sailed to Belize in 1926 and instantly fell in love with its soothing climate, unspoiled waters, and palm-studded islands. As a result of food poisoning he suffered in Trinidad, the baron was too ill to come ashore. He spent several months aboard his yacht, the Sea King, fishing in the harbor as he tried to recover his health. Bliss was impressed by the kindness and respect fellow sportfishermen and colonial officials showed him. He learned as much as he could about Belize without ever having the physical ability to come ashore. Before Baron Bliss died aboard his boat, he specified in his will that a trust fund of almost $2 million be established for the sole benefit of Belizeans. So far the interest generated from the fund has been used to help construct a public building in Belmopan, a Corozal health clinic, the Belize City water system, the Bliss Institute public library and museum, and many other civic projects. Baron Bliss also stipulated that a portion of the trust funds be used to stage an annual yacht regatta in Belizean waters. This is the focal event of the national holiday on March 9, honoring his contributions.

In the heart of Belize City, at the corner of Front and Queen Streets, is a large old colonial-style building that houses the main post office, as well as the Belize City headquarters of such ministries as the Department of Natural Resources. Here in the Paslow Building you may purchase the colorful Belizean stamps, among the most beautiful in the world. They depict brocket deer, storks, marine life, tapir, jaguar, macaws, and many other native animals. A special counter for stamp collectors is on the Queen Street side of the post office. Parcel post is now handled next door on North Front Street. Upstairs, on the right side of the Paslow, some of the best maps of Belize (divided into north and south sections) are available from a government office for about $10 each.

Facing the main post office is Belize City's Swing Bridge, reportedly the only such manually operated bridge still in service in the

Supreme Court building, Belize City, built in 1923 (Photo by Belize Tourist Board)

Americas. It was constructed in Liverpool, England, and has been cranked open for Haulover Creek's high-masted boat traffic since 1923. Daily, at about 6:00 a.m. and 5:30 p.m., policemen stop pedestrians and vehicles on either side of the bridge, while men insert long poles into a capstan and gradually open a passageway allowing vessels to pass upriver or out to sea.

Not far from the Swing Bridge, facing Battlefield Park (until recently called Central Park) on Regent Street, is the moderately imposing Supreme Court Building. Built in 1923 in classic British Colonial style complete with dome-topped clock tower, it stands on the site of the original settlement courthouse built in 1818. The courthouse has been rebuilt here twice: it was demolished in 1878, and destroyed again in a famous fire that took the life of then-governor William Hart Bennett in 1918. For a slice-of-life experience, step into a courtroom and watch the Belizean justice system in action.

Near the courthouse on Bliss Promenade (also called the Southern Foreshore) is the Baron Bliss Institute, which, with its modern-looking circular second floor, seems out of place amid the Victorian gingerbread of Belize City's oldest neighborhood. The institute displays (poorly) some ancient Mayan artifacts from Caracol and other Belizean archaeological sites. It also houses a public library, auditorium, and art gallery, as well as the National Arts Council. Slide shows, lectures, and seminars on science, history, conservation, and culture are held here. If you go, take a taxi. This area has become a tough neighborhood in recent years.

Headquartered on the south side of the Swing Bridge, near the busy intersection of Regent and Albert Streets, is Belize City's main public market, housed in a modern three-story building and offering good buys on fresh food and handicrafts. Another public market has operated from a warehouse on North Front Street, a few blocks west of the Fort George Lighthouse. Although it is scheduled to be torn down, as of mid-1995 this latter market was still the best place to purchase herbs from vendors whose wares include the bark from the negrito tree, used in the treatment of dysentery, and copal, a hard tree resin used by the Maya as incense. The stand operated by Miss Barbara, a legendary Belizean "granny healer," is highly recommended.

The oldest Protestant church in Central America is located at the far south end of Regent Street, across from Government House, itself a historical landmark. St. John's Anglican Cathedral is one of the oldest buildings in Belize. Built by slaves in 1812 from bricks brought over as ballast in the hulls of ships sailing from Europe, the church was the site of several coronation ceremonies for the Indian kings of the Mosquito Coast. These were members of an indigenous ruling class that once presided over the native tribes of what is now the Caribbean coast of Honduras, Nicaragua, and Costa Rica. Inside the church are dozens of plaques commemorating prominent Anglican colonists.

A few hotels, restaurants, travel agencies, and stores deserve special mention in these pages as some of our favorites in the city.

The Chateau Caribbean Hotel (6 Marine Parade) boasts a moderately priced ocean view with sea breeze, if you ask for a waterfront room. The restaurant and bar, which also feature a Caribbean view, are fairly good. On the more upscale side in the same district is the 106-room Radisson Fort George Hotel (2 Marine Parade), which has a well-stocked gift shop, fine restaurant, swimming pool, and comfortable bar. You can rent Avis cars here, and there's a full-service marina across the Marine Parade. For the budget traveler, the Eyre Street Guest House (7 Eyre Street) is recommended for no-frills accommodations with shared bath. The Bellevue Hotel, located on the waterfront at 5 Southern Foreshore, has modern rooms and a lively upstairs bar decorated like an old ocean liner. As mentioned in Chapter 4, the Bellevue is also a reliable departure point for a boat to Ambergris Caye. Away from the city center is the Kiss Hotel (Mapp St. and Freetown Rd.), which has clean rooms at moderate prices.

Mom's Restaurant (7145 Slaughterhouse Road) is one of the best places in Belize City for breakfast and lunch. Take-out and an early breakfast—both rare in Belize City—are available. The message board and sign postings are also worth a look.

Macy's Café (18 Bishop Street) serves Belize's inexpensive and ubiquitous main dish of rice and beans, with extras ranging from stewed chicken to freshly squeezed lemonade. Actor Harrison Ford stopped here during the filming of *Mosquito Coast* some years back and proclaimed Macy's his favorite restaurant anywhere. But not even a movie star's presence affects the laid-back atmosphere, friendly staff, and humble furnishings. There's a nice patio out back. Do the natural world a favor and resist the temptation to order wild game, which appears occasionally on the menu here and at other Belizean restaurants. When you eat gibnut, iguana, deer, turtle, and other rapidly-disappearing species, you encourage unregulated hunting and are contributing to an unhealthy imbalance in local ecosystems.

G G's Café and Patio (2B King Street) features a pleasant, romantic courtyard atmosphere, friendly service, and good food, particularly Creole-style grilled chicken. Again, we recommend you take a taxi, both coming and going, to avoid potential street crime. In recent years the somewhat upscale Grill, near the Ramada Royal Reef Hotel on Newtown Barracks Road, has produced good local seafood dinners. The Royal Reef, incidentally, is the biggest hotel in Belize and has several restaurants.

Dit's (50 King Street) has the best pastries and Creole cowfoot soup in town; and Fort Street Restaurant (4 Fort Street) is arguably the best place to eat in Belize City, serving excellent food, imaginatively prepared. The drinks are unusually good, too. The moderately priced Fort Street Guest House, which occupies six rooms above the dining area, is a long-time favorite of conservationists. American owners Hugh and Teresa Parkey are experts on things to do in and around Belize City.

For some of the biggest portions of the best modestly priced Chinese food in Belize City, visit the air-conditioned New Chon Saan Palace at 1 Kelly Street. Other recommended restaurants include Goofy's (6 Douglas Jones) and The Marlin (11 Regent Street West), serving Jamaican and Belizean cuisine, respectively. Good pizza is served at The Gourmet (13 Prince Street), along with delicious *liquados* (fruits drinks). They even deliver.

Romac's Supermarket, at 27 Albert Street, and Brodie's, directly across the street at the corner of Albert and Regent, come in handy for all those provisions you need for exploring the tropical forest. Brodie's has a pharmacy, a produce section, and an exceptionally good selection of Belizean books and magazines. You can stock up on

British colonial style guest house in Belize City (Photo by Richard Mahler)

even cheaper fruits and vegetables at the public market, about 3 blocks north, next to the Swing Bridge. Several family-run stands here sell inexpensive meals and snacks.

The downtown Mopan Hotel, at 55 Regent Street, is a moderately priced establishment with an attractive bar. The Mopan is run by Jean and Tom Shaw, longtime environmentalists who are happy to answer questions about Belize's "natural destinations." Another option, particularly for the traveler who enjoys boats and requires a beach nearby, is the modern Ramada Royal Reef Hotel and Marina on Newtown Barracks Road, which boasts all the amenities one would expect with a high price tag.

If you visit Belize City, you can finalize travel arrangements and also get those insider tips on people and places to visit in this diverse country. We recommend, particularly for the ecology-minded visitor, Jal's Travel, S & L Travel Services, 7 Candles Cab Service, and Tubroos Tree Adventures. See Inside Belize for addresses, phone/fax numbers, and details on each agency's specialty. Remember that it's a good idea to double-check flight times for air travel in-country, as well as to reconfirm your international departure.

For those who want a car for their visit, we recommend Crystal at 1.5 Mile Northern Highway (tel. 2-31600). The American owner offers a wide variety of slightly used cars, vans, and even motorhomes at reasonable prices (all major credit cards accepted). Newer model vehicles can be rented at the offices of Avis (corner of Fort and North Front Streets), Budget (771 Bella Vista), and National (126 Freetown Road and at the international airport), although prices are surprisingly high. Be advised that comprehensive insurance is not generally available in Belize, and the person renting the car may be held responsible for any and all damage, including flat tires.

If You Go: From Phillip Goldson International Airport, the 15-minute taxi ride into Belize City cost $15 in 1995. Rates are fixed by an informal cabdrivers' union—which squeezed out a hotel shuttle service a few years ago—so it does no good to shop around. Within Belize City itself, taxis—any vehicles with green license plates—are generally the best way to get around, unless you have your own car or have arranged transportation in advance. Remember, tipping of taxi drivers is not customary in Belize.

(See Inside Belize for listings of other hotels, restaurants, and services in Belize City.)

Altun Ha and Crooked Tree Wildlife Sanctuary

One of several rewarding day trips from Belize City can combine visits to a major ancient Mayan ceremonial center, Altun Ha, and to one of the premier bird sanctuaries in Central America, Crooked Tree Wildlife Sanctuary. Of course, you may want to spend more time at either Altun Ha or Crooked Tree, but it is perfectly feasible to visit both in a single morning and afternoon.

Stay alert on your way through the lowland pine savanna on the road to Altun Ha and Crooked Tree—the countryside along the Northern Highway is a rich habitat for many bird species. We once saw the Belizean "grand prize" for bird-watchers at Mile 11: a jabiru stork flew over the top of our vehicle, close enough that we could distinguish the bright red band on its neck. The jabiru is easy to identify since it is one of the largest birds of the Americas, with an adult wingspan of up to 10 feet. (See Chapter 7 for a more thorough description of the jabiru stork and other exotic animals of Belize.)

Other birds you might encounter on the Northern Highway are the roadside hawk (often perched on the telephone wire awaiting an opportunity to swoop down on an unwary rodent), or vermilion fly-catchers playing tag among low bushes bordering the drainage ditches. A great heron will likely greet you as it patiently stalks small fish in the many lagoons along the road. A large bird, the heron's white plumage makes it easy to spot against the dull silver-green of palmetto palms and brown savanna grass.

Altun Ha

The ancient Mayan ruins of Altun Ha are 31 miles north of Belize City on the old Northern Highway that passes through Maskall. (The new Northern Highway continues in a more westerly direction toward Crooked Tree Lagoon, reconnecting with the old highway at Carmelita). The Altun Ha site, 8 miles from the sea, was an important Mayan trading and ceremonial center. Here the sun was a focus of worship; Mayan priests were buried within one of the tallest structures, known as the Temple of the Sun God. Altun Ha means "stone water" in Maya, and this name refers to nearby Rockstone Pond, an ancient water catchment ingeniously dammed and lined with clay for irrigation purposes. Near this pond stands a temple in which archaeologists found artifacts the Maya obtained from the faraway city of Teotihuacán, on the outskirts of present-day Mexico City.

During its seventh-century height, Altun Ha became a focal point for the sacrifice of such valuables as jade jewelry and carved pendants, as well as offerings of copal resin. At the top of the Temple of the Masonry Altars, such precious items were smashed into small pieces and cast into an intense fire. Like many Mayan rituals, the origin and purpose of this sacrificial offering remain unclear.

Thirteen structures surround two main plazas at the site. The two tallest temples, Temple of the Sun God (the structure depicted on Belikin beer bottles) and Temple of the Masonry Altars, rise 60 feet above the grassy plaza floor. Altun Ha covers an area of about 5 square miles and includes an extensive swamp north of the plazas. It's believed that up to 10,000 people lived here during the Classic period of Mayan civilization, as late as A.D. 1000.

Visitors interested in birds are likely to be rewarded here. Brilliant green Aztec parakeets often streak by in tight formation, level with the tops of the temples. Ringed kingfishers rest on the summit of the Mayan structures before returning to the nearby swamp to fish. Tropical mockingbirds and brown jays squawk persistently at tourists. There are also trails into the bush for birders driven by the constant chorus of calls that echo around the two main plazas.

Altun Ha was first excavated by A. H. Anderson in 1957 and by W. R. Bullard in 1961, undergoing some of the most extensive fieldwork of any Belizean ruin. This rich ceremonial center remained archaeologically quiet until 1963, when quarry workers unearthed an elaborately carved jade pendant. This discovery triggered an intensive archaeological excavation from 1964 to 1971, spearheaded by David Pendergast with support from Canada's Royal Ontario Museum. Restoration work at the site was performed from 1971 to 1976 by Joseph Palacio and during 1978 by Elizabeth Graham. Altun Ha was the second Mayan ruin in the country, after Xunantunich, to be cleared and prepared for tourism. Crews from the Department of Archaeology now keep the grass neatly trimmed and groom some of the surrounding bush for visitors. Brochures and restrooms are available.

Perhaps Altun Ha's most famous historical footnote is Pendergast's discovery of a huge jade head replica of Kinich Ahua, the Sun God, in one of the last tombs to be excavated. The effigy was made in about A.D. 600 and owned by an elderly priest. At the time of its discovery, this priceless relic was the largest of its type ever recorded in the Mayan world: almost 6 inches tall and weighing nearly 10 pounds. The jade head can be viewed in the Department of Archaeology's vault in Belmopan. On rare occasions the Kinich Ahua replica is taken on exhibition tours with other artifacts; eventually it will be displayed in Belize's National Museum, which began construction in 1995. Jade found at Altun Ha probably came from Guatemala's Sierra de las Minas, since this stone does not occur naturally in Belize. Altun Ha's obviously important religious function as a sacrificial site remains unexplained.

Several phases of construction have occurred at Altun Ha, which was occupied from around 1000 B.C. until its abandonment 2,000 years later. You can easily detect this phased construction in the distinct sets of walls that are evident as you walk around the backsides of the plazas. Pendergast concluded that Altun Ha fell into disuse as the result of social upheaval. He found unmistakable evidence of desecration at several of Altun Ha's tombs, but believes modern-day looters were not the ones who destroyed the contents of tombs, buried crypts with soil, and displaced roof slabs. Pendergast reasoned that such activity, accompanied by violence, may have involved some form of peasant revolt among the Maya around A.D. 1200.

If You Go: From Belize City, take the Northern Highway about 20 miles and turn right just north of the village of Sand Hill, at the junction of the old Northern Highway (the sign is marked "Maskall and Orange Walk"). Proceed about 11 miles and turn left (just past Cowhead Creek) at the sign for the 2-mile connecting road to the Altun Ha parking lot. The drive from Belize City takes approximately 45 minutes, not counting stops to identify and observe birds along the way. There is no regular bus service to the site, although it is possible to hire a taxi or hitch a ride with a truck that brings goods to market in Belize City from the village of Maskall, about 10 miles north of Altun Ha. As at all Belizean archaeological sites, a fee of $1.50 per person is collected at the visitor registration center.

We recommend hiring a Belizean guide for the day, such as Winston Seawell at 7 Candles Cab Service in Belize City. Winston is a wealth of information about Belize, has reliable transportation, and gives an informative tour of Altun Ha. S & L Travel Services and Tours is also an excellent choice for some of the best, most experienced Belizean guides. If you are a serious student of the Maya, contact Mary Dell Lucas at Far Horizons Expeditions (see Inside Belize).

There are no accommodations at Altun Ha, but camping is allowed with permission from the caretaker. He also will permit free overnight parking for recreational vehicles. The only nearby hotel rooms are at the attractive (and expensive) Maruba Resort at Mile 40.5 on the old Northern Highway. Maruba Resort boasts a restaurant, swimming pool, an open-air Japanese-style hot tub, massages, cabaña-style accommodations, and tours of Altun Ha and other nearby ruins, such as Lamanai. Several low- to moderately priced guest houses are available in nearby Crooked Tree village; we recommend these for visitors who want to see both Altun Ha and the Crooked Tree Wildlife Sanctuary. The Paradise Inn is our favorite.

Crooked Tree Wildlife Sanctuary

Crooked Tree Wildlife Sanctuary is one of Belize's prime destinations for nature-lovers. Visitors from temperate-zone countries can easily see more birds in a single day than they are likely to see back home in a year. Even before you cross the causeway that connects to the freshwater island upon which Crooked Tree Village is located, you are liable to spot the American coot, northern jacana, snail kite, least grebe, white ibis, and rough-winged swallow. Hundreds of other different species have been recorded in Crooked Tree's lagoons and wetlands, but the richness and variety of habitats here suggest that many more birds are waiting to be "discovered." Mexico Lagoon, Spanish River, and Black River are some of the many excellent birding spots within the sanctuary's boundaries.

Not only is the variety of bird life tremendous at the Crooked Tree wetlands, especially during the February–May dry season, but the aggregate number of waterfowl is astonishing. Huge flocks of olivaceous cormorants, roseate spoonbills, egrets, and other species congregate here, taking advantage of the area's abundant food resources and safety as a resting spot on spring migration routes. The rare jabiru stork nests within the 3,000-acre sanctuary, and the limpkin, with its black body and strange-looking neck, is another frequently observed inhabitant. You may delight in identifying an elegant green-backed heron, sleek green-winged teal, ungainly wood stork, or brilliantly colored Yucatán jay.

Crooked Tree Wildlife Sanctuary was established voluntarily by the area's 750 residents in November 1984, with substantial financial assistance from the Wild Wings Foundation. But the Belize Audubon Society has made the most significant contribution to the success of Crooked Tree. During the early years, Audubon's management was accomplished exclusively by dedicated volunteers. Another group that has helped manage Crooked Tree's jabiru stork population is the

New Mexico-based conservation organization LightHawk. Using light aircraft that carry sharp-eyed spotters, flight missions are designed to thoroughly survey the sanctuary, to help perform an annual census for this imperiled species. Counts are made, locations of the giant birds are pinpointed, and nests are located. The collected data are then compared to information obtained from ground surveys, reports from villagers and visitors, and previous aerial surveys.

The sanctuary's well-maintained visitor's center and museum are located at the end of a 3-mile-long causeway, which runs between Crooked Tree Village and the paved Northern Highway to Orange Walk and Belize City. You are required to check in at the visitor's center before you explore the area. The center has informative displays that are designed to test your knowledge of the sanctuary's birds. The resident manager is happy to answer questions and assist in your explorations. Excellent maps are also available.

Donations to Crooked Tree Wildlife Sanctuary are encouraged and graciously accepted. This financial assistance keeps both the sanctuary and the Belize Audubon Society going. While no mandatory visitor fees are currently collected for this and other sanctuaries, monuments, and parks managed by Belize Audubon, plans to do so are periodically evaluated by the Government of Belize.

From sanctuary headquarters, you can follow several different nature trails. One is appropriately named after the northern jacana, a delicate bird that flashes yellow wings when it flies and is light enough to tread confidently on water hyacinth as it forages for small fish and mollusks.

Since 1993, an event has been held at Crooked Tree early each May which exemplifies positive action by foreign-owned tour companies whose revenue is derived from ecotourism. Alabama-based International Expeditions co-sponsors the Crooked Tree Cashew Festival, a communitywide celebration that includes music, dancing, feasting, story-telling, folklore performances, and, of course, demonstrations of the harvesting and preparation of local cashew nuts.

"By harvesting, processing, and selling cashews, residents have established a livelihood that enhances their natural environment, an achievement which they feel is cause for celebration," says Tom

Cashew fruit with nut in Crooked Tree Village (Photo by International Expeditions)

Grasse of International Expeditions. Cashew trees are native to the area, and their delicious fruits are used to make wine, jam, and sandwich spreads; they are sold in raw and roasted form as well. Mango products are also made and sold from the enormous, centuries-old trees that dominate the village. During the festival, birding trips are a possibility too. The success of the annual Crooked Tree Cashew Festival has made it possible to essentially turn the event over to the Crooked Tree community; however, International Expeditions continues to bring foreign participants to the event as a highlight of one of their many custom tour packages within Belize.

While tourism is the village's fastest-growing industry, its mostly Creole residents still engage in subsistence farming, livestock rearing, and fishing. The sale of cashew products throughout Belize and the rest of the world is an important boost to their economy. Crooked Tree community leaders and International Expeditions hope this program can serve as a model for other countries, communities and companies.

In 1994, the Belize Audubon's Crooked Tree management team was given some experienced assistance by Woodward Miley, on loan from Florida's Apalachicola National Estuarine Research Reserve. Miley established a baseline water quality monitoring program and a procedure for recording recreational and commercial fish catches, and made additions to the Sanctuary's management plan. Miley observed that a pressing need for Crooked Tree is to find a balance for the fish populations in the Sanctuary's lagoons that meets the needs of both wildlife and human residents.

For the best experience while visiting the Crooked Tree Sanctuary, we recommend contacting wardens Rennie Jones or Donald Tillett through the Belize Audubon Society in Belize, or phoning them at one of Crooked Tree Village's community telephones (tel. 2-44101 or 2-44333). During our last visit, there were very few boats in the village, so check with the wardens to make sure of boat availability before you visit. Unless you arrange in advance, you may be touring the Sanctuary on foot. The sanctuary headquarters has a two-way radio and its manager can help set up a boat tour. We recommend that you allow at least a half day to visit Crooked Tree and bring along a local guide. One rewarding boat trip takes you through Northern Lagoon to Spanish Creek. We also suggest that you ask your guide to periodically kill the engine and float quietly among the birds and other animals. One rewarding boat trip takes you through Northern Lagoon to Spanish Creek.

The most wildlife can be seen during April and May, when the water level is lowest. Mornings and evenings are peak activity times year-round. As you travel along the shore of Crooked Tree Lagoon, you will see Belize's largest contiguous stand of remaining logwood. The nearby village, one of the first ever in Belize's interior, was established because of the easy accessibility of this commercially valuable timber, still exported in small amounts. Logwood blossoms are lilac-shaped clusters of beautiful yellow flowers. On the way to Spanish Creek, your guide can also point out distinctively shaped bullet trees and dense stands of bamboo. Bullet trees are used to make boat gunwales: the wood is so hard that bullets cannot penetrate. Along this portion of the shoreline, the master of hovering flight, the snail kite, searches with neck craned downward for the abundant land snails that cling to logwood stems. The captured snails leave behind white, multichambered clusters of eggs, thus replenishing the food chain.

Calabash Pond, Revenge Lagoon, Western Lagoon, Southern Lagoon, Jones Lagoon, and Mexico Lagoon are other wild places encompassed by the Crooked Tree Wildlife Sanctuary. Morelet's crocodiles and several turtle species can be found here. You may spot a howler monkey or ocelot, both found in the Black River area. Indeed, there is so much to explore within this unique ecosystem that first-time visitors may quickly conclude that a half-day tour is, after all, entirely inadequate. Fortunately, there are several fine lodges and restaurants in or near Crooked Tree Village, most operated by locals.

If You Go: Crooked Tree Wildlife Sanctuary is roughly 33 miles northwest of Belize City and 3.5 miles west of the new Northern Highway. We recommend that visitors with a serious interest in birds arrange their trips in advance through S & L Travel Services (tel. 2-77593) or International Expeditions (800-633-4734). Overnight accommodations are provided by several rustic lodges and the homes of Crooked Tree Village residents. The latter are simple, inexpensive bed-and-breakfast arrangements in a rural atmosphere. Try the Raburn or Urrick family. Hotels include the Crooked Tree Resort (manager Sam Tillet offers guided boat trips), Paradise Inn (formerly Crooked Tree Lodge; owner Rudy Crawford also operates a boat chartering service), Bird's-Eye View Lodge, or Maruba Resort (in Maskall). Meals, which may include local fish, are available at these hotels and at the Corner's Inn Restaurant. Accessible by boat up the Spanish River is the unique and beautiful Chau Hiix Lodge (tel. 2-73787), operated by American expatriate Robert Brooks and catering specifically to bird-watchers.

Many local residents offer specialized services to visitors. Rudy Crawford at the Paradise Inn, for example, arranges horseback and carriage rides, as well as personalized bird-watching trips.

Buses from Belize City run daily to Crooked Tree. Check Venus Bus Lines (tel. 2-73354) or Batty Brothers Bus Service (tel. 2-72025 or 2-77146) for fares and schedules. Travel agencies arrange frequent tours. Taxis can also be arranged from Belize City or Orange Walk Town during the dry season. Expect to pay $75 and up for a round trip from Belize City.

The Community Baboon Sanctuary

In Belize, black howler monkeys are called baboons; therefore, the "baboons" being protected at this unusual private sanctuary have little in common with their African cousins of the same name. They are, in fact, Central American black howler monkeys, an endangered species found only in thick lowland forests from southern Mexico to Honduras.

Howlers—so named because adults (mostly males) emit a distinctive raspy, guttural growl that can be heard for a mile or more—are threatened in much of their rapidly shrinking range. The protected colony that can be seen by visitors on an easy day trip from Belize City numbered about 1,800 in mid-1995 and is considered one of the few healthy-sized populations in the region. And thanks to an innovative management scheme, the size of this group is increasing all the time.

What is most unusual about the Community Baboon Sanctuary and its interpretive museum is the fact that the project is voluntary, entirely reliant on the goodwill of interested subsistence farmers who work the lands immediately adjacent to the broadleaf jungle the howlers prefer. Although the sanctuary is both praised and admired by government officials, it is completely dependent on private lands and funding for its survival. Since the sanctuary's creation in 1985, the area's mostly Creole landowners have responded generously to the international scientific community's concern about the primate's dwindling habitat.

The current situation is a dramatic change from only 15 years ago, when the howler monkeys were frequent targets of Mayan Indians and Guatemalan refugees (who killed them for meat), as well as unscrupulous poachers (who sold them as pets). Both practices are

"Caution—Baboon Bridge" sign alerts travelers along road at the Community Baboon Sanctuary (Photo by Richard Mahler)

now against the law throughout Belize, where only licensed hunters are allowed to legally stalk wild game. The howlers have also been hard hit over the years by hurricanes, which destroy their treetop aeries, and by yellow fever, the same deadly disease that affects humans. But more significantly, they have been victims of deforestation. As arboreal vegetarians partial to wild fruits and flower blossoms, they need a thick forest canopy to survive.

To preserve this critical habitat along the Belize River, about 25 miles inland from the Caribbean Sea, nearly 100 farmers in an 18-square-mile area have agreed to maintain corridors of tall broadleaf jungle along the borders of their fields, to refrain from cutting such favored food trees as sapodilla, roseapple, fig, trumpet, and hogplum, and to protect 66-foot-wide strips of forest along the riverbank. These practices not only ensure that the monkeys will have a safe place to live, eat, and raise their families, but also help reduce erosion, minimize river siltation, and allow more rapid regeneration of the soil after slash-and-burn agricultural clearing. The smaller plots of cultivated land are now hedged in by thick vegetation that will quickly invade the area once it loses its productivity.

Organizers began asking their neighbors to sign conservation pledges in the mid-1980s, and so far not a single farmer has refused or withdrawn from the sanctuary. Locals have found that visitors help them out financially by hiring guides, patronizing businesses, and staying at informal bed and breakfasts that residents have set up in their homes. The women of the village often prepare hot meals for tourists, and the men take foreigners on leisurely canoe trips to observe the flora and fauna along the meandering Belize River. Also, several small stores sell food and drinks.

Like Bermudian Landing, seven other villages within the sanctuary are gradually attracting tourism business. They bear the sort of colorful names encountered all over Belize, including Double Head Cabbage, Scotland Halfmoon, and Flowers Bank. The howler population has expanded so vigorously that the preserve's boundaries now may also have expanded to include other villages.

"When I came here, I immediately noticed that the monkeys had a strong, viable community and the forest was relatively intact," recalls Robert Horwich, a zoologist from the University of Wisconsin who helped develop the plan for a voluntary wildlife sanctuary operated by local residents. "People seemed to genuinely like the howlers," notes Horwich, who still comes every spring to study the animals. "It struck me as logical to ask villagers to help preserve this habitat."

Backed by a coalition that includes the Zoological Society of Greater Milwaukee, the World Wildlife Fund, the Lincoln Park Zoological Society, the International Primate Protection League, and Belize Audubon, the Community Baboon Sanctuary now embraces a 20-mile stretch of Belize River watershed. The facility employs a full-time manager, two nature guides, and an education director. The latter takes the conservation message to classrooms throughout the country. Half the sanctuary's visitors are Belizean schoolchildren, most of whom had never seen a wild monkey before. (Since almost all of the reserve is on private land, visitors are asked not to stray from designated trails without a guide.) The natural history museum here is arguably the best in Belize.

Howler monkey troops, ranging from four to eight individuals, seem to appreciate the efforts being made to save them. Although the primates still spend most of their lives high in the tree boughs, they sometimes scamper along the ground within a few feet of lucky observers. The howlers' loud rasping call is used most often by dominant males to mark territorial boundaries between the troops they lead. The monkeys, including females, also howl when waking up in the morning and before going to sleep at night. Some locals swear that they also become vocal before the onset of big rainstorms. Howlers can reach up to 4 feet in length and weigh about 50 pounds when full-grown. Like other monkeys, they nurse their young, use their hands during feeding, and communicate by human-like facial expressions.

The black howler is one of only two species of primate found in Belize. Its primate cousin, the spider monkey, prefers wetter forests at higher elevations. In the entire world, there are only five other species of howler.

By 1992, the monkey colony along the Belize River was strong enough to withstand the transfer of some of its members to the Cockscomb Basin Wildlife Sanctuary, about 80 miles to the south. They may also be reintroduced to the Shipstern Nature Reserve and other protected areas. In these locations, a combination of hurricane damage, hunting, and yellow fever has wiped out indigenous troops of howlers during the past 30 years.

Another side benefit of the Community Baboon Sanctuary's success is the resurgence of other wildlife in the protected area. Nearly 200 bird species have been identified, along with dozens of different mammals, including jaguars, ocelots, paca, and deer. Researchers are also coming here to study the highly endangered hickatee river turtle, which is now holding its own within the sanctuary's borders.

Though modified by centuries of selective logging and small-scale farming, local forests still support about 100 tree species and scores of varieties of vines, shrubs, flowers, and herbs. Many wild orchids and bromeliads can be seen clinging to the trunks of tall trees.

The sanctuary is the winter home of many migratory birds that fly to Belize every year from as far away as Canada. Colorful year-round residents include parakeets, parrots, toucans, and tanagers.

Besides a close-up look at Belize's flora and fauna, a visit to the sanctuary also affords an intimate view of life in a rural Creole village, where little has changed over the decades. Until only a few years ago, for example, these villages lacked bridges, all-weather roads, telephones, and electricity. Many still do without the latter two. The residents are invariably gregarious and friendly, happy to share a funny story about their "baboons" over a glass of homemade whiskey or wine. *"Baboon ya de fu we,"* is a favorite Creole slogan in the villages along the river; it means, "We're for the baboons!"

If You Go: The Community Baboon Sanctuary is in north-central Belize, an easy day trip from Belize City. The site, about 30 miles from Belize City, can be reached by car in about an hour via the Northern or Western Highway. From either direction, take the Burrell Boom cutoff and follow the signs to Bermudian Landing. Note that there are only a few stores and no gasoline stations within 20 miles of the reserve. Several informal bed and breakfasts are available in the sanctuary and outlying villages. Campsites (on the museum grounds only) are $2 per tent per night. Meals cost around $4 each. Recreational vehicles can park overnight next to the museum for a small fee.

Although several commercial lodges operate near the Community Baboon Sanctuary, we urge you to stay with one of the local families that provide accommodations, meals, and guiding services as part of the sanctuary's local economic development plan. If you decide to stay, eat, or explore elsewhere, please try to patronize businesses that make contributions to the howler monkey project. We have been told that some facilities serve meals that make use of hickatee and other endangered species. While eating wild game is an age-old custom here, environmentally sensitive travelers will avoid this practice. The sanctuary's headquarters is a good source of information about reputable businesses in the area.

Three independent buses are operated by local residents (Oswald McFadzean, Sydney Russell, and Valentine Young) on imprecise schedules. They generally leave Belize City between noon and 12:30 each day (except Sundays and holidays) and return from Bermudian Landing at about 6:00 the following morning. Mr. Russell's orange bus runs Saturday but not Thursday, departing from the corner of Orange and Euphrates in Belize City at noon on Saturdays and

12:30 p.m. on weekdays. On Fridays and Saturdays, the buses fill up quickly, so don't be late. Taxi drivers from Belize City typically charge $75 and up for a round-trip to the howler sanctuary.

Specific directions on getting to the sanctuary by car or bus are available from the Belize Audubon office at the old Customs House in Belize City (tel. 2-77369). Belize Audubon can also make arrangements for groups interested in touring the area, as well as for overnight accommodations. As of mid-1995, the only direct contact with sanctuary headquarters was by two-way radio, which is sometimes unreliable. It is possible, however, to simply stop at the sanctuary office, buy a field guide, tour the sanctuary with one of the nature guides, arrange to stay overnight with a local family (about $10 per person), and eat home-cooked meals ($3 and up).

Guide fees are about $2.50 an hour or $25 a day. Canoe trips are also roughly $25. The free services of a local guide are included with the $15 purchase of a sanctuary guidebook, which is recommended.

Warning: Some visitors have complained in recent years about unauthorized, unqualified guides giving inadequate tours of the area or even abandoning them on trails. Check in at the visitor's center before hiring a guide, in order to make sure he or she is approved by the sanctuary's managers.

Because the jungle trails are often overgrown and muddy, rubber boots, long-sleeved shirts, trousers, hats, and insect repellent are advised. Always check with the headquarters and obtain a map before heading out.

Donations to the sanctuary's tax-deductible endowment fund are welcome. Checks should be made payable to Howlers Forever, Inc. and sent to Robert "Baboon Man" Horwich, RD 1, Box 96, Gays Mills, WI 54631. Donors of $50 or more receive a sanctuary-theme poster by artist Caroline Beckett, along with the group's quarterly newsletter.

The recently updated book *A Belizean Rain Forest: The Community Baboon Sanctuary* has been written by Robert Horwich and Jon Lyon for distribution to Belizean schools and interested individuals. It contains a wealth of information about Belize's flora and fauna, and can be ordered from the Howlers Forever address above for $12, plus $2 postage and handling.

The Belize Zoo and Tropical Education Center

One place where you are guaranteed to see native animals in their natural surroundings is the Belize Zoo. Most of us regard zoos as anything but a natural setting; however, as you know by now, things are done a bit differently in Belize. Instead of placing its animals behind bars in severe-looking cages, the zoo's managers have created an intimate, cozy atmosphere by putting their creatures in chicken-wire enclosures beneath a shady forest canopy. Each of the animals is referred to by its own pet name—from Sugar, the purring ocelot, to Rambo, the keel-billed toucan—and all are well cared for.

The Belize Zoo is located about 30 miles west of Belize City and 14 miles east of Belmopan on the Western Highway. This is another easy day trip from Belize City, as well as a good diversion en route to the Cayo District, Caracol, or Tikal.

The philosophy that permeates the zoo's exhibits is one of respect for all wildlife. Hand-lettered signs remind visitors that practices such as poaching and live capturing continue to threaten the survival of several unusual Belizean natives, including cats, macaws, and monkeys. In fact, many of the creatures held by the zoo are "pets" that were abandoned by their owners after they became too big, too wild, or too unwanted. Guides at the zoo are closely involved in a conservation outreach program designed to teach visiting Belizean schoolchildren (as many as 300 a day) about the natural wonders of their homeland.

A particular favorite is Belize's national animal, the Baird's tapir, which thrives at the zoo. Throughout Central America, this large but shy creature is in trouble: its future survival as a species is threatened by habitat destruction and hunting. The tapir, a relative of the hippo, is the largest of all native Belizean land animals, and adults may weigh up to 650 pounds. The zoo's female tapir, April, has endeared

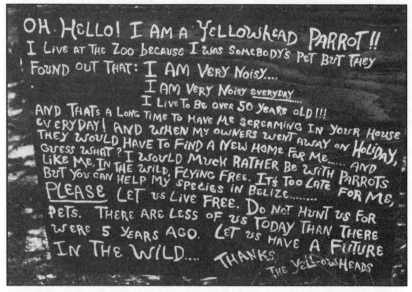

OH · HELLO! I AM A YELLOWHEAD PARROT!! I LIVE AT THE ZOO because I WAS SOMEBODY'S PET BUT THEY FOUND OUT THAT: I AM VERY NOISY.... I AM VERY NOISY EVERYDAY. I LIVE TO BE OVER 50 YEARS OLD!!! AND THAT'S A LONG TIME TO HAVE ME SCREAMING IN YOUR HOUSE EVERYDAY! AND WHEN MY OWNERS WENT AWAY ON HOLIDAY, THEY WOULD HAVE TO FIND A NEW HOME FOR ME..... AND GUESS WHAT? I WOULD MUCH RATHER BE WITH PARROTS LIKE ME, IN THE WILD, FLYING FREE. IT'S TOO LATE FOR ME, BUT YOU CAN HELP MY SPECIES IN BELIZE........ PLEASE LET US LIVE FREE. DO NOT HUNT US FOR PETS. THERE ARE LESS OF US TODAY THAN THERE WERE 5 YEARS AGO. LET US HAVE A FUTURE IN THE WILD.... THANKS. THE YELLOWHEADS

The sign in front of the yellowhead parrot cage at the Belize Zoo illustrates the pro-conservation philosophy of its founders (Photo by Richard Mahler)

herself to thousands of Belizean children, who have watched her frolic in her jungle paddock. April's pairing with a new mate reflects one of the major goals of the zoo—to give every animal a partner and thus ensure that future visitors will always be able to view each species at close range. Captive breeding programs for creatures such as the citreoline trogon and iguana have also been carried out at the Belize Zoo.

At least 100 other animals can be seen here, including the endangered scarlet macaw, jaguarundi, margay, jaguar, anteater, and great curassow. The assembly includes some 18 mammal species, 12 bird species, 6 reptile species, and 2 insect species. All live within areas that are as large and as close to their natural habitats as could be achieved by the zoo personnel.

The Belize Zoo was founded in 1983 by its director, Sharon Matola, after wildlife filmmaker Richard Foster's budget was cut and he was left with 17 animal "stars" that had no movies to appear in and no place to go. Matola, Foster's assistant, was told to disband the troupe of jaguars, coatimundis, peccaries, pumas, and other animals that had been trained to "act" in nature documentaries.

Instead of abandoning them, Matola boldly painted a description in front of each creature's enclosure and put a "Belize Zoo" sign in front of the compound. Success came only after she devoted thousands of hours to finding ways to feed and house the animals, while at the same time cultivating countrywide interest in their well-being. Matola's credo is manifest in the way she has always run the zoo: public awareness and education are critical to wildlife conservation. Her nature-oriented storybooks have become favorites of Belizean children who, in turn, are convincing their parents to adopt lifestyles that protect the country's environment. The zoo's education director has organized countrywide lectures that have made a noticeable impact on prevailing attitudes toward native flora and fauna.

Matola also organized and led scientific assessment teams to study the ecology of Belize's critical habitat areas, such as the Raspaculo wilderness and the Columbia Forest Reserve. A 1990 zoo-organized expedition to Columbia, a subtropical moist forest in southern Belize, yielded such treasures as an unusual type of Mayan pottery, an amphibian of the genus *Eleutherodactylus* that was new to science, and a bird that had never before been recorded in Belize (the common wood nymph [*Thalurania furcata*]).

The zoo site incorporates approximately 1,700 acres of land, with an actual animal exhibit area of about 30 acres. Such Belize-loving celebrities as actor Harrison Ford and musician/author Jimmy Buffett made donations that enabled the zoo to move to expanded, 28-acre quarters in late 1991.

A large waterbird aviary was opened in 1993, and future plans include a butterfly exhibit, a freshwater aquarium (with advice from the famous Monterey Bay Aquarium), and a reptile center. A biologist by training, Matola works constantly to improve the zoo and has taken advantage of Belize's thawed relations with Guatemala to acquire both a jaguarundi and a jaguar from that country.

The nearby Tropical Education Center is a sort of nature school for Belizeans, operated by University College of Belize, with early funding in part by Chicago's MacArthur Foundation. The property was previously owned by Dora Weyer, one of Belize's first conservation leaders and a founding member of the Belize Audubon Society. Weyer retired to the United States in 1989, and one of her conservation legacies is a 140-acre complex that has a self-guided nature trails, visitors' dormitory, lecture rooms, a library, and offices for its Belizean staff. Schoolchildren and college students who have never spent a night in the bush come here to spend a few days surrounded by nature. Solar energy powers the entire compound.

If You Go: The Belize Zoo and Tropical Education Center are clearly marked on the Western Highway at about Mile 29. Going west from Belize City, you will encounter the Tropical Education Center first on your left, then the old zoo site on your right, and finally the well-marked new zoo a little farther along, also on the right. The visitor center, which includes an excellent gift shop and playground, is about one-half mile off the highway on a dirt access road. To contact the zoo during business hours, call 92-3310 or 81-3004.

Taxis are easy to arrange from either Belize City or Belmopan. Many package tours also stop at the site. Expect to pay $70 and up for a round-trip.

Buses from Belize City run virtually every hour throughout the day. Check Venus Bus Lines (tel. 2-73354) or Batty Brothers Bus Service (tel. 2-72025) for fares and schedules. Drivers will be happy to pick you up and drop you off on the highway.

There are biting and stinging insects (uncaged) at the zoo, and a good repellent is strongly advised. We recommend keeping your arms, legs, and ankles covered while observing the animals, since wildlife tends to attract flying creatures that pester humans. Admission is $1 for Belizeans, $1.50 for military personnel, and $5 for foreign citizens. The zoo is open from 9:30 a.m. to 4:00 p.m. daily, except major holidays. Zoo memberships (starting at $25 for individuals) are available by writing to Box 474, Belize City. Supporters receive a newsletter about the Belize Zoo's ongoing activities, and contributions are used for conservation education.

Monkey Bay Wildlife Sanctuary and National Park

Located along the Western Highway about 2 miles west of the Belize Zoo and 31.5 miles west of Belize City, is Monkey Bay Wildlife Sanctuary. Adjacent to the property, across the Sibun River, is Monkey Bay National Park. Monkey Bay Wildlife Sanctuary was established on Earth Day 1990 as a privately owned and operated protected area encompassing 1,070 acres of mostly pine savanna, cohune palm, and tropical gallery forest, along with freshwater wetlands, lagoons, and river habitat. Monkey Bay National Park was legally established in May 1994 and together with the Sanctuary, comprises a 3,300-acre wildlands corridor spanning the Sibun River watershed.

Among the sanctuary's attractions are rolling jungle ridges, 2 miles of nature trails, and Sibun River frontage that includes a secluded bathing beach. The field research station and other facilities—all open to visitors—are part of an evolving permaculture design that integrates solar power systems, rainwater catchment, a biogas latrine, reforestation, composting, and raised-bed organic gardens into a nature-conscious living style.

Since its establishment by an Arkansas conservationist, observers at Monkey Bay have reported seeing at least 220 species of birds within the reserve's borders, including parrots, toucans, crakes, trogons, flycatchers, and cuckoos. Other wildlife sightings include jaguar, puma, deer, peccary, crocodile, iguana, tapir, and coatimundi.

Visitors might wonder why this particular name was chosen, since no monkey species are listed among the native denizens. Monkey Bay retains a name given to the property at a time when black howler and white-faced spider monkeys frequented this stretch of the Sibun River. A hurricane in 1978 destroyed the tall forest canopy habitat that these monkeys favor, forcing the remaining animals to retreat to the limestone karst hills visible on the southern horizon. However, on two occasions in 1993, monkeys were again observed near the sanctuary.

"We hope that with more recovery time, the forest here will again host these two endangered species," the sanctuary's co-founder,

Matthew Miller, told us. "In order to enhance this recovery process and provide an attractive and well-protected habitat, the Monkey Bay staff has actively been planting tropical forest trees, including mahogany, sapodilla, balsam, baboon cap, and velvet apple."

According to Monkey Bay's mission statement, the project's overall purpose "is to create a self-supporting economic entity so the sanctuary can, essentially, protect itself from conversion to another use," namely, agriculture, mining, and logging. Conservation and education organizations in Belize, Japan, and the United States are helping to further Monkey Bay's goals by expanding membership and organizing natural history-based study tours to Belize. Several North American high school and university groups participate in Monkey Bay's experiential-based learning programs, and visitation from Japan is also increasing. Belizean students visit Monkey Bay regularly for guided walking tours of the tropical forest. On neighboring lands, they learn about human impacts on the environment, including river mining and monoculture agribusiness.

A large wooden field research station at Monkey Bay (dubbed "The Barn") accommodates a classroom, library, and natural-history display room. It doubles as accommodations for visiting researchers and teachers. Monkey Bay is considered an ideal location for earth literacy and natural-history education programs, and offers home-stay opportunities with families in rural villages for visitors with a thirst for cultural immersion. Monkey Bay is also one of the few places in Belize where visitors are not only allowed, but encouraged to camp. Tenters are offered one of several large, thatch-covered raised camping platforms for a minimal per-person fee. Nature hiking, photography, picnicking, swimming, canoeing, and self-directed study are also available. Children of all ages are encouraged to visit. On-site arrangements, internship inquiries, or group study programs should be made through Matthew Miller or Marga Waals, Monkey Bay's resident managers. Contact Monkey Bay Wildlife Sanctuary at P.O. Box 187, Belmopan, Belize. (tel. 8-23180; fax. 8-23361).

If You Go: The well-marked dirt entrance road to Monkey Bay Wildlife Sanctuary is at Mile 31.5 on the Western Highway, about 45 minutes by car west of Belize City. Local buses will drop you off at the junction, and you can walk the short distance to the field station. A taxi from the international airport costs about $50. There is no admission fee to the sanctuary, and overnight visitors are welcome, although space is limited. Within walking distance of Monkey Bay is J.B.'s Kool Spot, a restaurant and bar (with occasional live music) popular with Belizeans and foreigners alike.

Stann Creek District

Until recently, the southern coast of Belize was ignored by the vast majority of visitors. Relatively isolated from the rest of the country by poor roads, rugged mountains, muddy swamps, and an almost perpetually damp climate, many of the region's attractions were (and, for the most part, still are) seldom seen and little developed. This situation is changing, however, as entrepreneurs move in and offer travel options ranging in scope from rugged rain forest treks (Belize's only true rain forests lie in the southern part of the nation) to luxurious sportfishing resorts on palm-studded beaches. Yet the most intriguing destinations in southern Belize continue to be its large tracts of unspoiled wilderness and long stretches of pristine coastline, plus an unusual mix of cultures that includes Mayan Indians, Garifuna (Black Caribs), Guatemalan refugees, Creoles, and U.S. expatriates.

The easiest ways to reach the far-flung coastal communities are by air (fast but relatively expensive) or boat (slower but cheaper). Other alternatives are private car or scheduled bus service. Daily buses fill the bumpy Hummingbird Highway that links Belmopan with Dangriga, continuing from Dangriga to Hopkins, Placencia, and Punta Gorda via the unpaved Southern Highway. (A gravel-surfaced shortcut, known variously as the Lagoon Road and the Manatee Cut-off, heads directly south from the Western Highway near Hattieville and rejoins the Hummingbird Highway outside Dangriga.) Although paved, the 52-mile Hummingbird Highway is scenic and uncrowded, but notorious for its bone-jarring potholes and muddy bogs. Allow at least 2 hours for the drive from Belmopan to Dangriga. Along the

Mayan children collecting firewood (Photo by Kevin Schafer)

way, you may wish to stop at the Blue Hole National Park, Five Blues Lake National Park, St. Herman's Cave (see Cayo District in Chapter 6 for descriptions) or the Hershey Chocolate Company's large cacao plantation. There are also a couple of large citrus plantations where, as at Hershey's, tours are available by appointment.

Midway along the Hummingbird Highway you enter the Stann Creek District, the more populous of Belize's two southern districts. Although Dangriga is its administrative center and largest town, several other communities are well worth a visit.

Gales Point

At the culmination of a dead-end, 15-mile dirt road that stretches through swampy terrain north of Dangriga, the village of Gales Point offers visitors a refreshing dose of rural Creole hospitality, some unparalleled nature attractions, and a great Belizean example of community conservation. Although it is not difficult to reach by road, the village is more frequently approached from the north by chartered boat via the Southern Lagoon, upon which Gales Point Village sits. Small craft can make an inland passage from Belize City (20 miles away) via the Burdon Canal (now a protected nature reserve) and Boom's Creek in only a couple of hours, navigating a complex maze of waterways. An alternative is heading directly south along the Inner Channel in open water and then following a narrow estuary across Manatee Bar into Southern Lagoon, also called Manatee Lagoon. A limestone escarpment on the northwest bank of this lagoon is the site of several caves that can be explored as an interesting side trip. We also recommend a boat ride up Soldier Creek (also called Plantation Creek), which has especially abundant orchids and other air plants.

The name Gales Point describes both a community of about 350 souls and a narrow 2-mile finger of land jutting up from the south end of Southern Lagoon. The village was founded by logwood cutters many years before Belize became a British colony and is inhabited mostly by Creole farmers and fishermen. The lagoons and estuaries near the village are full of marine life and represent one of the region's most important strongholds for the Caribbean manatee. These shy mammals, which look somewhat like walrus, feed on the thick grasses and other vegetation found in these lagoons. Local guides are happy to direct tourists to several manatee feeding areas where the gentle beasts are most often seen. The nearest feeding ground is a few hundred yards from the village.

Two extensive aerial surveys conducted in 1994 by volunteer pilots from the conservation group LightHawk—in collaboration with the Belize Fisheries Department, the Coastal Zone Management Unit, and scientists from the Mexican Centro de Investigaciones de Quintana Roo—yielded some interesting and encouraging results about Belize's manatee populations. These surveys showed a minimum manatee population of 264 for the region, which includes all of Belize and Chetumal Bay (just north of the border in Mexico)—the highest population of manatees in all of Central America. Aerial survey results indicating a high relative abundance of manatees in lagoons gives scientific proof to the importance of these lagoons as habitat for this endangered species. Southern Lagoon has historically been one of Belize's richest areas for this marine mammal.

In 1992, residents created the Gales Point Manatee Community Sanctuary to protect the manatee and develop conservation-oriented tourism. This cooperative venture, part of the government-mandated Manatee Special Development Area, pools local skills and resources to provide boat trips, wildlife observation, sportfishing, and cave exploration. About 15 residents provide boating and/or guiding services, while some 20 homes are open to overnight visitors. Other residents produce and sell handcrafted items such as tie-tie baskets and hats. Cashew and berry wines, as well as mango and cashew preserves, are made and sold locally. This visitor-related activity is designed to enhance Gales Point's base of subsistence agriculture without jeopardizing the community's rural character and beautiful environment.

Recently, local conservation efforts have focused on protecting endangered hawksbill turtles, since nearby Manatee Bar is one of the few known nesting beaches for this endangered marine reptile in all of Central America. With assistance and training from Wisconsin-based Community Conservation Consultants, area residents have installed wire mesh to protect nesting hawksbill turtles from predation near Manatee Bar. As a result of this community-driven work, some 12,000 turtle hatchlings made it into the Caribbean in 1994.

With the help of international organizations, residents have installed buoys and signs to help protect the manatee from speeding boats, planted disease-resistant coconuts, and installed improved sanitation facilities to maintain water quality in the lagoon. These seemingly small efforts are critically important to the long-term viability of small communities like Gales Point, which have predicated much of their future on the growth of natural-history tourism.

Boat excursions from Gales Point take visitors past small cayes in the various bodies of water—particularly Bird Island in Northern Lagoon—that are important breeding grounds for iguanas, crocodiles, and waterbirds, including the white ibis and boat-billed heron. Aquatic flora and fauna are abundant here, since a tremendous amount of nutrient-rich runoff flows through these passageways en route from the Maya Mountains to the Caribbean Sea. The tangled mass of mangrove forests along the shoreline is an important nursery for young shrimp, crabs, lobster, and fish. Wildlife in the area includes deer, peccary, armadillo, gibnut, and various cats.

If You Go: Upscale accommodations are provided by the Manatee Lodge (co-owned by the Hidden Valley Inn), oriented to sportfishermen and nature lovers. Remodeled in 1993, the 12-room facility offers boat tours to manatee breathing holes and a turtle nesting beach. Foreign anglers are attracted to the several species of game fish that abound in these waters, notably tarpon, snook, and cubera.

Simple bed-and-breakfast accommodations and tent sites are available through the Gales Point Bed and Breakfast Association, with no advance reservations required. Call the village's community telephone at 5-22087. A planned seven-room waterfront lodge, the Gales Point Cooperative Hotel, may be open by the time you visit.

Tour operators arranging trips to the area include the recommended S & L Travel and Jal's Travel in Belize City, Pelican Beach Resort in Dangriga, and Ricardo's Beach Huts on Bluefield Range Caye. Competent local boatmen include Allen "Passo" Andrewin and his brother, Mose. For a truly unusual cultural experience, visitors may wish to enroll in the highly recommended Maroon Creole Drum School, operated by Emmeth Young, one of the best drummers in Belize. Young offers camping on his land (meals included) for a modest fee and charges $5 an hour for expert instruction in making and playing the traditional Belizean drum. You'll learn a good deal about Creole history and culture in the process. Advance reservations are preferred, since Young performs in Belize and other countries from time to time. Write him c/o Gales Point Village, Belize District, Belize, C.A.

Oceanic Society Expeditions offers trips in which participants are asked to help scientific researchers assess the distribution and habitat use of resident manatees, and to protect hawksbill turtle hatchlings from predators. Guests stay in village guest quarters and campsites, taking meals with local residents. The nine-day expedition includes a trip to nearby Ben Lomond Cave.

Dangriga

The name of this busy port town was changed from Stann Creek to Dangriga some years ago to honor the proud Garifuna people who make up the majority of its 9,000 residents. The name means "standing water" in the Garifuna language, a reference to the brackish pools that sometimes form when the rain-swollen Stann Creek overflows its banks on its way through town toward the Caribbean. Dangriga was settled by European traders and farmers in the late 17th century, then became an important shipping center during colonial times.

The Garifuna (also known as Black Caribs or Garinagu, which means "Garifuna people") are a distinct and close-knit ethnic group of mixed West African and Caribbean Indian ancestry who arrived here in great numbers beginning in 1823, after civil unrest along the Honduran coast drove them north. The Garifuna history begins many years earlier, when shipwrecked slaves escaped to the British-controlled islands of Dominica and St. Vincent in the West Indies. These West Africans (mostly males) intermingled with aboriginal Red and Yellow Caribs (mostly females), sharing many customs and rituals as the years progressed. Their mixed-blood offspring developed impressive skills in fishing, farming, and hunting. They also remained staunchly independent, refusing to bargain with the Europeans who tried to subdue them and take over their lands. For several decades they successfully resisted colonization. Finally, in 1795, the Garifuna chief was killed by an English soldier's bullet. His conquered people were rounded up and shipped off to the Bay Islands off Honduras, at that time a part of the British empire. Over the next 25 years, small bands of restless Garifuna wandered up and down the Central

American coast, establishing settlements in what are now Belize, Guatemala, Costa Rica, and Nicaragua, as well as mainland Honduras.

On November 19, 1823, a large group of Garifuna from the Bay Islands joined about 200 others who had settled at the mouth of Stann Creek some twenty years earlier. A Puritan trading post had been built on this spot and the traders called these structures "stands." Over time, this term was locally corrupted into "stann," and the revised name stuck. The date of the mass Garifuna landing, November 19, is still celebrated loudly and enthusiastically each year as Settlement Day, a Belizean national holiday.

Because Dangriga is one of the largest Garifuna communities among the many now spread along the coastline of four Central American nations and the Windward Islands, a visit here provides an excellent opportunity to learn about a fascinating Afro-Indian subculture that is little known outside Belize. The ideal time to come is on Settlement Day and, if possible, the week leading up to the November 19 celebration. Hundreds of Garifuna from throughout Central America and the Caribbean flock to Dangriga for the festivities. The streets are alive with dancing, drumming, and impromptu music concerts. (At other times of the year, several nightclubs offer indigenous music and dancing.) Feasts and celebrations last far into the night. Scheduled events include a reenactment of the arrival of Garifuna leader Alejo Beni and his boats from Honduras, plus a fascinating religious ceremony in the Catholic church which combines European, African and Carib rituals. (Most Garifuna—like most Belizeans—now consider themselves at least nominally Roman Catholic.) The ceremonies are performed in the Garifuna language, a unique mixture of West Indian, West African, Spanish, English, and French words. Interestingly, there is a long-standing gender difference in grammar, with males following more of an African pattern and females following more of a Carib pattern.

Many outsiders, including Belize's early white colonists, have contended that the traditional spiritual beliefs of the Garifuna are akin to Haitian-style voodoo, which is only partially true. The central focus of Garifuna religion is the mysterious and magical practice of *obeah*, originating in West African traditions brought to the Americas during the 1600s. Through the use of fetishes, amulets, symbols, and rituals, followers believe spiritual energy—both positive and negative—can be directed to individuals. Indigo crosses on the foreheads of small children, for example, keep away bad spirits, and the blood of sacrificed animals (usually chickens or pigs) wards off evil. A small cloth doll stuffed with black feathers, called a *puchinga*, may be buried under an enemy's doorstep to bring about tribulation, illness, or even death.

At the opposite end of the spectrum, a kind of white-magic healing ceremony and feast of reconciliation known as the *dugu* is also used to rid the community of evil spirits. This ritual, rarely observed by outsiders, takes place over the course of a full week and is accompanied by animal sacrifices, hypnotic music, and nonstop dancing.

Through the intercession of a *byei*, or shaman, the Garifuna believe they can communicate with the dead, thereby tapping into the power of their ancestors. Some expatriate Belizeans come from as far as the United States and Canada to attend special ceremonies, called *gubida*, whereby contact with the deceased is used to cure sick relatives or avenge evildoings.

Practitioners of obeah believe they can make contact with the dead whenever certain ceremonies are performed with the accompaniment of monotonous, trancelike drumming, singing, and dancing. These performances may last all night, or even days on end, without a break. Ethnomusicologists have noted that the rhythms and call-and-response patterns of the Garifuna are very similar to those used in the religious and social rituals of West Africa, where they presumably originated. The practice of playing with sticks is also African.

The Garifuna's devotion to their culture has set them apart from other Belizeans, particularly those of European descent. So fearful were the early colonials of Garifuna practices that traders from Dangriga and neighboring villages were officially barred from staying overnight in Belize City. Those bringing their produce and handicrafts to the public market were ordered to be out of town by sundown. As recently as the 1960s, Garifuna were afraid to hold dugu ceremonies in Dangriga for fear local magistrates might disapprove. This situation has changed dramatically and the Garifuna are now widely respected, constituting a large percentage of Belizean school-teachers, civil servants, and physicians.

It is in arts and crafts that the Garifuna particularly excel. Their drum-makers are revered for a perceived ability to induce the obeah magic through the music of their instruments. Dances are performed to the beat of three drums of varying sizes, traditionally made out of carved cedar trees or sea turtle shells. Some of the younger Garifuna have incorporated these ceremonial instruments into reggae and calypso musical stylings, giving birth to a distinctive style of music known as "punta rock," now popular throughout Belize. More traditional groups that perform in Dangriga include the Turtle Shell Band and Warribaggabagga Dancers. The opportunity to see a performance by the latter, critically acclaimed group, which has toured throughout the world, should not be missed.

On Settlement Day, Dangriga's main street (St. Vincent) is closed to traffic so that musicians, costumed dancers, and revelers can parade with abandon, carnival-style. In the weeks leading up to Christmas, garishly painted and masked John-Canoe (also spelled Yan-kunu) dancers perform in the streets for gifts of rum, money, and candy. The dance is performed only by men, who imitate the strident movements of a slave master. At midnight on Christmas Eve, the town echoes with the deep blast of several hundred hollow conch shells blown simultaneously.

These vivid community rituals are favored subjects of several well-known Garifuna painters, residents of Dangriga, whose studios are open to visitors. Most have adopted a kind of folk-primitive realism recalling the simple artwork of Haiti. The paintings emphasize bright colors, flat perspective, and festive or rural themes. Pen Cayetano's studio closed in 1992, but fellow painter Benjamin Nicholas—probably the most famous Belizean artist—still welcomes visitors at his 27 Oak Street gallery, near the Bonefish Hotel. Nicholas' paintings are on display in public buildings and offices throughout Belize. Accomplished drum-maker Austin Rodriguez has a similar studio at 32 Tubroos Street, where he sells baskets, masks, and reed purses, as well as fine drums (priced from $50 and up). Next door to Rodriguez is a boatbuilder who carves dories out of a single tree trunk. PJ's Gift

Shop (21 St. Vincent) and the Treasure Shop (64 Commerce St.) are recommended for smaller handicrafts. Be sure to visit Melinda's Historical Museum (21 St. Vincent, tel. 5-22266), which displays Garifuna artifacts such as the mahogany badaya bowls used in making cassava flour. The museum is open ($1 admission) from 9:00 a.m. to noon and 2:00 to 5:00 p.m. daily except Thursday and Sunday. Studio and gallery hours vary from place to place.

While visiting Dangriga, try to sample some traditional Garifuna cuisine, which vaguely resembles the "soul food" of the American South. Home-brew cashew wine and "local dynamite" (a mixture of raw coconut milk and Belizean rum) are popular lubricants, along with chicory-flavored coffee. Endless varieties of cassava bread—all delicious—can be purchased from the smiling housewives who make them from scratch. The preparation of such breads, using a flour made from potato-like cassava roots that have been strained and ground by hand, is a time-honored Garifuna practice which takes at least two days to accomplish. The cassava's importance to local people cannot be overstated, and in fact the word "Garifuna" roughly translates as "the cassava-eating people." Other popular dishes are hudut, masked plantain (also called "plantain fu-fu"), and boiled fish in coconut sauce (known as "fish sere"). Not to be missed are the sweet oranges and grapefruits grown on nearby citrus plantations and in backyard gardens.

If You Go: With a couple of notable exceptions, Dangriga's hotels are generally modest and have few amenities. Travelers have recommended Pal's Guest House, Río Mar Hotel (which arranges lodging and boats for Tobacco Caye visitors), Soffie's Hotel, Hub Guest House (next to the bus depot), Riverside Hotel, and Bonefish Hotel (owned by the Zabaneh family, which also runs the Blue Marlin Lodge on South Water Caye). The cheapest of the lot is the Dangriga Central Hotel at 199 Commerce Street; and the most upscale are the Bonefish, at 15 Mahogany Street, and Pelican Beach Resort, at the north end of town next to the Dangriga airstrip.

There are several Chinese cafés, a classic fishermen's diner (The Ship's Mate) and a handful of other restaurants: try Burger King (no relation to the franchise) or the Pelican Beach for the best selection.

Dangriga also has bars, banks, gas stations, and general stores. Punta rock can be widely heard on holidays or at one of several nightclubs: the Wrong House, Son-Flo Disco, and Dada's Disco. Tourist information is cheerfully dispensed at PJ's Gift Shop, and airplane tickets can be purchased at The Treasure Chest, which doubles as a souvenir store and travel agency.

About a mile south of Dangriga is the enormous citrus processing facility at Commerce Bight, where a large pipeline sends fruit concentrate directly to the holds of oceangoing vessels anchored offshore. Along this stretch of private beach are a few campsites that can be leased from either of the two owners, Mr. Williams and Mr. Sue, for a reasonable fee.

Because of its location and services, Dangriga is a good base for excursions to the southern cayes and atolls or to the nearby Gales Point Manatee Community Sanctuary, the Cockscomb Basin Wildlife Sanctuary, the Garifuna village of Hopkins, and the Mopan Indian village of Maya Center. Accommodations on Tobacco and South Water Cayes, along with the nearby biological research stations on Carrie Bow and Wee Wee Cayes, are easily reached by boat from Dangriga. Inquire at the Río Mar Hotel, near where Stann Creek enters the sea.

Several bus companies, notably the Z-Line, have daily departures to and from Dangriga via the Hummingbird and Southern Highways. The town is about 35 miles by boat from Belize City, 105 miles via the Hummingbird Highway (through Belmopan), or 70 miles via the Lagoon Road cutoff. (As of mid-1995, buses were not operating on the cutoff route.)

The moderate-to-expensive Pelican Beach Resort—a former dance hall—is a favorite of many travelers, particularly those interested in the environment. A two-story wooden colonial building with high ceilings and a wide veranda that overlooks the Caribbean, this is a comfortable jumping-off point for excursions to the barrier reef or interior. From their location on a sandy beach adjacent to the airport, the Pelican's friendly, well-informed staff also arranges trips to the Cockscomb Basin, various Mayan ruins, Gales Point, Sittee River, Hopkins, and the barrier reef. Local tours of the town of Dangriga and nearby citrus plantations are also available. The resort is run by members of the Bowman family, a pioneering Belizean clan that has contributed to many of their nation's conservation achievements. Your hosts are Belize Audubon board member Therese Bowman Rath and her American husband, nature photographer Tony Rath, whose photographs and videotapes are on sale here. Tony's periodic slide shows at the Pelican are not to be missed.

Melinda Farm

A pleasant day trip from Dangriga is the 400-acre Melinda Farm, located in the foothills of the Maya Mountains. This verdant plantation is the home of Marie Sharp's (formerly Melinda's) Hot Pepper Sauce, a neon-orange condiment made from the spicy habañero chili pepper. (Products sold under the Melinda's label are now manufactured and distributed by a Costa Rican competitor.) Praised by connoisseurs as nature's hottest pepper, the tiny habañero grows only along the Yucatán peninsula and in a few other subtropical locations.

Marie and Jerry Sharp began making their hot pepper sauce atop a kitchen stove in 1983, and now the fiery product is one of Belize's most popular exports, gracing tables throughout the world. Their farm also produces oranges, Surinam cherries, papayas, mangos, guavas, pineapples, and passionfruit, most of which are used in the Sharps' extensive line of dried fruits, jams, and jellies. Their cottage-style factory relies on recipes personally developed by Marie and tested on discriminating Belizean palates. The farm, located at No. 1 Stann Creek Valley Farm Road, is open to visitors by appointment: call 5-22080 (fax 5-22299) or arrange through the Pelican Beach Resort in Dangriga. In the U.S., products can be ordered by calling (305) 477-2616. When ordering hot sauce, be sure to specify low, medium, or high "heat levels."

Hopkins

Situated on the sandy, palm-shaded inlet of a small bay some 8 miles south of Dangriga, Hopkins is a relaxed Garifuna fishing village of about 1,000 people. It can easily be reached by private boat or by following a 4-mile unpaved road from the Southern Highway. This route crosses a marshy landscape that is particularly rich in bird life.

Even the majestic jabiru stork has been sighted here, so keep a sharp eye out as you head for the village.

In Hopkins, life is simple and unhurried. People walk everywhere, using sandy paths that parallel the beach. There was no electricity or television here until 1992, and most residents subsist on small-scale fishing and farming. Women still tend the family garden plots and sing together as they weave red baskets or grate cassava roots on wooden slats. The men hand-carve their dugout canoes and weave fishnets out of hemp cloth. Children chase each other on the broad beach, build sand castles, and splash about in the aquamarine water.

At the end of each day, the fishermen of Hopkins haul their brightly painted dories beneath the coconut trees and join their families for the evening meal inside one-room houses, many of traditional thatch-and-pole construction. Homes are clustered together, with marvelous views of a gently curving bay to the east and misty jungle mountains to the west.

Eager to see Hopkins remain a self-sufficient traditional village and at the same time provide employment for its young people, a group of women have formed a tourism cooperative that operates the rustic Sandy Beach Lodge there. The lodge's several neotraditional cabañas, built with the assistance of the Barbados-based Caribbean Council of Churches, have been open since 1987 and provide an important source of income to the friendly people of Hopkins. Meals are also served at Sandy Beach, cooked Garifuna-style by local women. Entrepreneurs—many of them American and European expatriates—recently have built several accommodations, bars, and restaurants in the village. Overnight options now include the Tropical Paradise Hotel, Hopkins Guest House (offering canoeing, camping, and rafting), Ransom's Seaside Garden (which also rents bicycles and kayaks), and the Caribbean View Hotel. For advance bookings at any of the above, call the community telephone at 5-22033.

Houses in Hopkins can also be rented for about $10 a night (try Mama Nuñez, a friendly woman and wonderful cook). Informal camping along the beach costs about $5 a night, with prior consent. Inquire at Hopkins Guest House, The Sand Bar Restaurant (run by Canadian expat Jean Barkman), or Lebeha Restaurant (operated by a

Swiss woman). Local women are happy to fire up their oil-burning stoves to make meals for casual and overnight visitors. Meals usually include fresh fish, rice, beans, citrus fruit, coconut, and the ubiquitous cassava bread. At night, you may want to take in the Ayumahani Band, which performs often at the Laru Beya Bar, where the main road from Dangriga enters the village. There is a grocery store in Hopkins and by the time of your visit, one or more upscale resorts—under construction in 1995—may have opened.

Getting to Hopkins usually involves an inexpensive, half-hour bus ride from Dangriga or Placencia via the Z-Line. If the schedule isn't convenient, try hopping aboard one of the daily supply trucks heading south from downtown Dangriga at 2:00 p.m. or arranging private transportation via the Southern Highway. Many tour operators will gladly make an excursion to the village when traveling to or from either the Cockscomb Basin Wildlife Sanctuary or the Possum Point Biological Station (both are easy day trips from Hopkins). Better yet, take the quick boat ride from Dangriga with one of the locals, setting out from the Stann Creek bridge. En route you can often arrange accommodations with the boatman, since everyone in Hopkins knows everyone else.

Sittee River, Possum Point, and Wee Wee Caye

About 5 miles south of Hopkins, on the banks of the picturesque Sittee River, is Possum Point Biological Research Station. The 22-acre nature reserve is owned by Paul and Mary Shave, American expatriates who lease government-owned Wee Wee Caye (9 miles east) for use as a marine laboratory and education center. The couple also manage Bocatura Bank Campground, located on a 4-acre plot about a mile downriver from Possum Point. Although these operations cater primarily to natural-history study groups, individuals and small groups of kayakers, fishermen, and birders are accommodated (by reservation only) on a space-available basis.

The research station enjoys a lush setting, surrounded by broadleaf forest at a sharp bend in the river. It is named after the many opossums found here when the lab and surrounding cottages were being built in what was then thick bush. Wildlife still abounds and bird-watchers will be especially rewarded: Possum Point has well over 100 species of "yard birds." The call of the jaguar can sometimes be heard as the cat passes through the property at night. Possum Point and Wee Wee Caye embrace studies in coral reef ecology, botany, herpetology, entomology, ornithology, and mammalogy, as well as general tropical biology.

Possum Point dorms and bungalows can accommodate up to thirty people, with room for another 15 among the raised tent platforms and two cottages of Bocatura, 5 miles from the river's mouth. Wee Wee Caye has seven cottages, and the tiny island is a wonderful place to snorkel, swim, and relax. The Shaves have taken great pains to preserve the mangroves, where a number of wowlas (boa constrictors) make their home, feeding on lizards, iguanas, and small birds. Paul Shave, a marine biologist, has counted 46 species of coral and ten species of crab in the immediate area of Wee Wee Caye. Bring plenty of insect repellent, as the tiny island's no-see-ums can be fierce.

The peaceful Creole community of Sittee River Village makes an interesting side trip and offers several places to stay, including Sittee Fish Camp, Mrs. McKenzie's Guest House & Campground (meals served), and Toucan Sittee (which rents bicycles and canoes). The ruins of the 19th-century Serdon sugar mill are preserved as a park not far from the village on the road to the Southern Highway; you'll notice how the jungle has quickly reclaimed some impressive machinery, including the rusty hulk of a steam engine.

A few miles south of Sittee River along the Caribbean coast, Sapodilla Lagoon has an abundance of orchids, and howler monkeys have been spotted nearby at False Sittee Point. Trips can be arranged from Possum Point to these destinations and Boom Creek, a jungle tributary of the Sittee River. Not visited by the authors but recommended by other travelers is the Black Cat Lodge & Nature Reserve, providing simple accommodations and meals at Sapodilla Lagoon, at the end of a dirt road that branches off the Southern Highway.

Seine Bight Village

Even smaller and more laid-back than Hopkins, the Garifuna community of Seine Bight is about 30 miles south of Dangriga on the idyllic Placencia Peninsula. Until the mid-1980s, the village could be reached only by boat (a 4-hour trip from Dangriga by dugout canoe). Since then, daily buses and private auto traffic have dimmed its status as one of Belize's most isolated coastal communities. Nevertheless, the peninsula still feels like—as one visitor put it—"the island you can drive to."

Seine Bight is said to have been founded by pirates in 1629 and later inhabited by French fishermen deported by the British from Newfoundland when England took control of northeastern Canada. Like Hopkins, the residents occupy small palm-thatch houses atop high stilts (to keep away insects, rodents, snakes, and floodwaters). They follow traditional Garifuna patterns: women take care of children and subsistence gardens, while the men hunt and fish. Seine Bight looks like a postcard, tucked along a narrow beach about 5 miles north of the Creole/Garifuna community of Placencia. Beachfront accommodations here include the expensive Nautical Inn Adventure Resort (north of the village) and Serenity Resort (an alcohol-free lodge a short distance to the south). A few miles north of Seine Bight is the cabaña-style Singing Sands, a more moderately priced facility. All offer the usual reef and interior trips. Souvenir hunters will want to check out Lola's Art, a gallery featuring local craftwork, at the north end of the village.

Seine Bight can be reached either by way of the daily Z-Line bus shuttling between Placencia and Dangriga or by private car or bicycle. It is a pleasant 2-hour walk (3 miles) up the beach or dirt road from Placencia.

Placencia

Straddling a sandy, palm-forested spit of land at the tip of an 11-mile peninsula, Placencia (also spelled Placentia) is one of the oldest continuously inhabited villages in Belize. Its 400 or so residents brag that their small settlement was founded by English buccaneers in the early 1600s, and artifacts discovered beneath their homes suggest this was the location of several fierce battles between British and Spanish sailors. There is also ample evidence that Placencia was a Mayan fishing camp long before the Europeans arrived. For the last few centuries, it has been home to a close-knit cluster of mostly Creole families whose ancestry includes Garifuna warriors, freed African slaves, and Scottish pirates.

Much of Placencia's considerable charm can be attributed to its scenic locale. A long and gently curving beach—arguably the prettiest in Belize—graces the village's windward side. A few hundred yards opposite this wide strip of talcum-powder sand is Placencia Lagoon, a placid waterway harboring abundant marine life. Since the southernmost tip of the settlement borders the Caribbean, the illusion is that of being on a tropical island, with only the north connected to mainland Belize. Before a dirt road was hacked through the swamps, Placencia might as well have been an island, since the only access was by boat.

One unusual feature of Placencia is its main "street," a concrete sidewalk which stretches for about a mile through the center of town. (Vehicles are relegated to a single unpaved road that skirts the western edge of the village.) Placencia's unhurried ambiance is reminiscent of Caye Caulker, with smiles and friendly exchanges the norm among locals and visitors alike. One of the friendlier social centers along the walkway is The Flamboyant Restaurant (formerly Jene's), opposite the Seaspray Hotel and D&L Resort. Three delicious, reasonably priced meals a day are served under the filigree shade of a flamboyant tree. An afternoon snack may also be procured from Miss Lilly, who sells delicious homemade cassava and coconut bread from her front door (behind Hortense's Market). Baker John Whylie (behind Wallen's Market) makes excellent pastries, and Daisy's Ice Cream Parlor (in the center of town) serves Placencia's finest homemade ice cream. With a wide range of inexpensive and reasonably good restaurants and bars to choose from, visitors will not lack for food and drink.

Along the 3-mile Placencia beachfront, dozens of guesthouses and lodges snuggle beneath the palm trees. The azure water is surprisingly deep here, and dolphins occasionally frolic very close to shore. (The depth and tricky currents can make swimming hazardous at times.) Soothing trade winds usually keep biting insects at bay.

Up the coast a short distance are several upscale resorts offering rooms, meals, tours, and equipment for snorkeling, diving, windsurfing, kayaking, or fishing. They can also arrange nature trips to nearby Lark and Laughingbird Cayes, or to such far-off destinations as the Sapodilla Cayes. Recommended full-service hotels here include Placencia Cove Resort, Turtle Inn, Kitty's Place (which also accommodates campers), and the Rum Point Inn. The latter, 2 miles north on a secluded beach, is operated by Corol and George Bevier, early supporters of the Belizean environmental movement and knowledgeable tour guides. Their son, Wade, joined the business not long ago; he is an experienced photographer and naturalist active in the Placencia chapter of the Audubon Society. He also maintains a working color slide-photo processing lab and knows a great deal about local marine fauna. The Rum Point compound includes a gourmet restaurant, a well-stocked library, and dome-shaped garden cottages.

Within the village itself, we recommend the D&L Resort (contrary to the name's implication, this is a relatively modest five-room hotel in the center of town), the aforementioned Sea Spray (run by postmistress Janice Leslie), and the Paradise Vacation Resort (also more basic than the name suggests). The most economical option in Placencia is pitching a tent at Clive's Campground, at the northernmost end of the sidewalk. Clive also rents a few basic cabins.

Sportfishermen have discovered Placencia, with good reason: the tarpon and bonefish opportunities here are superb. Several resorts and businesses now cater exclusively to anglers, and there are a number of topnotch fishing guides based in Placencia.

There are several popular night spots in the village, where an inexpensive bottle of local rum goes a long way. Favorites include the Cozy Corner, Dockside Bar, Mike's Caribbean Club, Tentacles, Sonny's, and the Crab Shell Restaurant. Live music, drumming, and dancing are sometimes available weekend nights at the Cozy Corner and Flamboyant Restaurant.

By and large, Placencia is a tranquil, informal place where you can easily fit in by doing nothing. If you change your mind, it's an excellent departure point for the lesser-known southern cayes or the interior nature parks and Mayan ruins. Bird-watching and beachcombing are especially rewarding here, and the nearby lagoon is an important breeding area for saltwater crocodiles, marine turtles, and the elusive manatee. One highly recommended boatman and tour guide is Cagey, who can take you fishing or on a fabulous natural history tour (tel. 6-23161). We also recommend Samuel Burgess Guide Service, next to the B&J Restaurant.

The hub of activity in Placencia—such as it is—can be found at the very tip of the peninsula, where the pier, marina, gas station, bus stop, BTL phone, and fishing co-op are all located. Boats leave here frequently for nearby Big Creek (a 15-minute trip for about $10), from which airplane and bus connections go both north and south. (In recent years convenient daily bus and plane service has finally come to Placencia, so there's little reason to shuttle to Big Creek for this purpose.)

Placencia's one-room post office, a stone's throw from the pier, also dispenses airline and bus tickets. Janice, the friendly and well-informed postmistress, will happily place phone calls and find you a room or camping spot. If you want to charter a boat, reserve a tour, or sample some cassava bread, this is a good place to start.

The Placencia airstrip is north of Kitty's Place, about 2 miles from the village. A taxi usually awaits deplaning passengers or you can arrange with your hotel to be picked up. We recommend some patience here: Placencia does not operate at an urban pace, and that's part of its charm.

Laughingbird Caye National Park
A small, coconut-studded island about 12 miles southeast of Placencia, Laughingbird gets its name from the large number of laughing gulls that once used it as a rookery. Overuse by humans caused the gulls to abandon the island completely, although a few have returned since 1990, along with brown pelicans, green herons, and melodious blackbirds. In recent years this has been a popular destination for day-tripping picnickers, snorkelers, divers and sea kayakers, who placed Laughingbird on their regular route. The government has taken steps to minimize this disruption, and in the interest of conservation you may wish to drop anchor elsewhere.

Laughingbird Caye, the southernmost island in the Inner Channel, is only about 120 yards long by 10 yards wide. Its unusual shape, an angular atoll on a continental shelf, is called a "faro" formation. Like true atolls, faroes are steep-sided and widely separated from other land formations. Trips to Laughingbird and the nearby (and equally idyllic) Silk, Bugle, Colson, and Lark Cayes can be arranged in Placencia. Wippari Caye, Little Water Caye, and Ranguana Caye have overnight accommodations; with Nicholas, Lime, and Hatchet Cayes slated to host resorts by 1996 (see Chapter 4 for details on offshore Belize). Many of the cayes on the southern part of the reef also have part-time fishing camps, and a handful have full-time residents.

Big Creek, Independence, and Mango Creek

The small villages of Big Creek, Independence, and Mango Creek dot a 7-mile branch of the Southern Highway directly across the lagoon from Placencia. They are about 40 miles by road south of Dangriga and slightly father north of Punta Gorda.

Big Creek has been developed as an important port servicing the deep-water cargo ships that come here to load bananas, mangos, pineapples, citrus fruits, and other cash crops. Until the late 1980s, shallow-draft boats and barges had to shuttle small loads of these exports to Puerto Barrios in neighboring Guatemala. Dredging has made this a major industrial center for Belize.

Big Creek is home to the Billbird Hotel (formerly Toucan Inn), a remodeled barracks for employees of Big Creek's largest banana company. The Billbird is known for its Irish food and the English pub atmosphere of its Tipsy Toucan bar.

Immediately north of Big Creek is the tiny settlement of Independence, and a short distance beyond that is Mango Creek (many people now consider all three villages as the same community and use their names interchangeably). Mango Creek has an important Z-Line bus stop (transfer here for private boats to Placencia) at the unexceptional Hello Hotel and Café, where passengers are allowed time to eat a meal. The Hello is owned by Antonio and Beth Zabaneh, who also own the adjacent Zabaneh Grocery Store and are experts on boat trips that can be arranged from here to Glover's Reef, Guatemala, and Honduras. (For those leaving Belize from Mango Creek, the nec-

▲ Pelicans roosting at sunrise
▼ Conservation education at the Belize Zoo

Mayan children

▲ Mayan pots discovered in Vaca Plateau cave
▼ Iguana hunters   ▼ Tropical forest destruction

▲ Scarlet macaw
▼ Baird's tapir

▲ Black howler monkey
▼ Jaguar

▲ West Indian manatee
▼ Calliandra flower

▲ Heliconia flower

▲ Barrier reef of Belize from the air
▼ Rendezvous Caye from the air

▲ Keel-billed toucan   ▲ Black orchid and toad
▼ Creole children along the Northern Highway

▲ The Blue Hole, Lighthouse Reef
▼ Snorkeling at Lighthouse Reef

essary passport exit stamp can be obtained from the village police station.) The James bus line stops a short distance away, in front of Marita's Restaurant.

Monkey River Town

This sleepy Creole/Garifuna fishing village is about 10 miles by boat south of Mango Creek, tucked behind mangrove forests at the mouth of the slow-moving Monkey River. This lowland waterway drains the Bladen and Swasey watersheds, which now enjoy protected status as important sources of irrigation water and sanctuaries for wildlife. The Paynes Creek/Monkey River Wildlife Sanctuary encompasses 28,000 acres south of the village and north of Punta Ycacos. The area is gradually being developed for natural history research and tourism. An overgrown dirt road (impassable in wet weather) also connects Monkey River Town with the Southern Highway, about 15 miles to the north.

For a prearranged fee, guides from Placencia or Big Creek will turn a visitor loose in the Monkey River estuary with canoe, returning in a few hours—or days—for the powerboat trip back to home base. Some of these guides will also be happy to take visitors up the river itself, where many species of birds and, yes, even spider monkeys can be seen.

Recent visitors describe the village itself as something of a ghost town, its population drained by a lack of jobs and the desire to live in a less isolated community. The few remaining residents struggle along through subsistence farming, fishing, and hunting. Over the years, Monkey River Town has been hard hit by natural disasters: a blight destroyed the banana industry, and trappers sold most of the local crocodiles for their skins. During April, the village briefly comes alive again with a celebration centered around the iguana egg-laying season. People from throughout the area descend on Monkey River Town to eat freshly killed iguanas and their eggs, which are considered a tasty delicacy. Efforts are now under way to develop forms of low-impact tourism that would provide more jobs for residents while preserving the environment. In 1994, William and Ena Anderson opened Ena's Hotel, which has basic rooms and serves simple but wholesome meals. There are no other restaurants in Monkey River Town and only one small grocery. Camping is possible, by permission, on a sand spit at the edge of the village.

Toledo District

Heading south from the citrus and banana plantations of the Stann Creek District, travelers enter the most sparsely populated and undeveloped region in Belize. The Toledo District is (barely) connected to the rest of the country by a single dirt road—the Southern Highway—and one commercial airstrip at Punta Gorda. Public transportation consists of one biweekly (James Line) and two daily (Z-Line) buses and a half-dozen daily domestic airline flights (Maya and Tropic), plus twice-weekly flights to Guatemala. There is also a ferry twice each week (Tuesday and Friday) to and from Guatemala.

Much of the area is still without electricity, indoor plumbing, hot water, or roads. In fact, the majority of its residents are subsistence farmers—including 10,000 Kekchí and Mopan Maya—living in wooden, thatched-roof huts or small cement-block houses. The per capita annual income here is estimated at less than $750. Obviously, a trip to the Toledo District is not for everyone. Although there are a growing number of hotels with modern amenities, most lodges and guesthouses are decidedly rustic. (See the Inside Belize section for a list of recommended accommodations.)

Travel within the area is manageable during the dry season (February through May) but can be problematic the rest of the year. This part of Belize averages over 150 inches of rain annually; therefore, its many rivers and creeks can be difficult to ford during a downpour. There are few gas stations, grocery stores, or restaurants. In short, tourist services are minimal.

Yet a visit to the Toledo District is a must for those who wish to get a firsthand look at the Kekchí (sometimes spelled Ketchi), Mopan, and Garifuna cultures, and to experience small-scale tourism as a strategy for ecosystem conservation. The district also features

Belize's only true rain forest and some of its most unusual Mayan ruins and caves.

Punta Gorda

Even in the Toledo District capital of Punta Gorda, some 200 miles south of Belize City, the pace is slow. In the middle of this sprawling town of about 2,400 people, chickens roam freely between clapboard houses and patches of uncut vegetation. Freshly caught turtles and fish are dressed on the shoreline. Wheelbarrows full of produce roll along the broad streets. Uniformed schoolchildren play in front of unpretentious churches; adults gossip on street corners as they go about their errands. There is virtually no automobile traffic to dodge, and the silence at night can be deafening.

If you fly to "P.G.," as the community is known locally, a spectacular view of the Caribbean and, on clear days, the mountains of Guatemala will greet you as you walk from the airport to downtown—which happen to be only a few steps apart. The five tree-shaded principal streets of Punta Gorda run parallel to the coast and are unpaved. This tranquil façade belies a colorful and sometimes violent history.

P.G. is believed to have been founded by Puritan traders in the 17th century, then occupied off and on by English pirates and Spanish soldiers, who gave it a name that translates as "large point," a reference to the bluff upon which Punta Gorda sits. Throughout most of the colonial era, it was primarily a fishing village. In 1867, a group of disaffected Civil War Confederate Army veterans and their families settled on unoccupied land nearby and tried to re-create their Deep South lifestyle around a group of sugarcane plantations. Chinese, Creole, and East Indian laborers were brought in to cut the cane and clear the forest. Over the next 40 years, a dozen sugar mills were built. But by 1910, the Toledo Settlement, as it was known, had failed, and most of the Americans returned to the United States. The name and townsite (plus many descendants of the conscripted laborers) remain. Although Punta Gorda is still an important fishing port (especially for sport anglers), it has been converted into a market town and service center by gradual improvements in transportation and the influx of peasant farmers from nearby Guatemala. There are also many traditional Garifuna and Creole farms along the coast, primarily growing cassava, beans, maize, and rice. The town itself has an interesting ethnic mix that includes Maya, Garifuna, Creole, East Indian, Chinese, European, and Lebanese residents.

According to a 1994 census, almost 50 percent of Punta Gorda's population is Garifuna. These people have had a difficult time keeping their unique culture alive, and the modern world provides few financial and social incentives for them to do so. Their rich and varied language is not taught in the schools, and the difficulty of finding steady employment is ever-present. Farming once was a part of the Garifuna culture in the Toledo District, but today such traditions as the baking of cassava bread are practiced by only a few families. Many families have at least one member now living in the U.S. or Canada.

Until 1994 a considerable number of British soldiers were stationed in P.G., which bolstered the local economy. Although the Brits are mostly gone, United States taxpayers continue to support a large Voice of America radio station south of the town, which beams programming throughout Central America. The facility is for sale, but still operated by the U.S. Information Agency. You can see the flashing navigation lights atop the compound's 20 tall antennas and tune in its broadcasts on shortwave radio.

Punta Gorda is a good base for trips to Toledo's more than thirty Mayan villages and several major ruins, along with jungle rivers, caves, diving, snorkeling, and sportfishing grounds. Excursions can also be made to the southern end of the barrier reef, although its islands are so far offshore that it may be easier to head for them from Placencia or Dangriga. Recommended interior destinations include the Maya's sacred Hokeb Ha Cave (also called Blue Creek Cave), the awesome opening of a 5-mile-long underground river. The water flowing from this passageway is crystal clear and perfectly suited to a refreshing swim on a hot day. Access is by a well-marked riverside trail from Blue Creek Village, about 21 miles northwest of Punta Gorda. Local guides Bobby Polonio and Alfredo Romero also offer treks to sugar mill ruins and chicle camps.

Travelers with a special interest in rain-forest ecology and Mayan culture can stay at a comfortable field station and lodge near Blue Creek, maintained by International Zoological Expeditions. The biodiversity here is probably unsurpassed in all of Belize; a special treat is IZE's canopy walkway, which zigzags its way through the 100-foot-high forest "ceiling" (home to more than 80 percent of rain forest organisms).

For those with offshore interests, Timeless Tours runs 7- to 12-day camping excursions to cayes and jungle rivers aboard its 38-foot schooner Juanita, based in P.G. harbor. The sailboat goes as far as Wild Cane Caye (the site of a Mayan ruin), the Snake Cayes, and Livingston, a Garifuna town in Guatemala. Charter by Land/Sea schedules boat and interior trips from its office located at 12 Front Street (tel. 7-2070).

We recommend spending at least two or three days in the Toledo District to experience this seldom-seen corner of Belize. Many of Belize's long-time visitors say that P.G. and the rest of the Toledo District remind them of what the rest of the country was like 20 years ago, before television, consumerism, and drug trafficking made their impact.

One of the greatest challenges facing the Belizeans of Toledo is the need to ensure that local people—in this case mostly Kekchí Maya, Mopan Maya, Garifuna, and Creole—benefit from increased tourism and are given incentives to protect the natural and cultural resources of the region. Complicating the matter are some daunting environmental problems facing the area's subsistence farmers. Natural habitat degradation has been especially heavy here, mainly because of new road construction and the collective impact of forest destruction by commercial logging and the kind of slash-and-burn agriculture practiced by a growing native Mayan population and Guatemalan immigrants. However, as of mid-1995, at least two noteworthy locally initiated projects were underway in Toledo, seeking to combine tourism, sustainable agriculture, cultural revitalization, and environmental conservation: the Toledo Host Family Net-work/Indigenous Experience Program and the Mayan Guest House & EcoTrail Program.

These two programs both encourage foreigners to visit traditional

Don Chama entertains visitors at the Nature's Way Guest House in Punta Gorda (Photo by Steele Wotkyns)

Mayan villages, but in fundamentally different ways. The Host Family Network places tourists in the actual homes of Mayan Indians, where guests observe and participate in daily village life. In contrast, the Guest House Program arranges visits to many of the same villages, but tourists stay in structures that are separate from Mayan homes and built specifically for use by foreigners. Under both schemes, visitors eat meals prepared by local residents and take outings guided by villagers. (Although the Maya of Belize converse among themselves in their own languages, most are also fluent in English, which is not the case in neighboring Guatemala, Honduras, or Mexico.)

"We don't look at these programs as rivals," says Alfredo Villoria, one of the coordinators of the home-stay endeavor. "We think they are complementary. Some folks want to stay in a guesthouse and some want to stay with families. We let them exercise that choice."

A Mayan family prepares tortillas in their San José Village home (Photo by Mayan Homestay Network)

Mayan Guest House Program

Since 1991, several rural villages have constructed small guesthouses, designed and marked nature trails, and started introducing travelers to Mayan customs. As of mid-1995, guesthouses were completed and operational in five communities: San Pedro Columbia, San Miguel, Santa Cruz, San José, and Laguna. A sixth facility is scheduled to open Barranco, the only village on the coast. Accommodations and meals are basic, and there is no electricity or indoor plumbing, but the overall experience cannot be duplicated. Laguna Village completed its guesthouse ahead of the others and offers the widest range of activities for tourists, including guided nature walks and exploration of a Mayan ceremonial cave where ancient paintings can be seen.

"These people are very quiet, gentle, and vulnerable," North American visitor Louise Foster observed, in an account of her Laguna experience, published in *The Belize Review*. "They are excited about reviving their traditions and sharing them with outsiders. It is a fragile situation; they can so easily be exploited and hurt."

Laguna is a Kekchí Maya agricultural center located about 10 miles from Punta Gorda. The population is descended from immigrants who originated in the Alta Verapaz highlands of Guatemala and came to Belize to escape brutal oppression. Kekchí people have a strong tradition of cooperation, particularly in farming and building,

Laguna's thatch-roofed guesthouse accommodates up to eight visitors and includes a veranda, a separate bathhouse, and outhouses. Guests are treated to a spectacular view of the rain forest-covered limestone karst hills nearby. Since the lodge does not have a kitchen, visitors eat in small groups at different households each day. Guides take guests on carefully tended footpaths, where the native medicinal plants are marked in various languages. A recommended stop is the arts and crafts center, where tourists can buy handmade baskets and other Mayan craftwork directly from the village cooperative.

The Mayan Guest House Program is coordinated as a profit-making venture by American expatriate William "Chet" Schmidt, who owns and operates Nature's Way Guest House/Belize Adventure Travel in Punta Gorda. Schmidt has worked with local villagers to devise a system that integrates ecosystem conservation, appropriate-scale tourism, and environment-friendly farming. Its intention is to minimize stress levels on the natural and cultural resources, while employing the maximum number of villagers. Part of the profits are used to support sustainable agriculture, a community fund, local government, and the construction of clinics. Rates are about $20 a night, plus about $3 for each meal and $10 for guided tours. (Visitors are strongly encouraged to fill out a written evaluation of the program before they leave.)

The Guest House Program was originally designed to incorporate an important but controversial strategy—controlling tourists' access. In an attempt to minimize stress levels on the natural environment and not overburden local Maya with massive infusions of outsiders, organizers can arrange for individuals and small groups to be cycled in and out on a rotating basis. Each village thus gets its share of tourists, but the overall demands on local people and resources are kept low.

Toledo Host Family Network/Indigenous Experience Program

Catering to overnight visitors who wish to stay in the actual homes of Mayan villagers, Alfredo and Yvonne Villoria are working in cooperation with the residents of several communities to provide intimate contact with the daily lives of Toledo's aboriginal people. A growing number of local Maya have volunteered to participate in the program, which provides them with extra income and the chance to share their culture with interested outsiders. Participating villages include San Antonio, Santa Cruz, San José, Na Luum Ca, San Pedro Columbia, Silver Creek, and Santa Elena.

The home-stay program is offered through the Villorias' business, Dem Dats Doin, which operates out of the couple's rural farm and their Toledo Visitors Information Center in Punta Gorda. For a $5 fee, tourists are connected with a Mayan family that will provide meals, a hammock (with sheet) to sleep in, illuminating conversation, and a close-up look at their activities, such as corn preparation and land tilling. Guided trips are made to nearby ruins, caves, and nature trails. Visitors pay their host families about $7 a day for room and board. Because of the time it takes to coordinate a home-stay, it's best to make reservations with Dem Dats Doin well in advance and to specify which Kekchí or Mopan village you would like to visit. Mail inquiries (to Box 73, Punta Gorda) should include $2 to cover reply postage and materials. You can also can also directly contact the alcalde (chairman) in each village to arrange a home-stay on your own.

The Villorias also offer tours of their own "low-impact" farm and nursery, 1 mile from the San Pedro Columbia village (about 3 miles from P.G.). Using biogas methane generators, photovoltaics, predatory insects, permaculture, and other "appropriate technology," the couple has approached energy self-sufficiency, and they now grow most of their own food. Guided tours are $5 and last up to 2 hours. Guests may stay overnight and take meals here for a modest fee, but this should be arranged in advance.

Temash-Sarstoon Nature Reserve

If you want to see some of the tallest and oldest mangrove forests in all of Central America, a trip up the Río Temash fills the bill. This

Mayan villagers washing dishes in a stream near San Pedro Columbia village
(Photo by Mayan Homestay Network)

river and the neighboring Sarstoon are two of four major watercourses that drain into the Caribbean from the Toledo District. In 1992, the Government of Belize protected much of this precious watershed through its creation of the 41,000-acre Temash-Sarstoon Nature Reserve.

As you speed from Punta Gorda in a hired boat—there is no public transportation in the area—you will pass such scenic coastal destinations as Orange Point, the Moho River, and Mother Point. The tall forest canopy along the coast contrasts with brighter green cascades of mangrove and forest stands that have been disturbed by the periodic hurricanes that batter the mainland.

We recommend that you hire an experienced boatman and guide for this adventure, or any other trips up the wilderness rivers of Belize. The need becomes apparent as you maneuver past dangerous sandbars and tangled mangrove thickets. In this instance, a well-informed local is also extremely helpful to the amateur naturalist once you're past the verdant tunnel entrance of the Temash's delta. Comfrey palm swamp is found around the estuary of the Temash River, possibly the only place in the country where this habitat type exists in such abundance. The entire area is officially classified as a tropical wet-transition to subtropical forest and harbors much wildlife. Even the usually short palmetto palms tower overhead here. The deeper you penetrate this wide river, passing Conejos and Sunday Wood Creeks, the bigger the trees become. The tangle of vines and understory is almost impenetrable. Dense stands of Santa María and sapodilla trees are broken by a swampy maze of red mangrove. And then you begin to see the river's premier natural attraction: black mangrove trees that tower above the Temash, sometimes reaching more than 100 feet.

The presence of many fish-eating birds and local anglers attest to the Temash's richness as a fishing area. Large snook and tarpon cruise in the river, which reportedly reaches a depth of more than 100 feet. Sportfishing guides in Punta Gorda and other coastal towns can arrange excursions to this rich aquatic environment.

Farther north, the Columbia branch of the Río Grande drains the nearly 103,000 acres of uninhabited wilderness known as the Columbia Forest Reserve, one of the last remaining large tracts of intact forest in Central America. Recent explorations of the reserve have revealed sinkholes up to 800 feet deep and ¼-mile wide, plus many sacred Mayan caves containing ancient artifacts. Access is difficult, however, and prior permission from the Department of Forestry is required.

If You Go: As of mid-1995, Maya Airlines had four daily flights to and from Belize City to Punta Gorda; Tropic Air had two flights on the same route. Maya also has Monday and Friday flights out of P.G. to and from Puerto Barrios, Guatemala.

The Z-Line bus runs twice daily to and from Dangriga and Belize City (Z-Line Bus Service, 53 Main St., tel. 7-22165), and the James Line makes the same trip Tuesdays and Fridays. The inexpensive but bumpy Belize City trip takes about 10 to 12 hours, via the rough Southern and Hummingbird Highways. A number of local buses and supply trucks carry passengers on semiweekly schedules to surrounding villages, with the heaviest traffic on Wednesdays and Saturdays (Punta Gorda's market days).

Temash River, southern Belize (Photo by Steele Wotkyns)

A passenger ferry provides Tuesday and Friday service from P.G. to Puerto Barrios, Guatemala. The boat arrives from Guatemala at about 9:30 a.m. and leaves at noon. There are easy connections from Puerto Barrios, a major shipping port, to interior Guatemala and

Honduras. (The boat no longer stops in Livingston.) The crossing takes about 2¹/₂ hours and costs about $6.50 each way. You must have your passport stamped before embarking; the Belize immigration office is at the foot of the municipal wharf. Ferry tickets can be purchased in advance at Godoy's Shop in Punta Gorda (tel. 7-2065, 24 Middle St.). Bring your own food and water; neither is available on board. Quetzales, the Guatemalan currency, can be obtained at Grace's Shop or from arriving ferry passengers (the P.G. bank does not handle quetzales). Guatemalan visas are not available here or in Puerto Barrios. Because the ferry departs for P.G. at 7:00 a.m., passengers heading to Belize from Puerto Barrios should buy their tickets and have their passports stamped by Guatemalan immigration the afternoon before departure.

A Punta Gorda institution that provides many tour options and much information about the Toledo District is the Nature's Way Guest House, located at the south end of town at 65 Front Street (tel. 7-22119). Sleeping quarters are basic: clean rooms with bunks and shared baths. Proprietor Chet Schmidt can arrange visits to many attractions, including Mayan villages and a remote campsite down the coast, and has a reliable boat for trips up jungle rivers and to offshore cayes.

The Toledo Visitors Information Center (open daily from 8:00 a.m. to 11:30 a.m., except Thursday and Sunday), is operated next to the main pier by Alfredo and Yvonne Villoria of Dem Dats Doin. Besides extensive information on Toledo attractions, the Villorias can arrange inland tours and boat charters. The center maintains a message center, bulletin board, and paperback book exchange as well. Information is dispensed free of charge.

Another information resource in P.G. is the Toledo Explorer's Club (46 José María Nuñez St.), which answers visitors' questions and arranges custom-guided camping expeditions to remote villages, rivers, caves, and cayes. Basic rooms are provided in the group's "clubhouse."

Other recommended accommodations in Punta Gorda include the moderately priced Mira Mar Hotel (including a bar, restaurant, and pool hall at 95 Front St.), Mahung's (11 Main St.), Punta Caliente

(108 José María Nuñez St.), and the Saint Charles Inn (23 King St.). The most upscale place in P.G. is The Traveler's Inn, located above the Z-Line bus station (53 Main St.) and operated by the Zabadeh family, Z-Line's owners.

Restaurant choices are rather limited, but there are several acceptable Chinese cafés, and the larger hotels serve a variety of cuisines. Our favorite eatery is Man Man's Five-Star, an authentic home-style Garifuna restaurant, located on Far West Street near the corner of King. The chef is an elderly but energetic gentleman who serves enormous, modestly priced meals at a single table in his small house. Eating and visiting with Man Man is the kind of experience that makes Belize such a special place. Also try Punta Caliente, at 108 José María Nuñez Street, for regional dishes and friendly service. The best breakfasts in town are served at Granny's and Nature's Way, both on Front Street. Punta Gorda also offers a good bakery, well-stocked grocery store, and a happy expatriate American named Danny who rides around town on a bicycle selling pizza (he's the one wearing a U.S. Postal Service uniform). Nightlife is limited to a handful of bars and restaurants, or you can look overhead and see one of the most amazing starscapes in the country.

Wednesdays and Saturdays are market days in P.G., and this is a good time to inspect the handcrafted wares of Mayan artisans from local villages and Guatemala. An amazing selection of exotic fruits and vegetables is on sale. The market is on Front Street, with handicraft booths spilling over onto adjacent Queen Street.

See the Inside Belize section for lodging in outlying villages of the Toledo district.

6

The Interior

Until the late 1980s, few of Belize's visitors ventured west of the Belize Zoo unless they were heading across the Guatemalan border to Tikal. The conventional wisdom was that, except for the capital of Belmopan and the Mayan ruins of Xunantunich, there was not much to see in the country's interior. We have talked to some travelers whose only memory along the Western Highway is of the roadside Belize City cemetery and unsightly municipal garbage dump, since closed down. Fortunately, the interior's infrastructure has improved to the point where many rewarding destinations can (and should) be added to any visitor's itinerary. Besides the country's most extensive collection of Mayan ruins and a growing number of comfortable lodges, Belize's interior offers the best opportunity to encounter the marvelous flora and fauna of a relatively undisturbed subtropical forest. Although some of the nation's newest sanctuaries and reserves offer virtually no access to the casual visitor, others provide an "up close and personal" experience you are not likely to forget. In addition, there are caves, rivers, horse paths, waterfalls, ruins, nature trails, and campsites galore, just waiting to be discovered—in some cases quite literally, since much of the interior remains virtually untouched by humans.

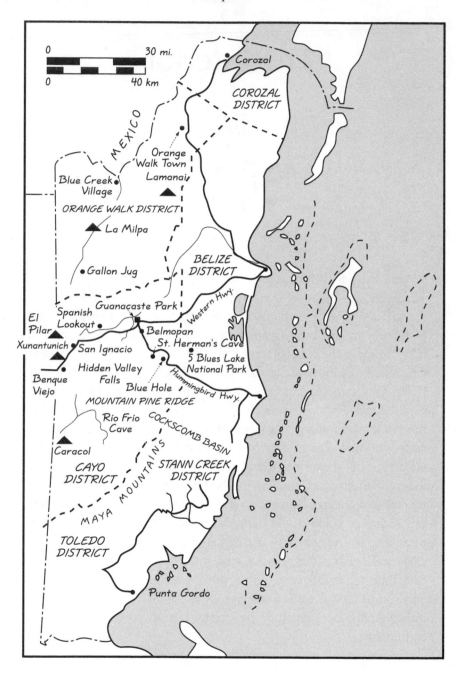

The Interior

Cayo District

With an estimated 1995 population of 40,000, Cayo (Spanish for "small island") is the second-largest and fastest-growing district of Belize. The capital city of Belmopan lies at the district's eastern edge, and Benque Viejo anchors its western border with Guatemala. In between these two small towns, visitors find some of the nation's richest farmland, at times so carefully manicured by Mennonites that it looks more like the rolling hills of rural Pennsylvania than Central America. Besides cattle, poultry, and pigs, Cayo farmers raise corn, sorghum, beans, fruit, and various vegetables for both domestic consumption and export. Significant amounts of pine, rosewood, Santa María, cedar, and mahogany are harvested by local lumber interests.

One of the district's most important industries is tourism. Travelers have much to choose from here: Mayan ruins, jungle trails, horseback rides, white-water rivers, bird-watching, canoe trips, and such natural wonders as cascading waterfalls and limestone caves. Cayo's flora and fauna are varied and plentiful. Such attractions have been enhanced in recent years by development of an infrastructure that caters to the needs and interests of even the most discriminating visitor, offering everything from wilderness campgrounds to luxurious villas.

With 8,000 residents, San Ignacio, 22 miles west of Belmopan and 9 miles from the Guatemala border, is the largest town in the Cayo District and a fine place to have a meal, mail a postcard, fill the gas tank, fix a flat tire, exchange currency, and load up on supplies. There are many pleasant hotels in San Ignacio, although most visitors prefer to find accommodations in the surrounding countryside. The town is laid out on a series of bluffs alongside the Macal River, at an elevation high enough to be noticeably cooler and less humid than the coastal plain. The people are friendly and happy-go-lucky, pointing with pride at their Hawkesworth Bridge: a scaled-down version of the Brooklyn Bridge erected in the late 1940s and still the only suspension span in the country. (Until 1992, the one-way bridge also boasted the only traffic signal in Belize.) Locals will also steer you to the partially restored Mayan ruin of Cahael Pech, just up Main Street at

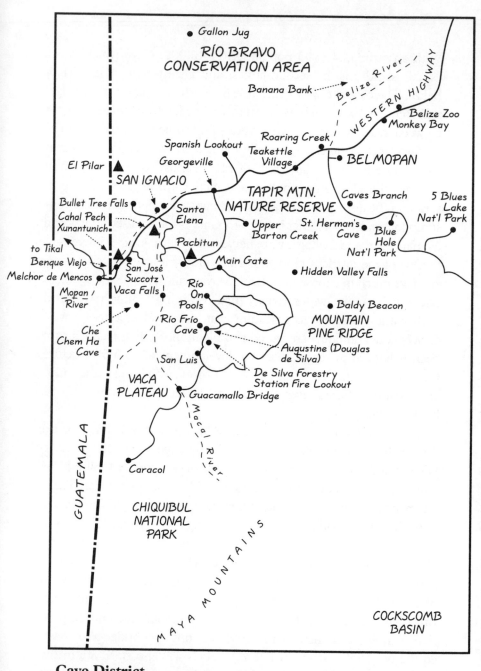

Cayo District

Canoeing on the Macal River (Photo by Richard Mahler)

the crest of a hill, and to Serendib, a Sri Lankan restaurant justifiably revered for its spicy curry. Another good dining spot and social hub is Eva's Restaurant (9-22267), across Burns Avenue from Serendib, run by English expatriate Bob Jones and his Belizean wife, Nestora. Wide-ranging travel tips and assistance are cheerfully dispensed at Eva's, the unofficial tourist information center for western Belize. Among other noteworthy stops are the well-stocked souvenir shop and bookstore next to Eva's; the Bel-Brit Bar, an English-style pub also located on Burns Avenue; the Blue Angel Club, a popular nightclub on Hutson Street; and the Cahael Pech Tavern, San Ignacio's liveliest dance hall. We also recommend the Sand Castle, next to the bus stop, for the best food and drink in town.

Other Cayo District towns include Santa Elena, San Ignacio's sister city across the suspension bridge, and Benque Viejo, which practically straddles the Guatemalan border. Both communities are largely Spanish-speaking, and you are likely to encounter marimbas, fiestas, and colorful social customs centered around Catholic holidays and the rituals of baptism, confirmation, and marriage. Many inhabitants are descended from Guatemalan immigrants who crossed the border into Belize to escape political persecution and economic exploitation.

Until the late 1980s, the Western Highway was unpaved beyond San Ignacio; rural residents here were very isolated. Many still make do without electricity, telephones, and indoor plumbing.

Tucked into the folds of the lush green hills are a dozen or more "cottage" resorts ranging from rustic to elegant, each catering to the visitor who wants to get away from urban distractions in a wooden bungalow or palm-thatched cabaña. Some of these charming retreats are located on working farms or ranches, while others are exclusively dedicated to a kind of gracious, low-key tropical tourism that brings to mind images of the African veldt or Costa Rican jungle.

Each lodge is slightly different in style and character, with its own set of advantages and disadvantages. Some specialize in horseback riding or canoeing; others cater to forest trekkers and bird-watchers. Still others can arrange strenuous camping trips in the unexplored wilderness or investigations of little-known caverns. All, however, supply meals and other basic amenities to their guests, and most can set up tours of the nearby Mayan ruins at Xunantunich, Caracol, Cahael Pech, and Tikal. A few even have reciprocal agreements with resorts on the coast or cayes that allow visitors to package a "surf and turf" holiday. Rates and accommodations vary widely, from budget to five-star, depending on such variables as location, meals, services, and transportation costs.

Most Cayo resort operators take individual preferences into account, making breakfast at 5:00 a.m. for eager bird-watchers, for example, or eliminating the meal entirely for late risers who wish to sleep in. If you want to be chauffeured, they will pick you up at the Belize City airport, San Ignacio bus stop, or almost anyplace else. Charters can now be made to the Cayo airport at Central Farm or Blancaneaux strip in the Mountain Pine Ridge. If you have your own transportation, operators will be happy to give you detailed instructions and maps to whatever destination pleases you.

Some of the more established cottage resorts with good reputations among experienced travelers include the Maya Mountain Lodge (encompassing a forest preserve on the Cristo Rey road); Chaa Creek Cottages (offering Mayan-style cabañas and a butterfly farm on a

Typical cabaña-style bungalow of Cayo District cottage resort, this one at Chaa Creek (Photo by Richard Mahler)

bluff above the Macal River); Mountain Equestrian Trails (a 150-acre, 20-horse ranch catering to nature lovers); Nabitunich (a cattle ranch near the Xunantunich ruins where you can simply relax and watch the Mopan River flow by); Windy Hill Cottages (yet another ranch, this one with elegant rooms and swimming pool); Banana Bank Ranch (operated by former Montana cowboy John Carr and his artist wife, Carolyn); Parrot's Nest (a fascinating collection of tree houses built above the river near Bullet Tree Falls Village); Crystal Paradise Resort (operated by a Mayan-Creole family and offering bird-watching, horseback riding, and boat trips from Cristo Rey Village); Las Casitas (a cluster of rustic bungalows at the confluence of the Belize and Mopan rivers); and Ek'Tun (a remote but luxurious hideaway perched above the Macal River).

Several of the Cayo resorts have become actively involved in projects that combine conservation and sustainable economic development. Mountain Equestrian Trails (MET), for example, has joined with neighboring private landowners to establish the 3,500-acre Slate Creek Preserve, a limestone karst area covered with moist broadleaf forest and home to such endangered fauna as the keel-billed motmot and Baird's tapir. Mountain Equestrian Trails owners Jim and Marguerite Bevis also are involving residents of the nearby immigrant village of Siete Millas in handicraft production, nature-oriented tourism and environmentally sound farming as an alternative to slash-and-burn agriculture, which threatens the Slate Creek watershed and other tracts of unspoiled wilderness. A Belizean of American descent, Jim Bevis hires well-informed local guides to lead visitors on horseback to remote area caves, waterfalls, and ruins. These highly recommended trips are tailored to equestrians of all abilities, including novices. Visitors may camp out or stay in beautifully appointed bungalows at the ranch. Other MET expeditions, conducted in association with The Divide Ltd. (Neil Rogers), combine camping and hiking to such unusual destinations as Puente Natural and Las Cuevas, deep in the Chiquibul forest. MET's Jim Bevis also co-leads a "Maya Mountain Traverse" through virtually unexplored wilderness as part of a trek offered by Ecosummer Expeditions (see Inside Belize).

The operators of Maya Mountain Lodge, located about one-half mile south of Santa Elena, also show genuine concern for the future of Cayo and its people. Owners Bart (vice president of the Belize Ecotourism Association) and Suzi Mickler are developing a ceramic handicraft industry using local artisans, teachers, and materials. They began holding ceramics classes in 1993 with the goal of more evenly distributing the economic rewards of tourism among all Belizeans. Thanks to their efforts, many residents of nearby San José Succotz are now making and selling Mayan-style ceramic art objects. Besides the usual sightseeing trips, Maya Mountain offers guided horseback trips, canoe rides, mountain biking, birding, Mennonite visits, and nature treks (with accompanying guidebooks prepared by biologist Bruce Miller and Suzi Mickler, who holds a master of science degree in education). The facility maintains an educational field station and reference library for cultural, archaeological, and wildlife studies. Maya Mountain is also one of the few Belize lodges that encourages families to visit, and provides a growing number of activities for parents and their children. The lodge holds special week-long workshops during the summer for various interest groups, including artists, families interested in ecology or multiculturalism, and teachers studying tropical ecology or Mayan culture. Professional biologist and author Jim Conrad is a consultant and tour guide here, presenting entertaining and informative lectures one or more nights a week. A former chicken ranch, Maya Mountain grows much of its own food and has established a private nature reserve that includes an unexcavated Mayan ceremonial site. The lodge can arrange home-stays in Gales Point, Bermudian Landing, and several other Belizean villages.

A favorite of many travelers is Chaa Creek Cottages, established many years ago by British expatriate Mick Fleming and his American wife, Lucy. Guests stay in Mayan-style cottages or a campground set beneath tall tropical trees or camp out on a bluff above the Macal River. Visitors are serenaded by exotic birds every morning; there is no glass in the windows because Chaa Creek, like much of Cayo, has almost no biting insects. Several nature-oriented tour operators regularly bring their tours here because of the resort's high standards and commitment to environmental awareness. In 1994, Chaa Creek started a butterfly breeding farm, where visitors can see such brilliant species as the "Belize Blue" being raised for sale to indoor butterfly parks around the world.

The authors recommend several low-key Mountain Pine Ridge resorts that also specialize in natural-history tourism. These facilities are set in beautiful natural surroundings and afford easy access to the area's rivers, forests, caves, waterfalls, and Mayan ruins.

The Blancaneaux Lodge, set on a lush 50-acre compound owned by movie director Francis Ford Coppola, reopened in 1993 in a forested area crisscrossed by white-water rivers and nature trails. Rates are beyond the reach of budget travelers, but the accommodations and meals are first-rate. Tours are arranged to destinations throughout the area (including the spectacular Five Sisters Falls, where another luxury lodge is located). Guests arrive either via Blancaneaux's airstrip or 16 miles of dirt road from San Ignacio. Coppola has supervised the construction and furnishing of several beautifully appointed Mayan-style cabañas and villas, set in gardenlike surroundings beneath tall pine trees. Guests in each of the 23 rooms can look down on the idyllic Privassión River, where a large pool (suitable for swimming) is used to generate electricity through an unobtrusive hydroelectric turbine. Coppola imported a wood-burning oven from Rome to make pizza at Blancaneaux, and his dining room—open to the general public—also features fine wines from Coppola's own Napa Valley winery, as well as his Italian family's imaginative pasta recipes. Much of the food is grown in an organic garden adjacent to the lodge. This may well be the best restaurant in Belize. As if this weren't enough, there is a certified resident masseur, Rick Garzaniti, who specializes in neuromuscular massage. (Don't expect to see Coppola during your visit; he spends only a few weeks here each year.)

Located about a mile away from Blancaneaux, the more moderately priced Pine Ridge Lodge offers caving (including three newly rediscovered Mayan ceremonial caves), hiking, river trips, birding, mountain biking, and equestrian and archaeological explorations. This comfortable, bungalow-style hotel also operates a small restaurant that serves excellent meals, often prepared by Vicki or Gary Seewald, the American owners. There are well-maintained nature trails through the nearby pine forest and jungle, where you'll see wild orchids, possibly deer, and maybe even a jaguar. A nice feature is the "hammock room," a screened-in, high-ceiling shelter where you can curl up with a glass of fresh, cold limeade and read a book. Ask about off-season (summer) rates.

An unusual combination of options is offered by the Hidden Valley Inn, located a few miles away from the Pine Ridge Lodge on the Coona Cairn Road, which continues to Thousand-Foot Falls (on the Inn's property). Maintained by the Georgia family that owns 18,000 acres of the pine ridge and adjacent subtropical jungle, visitors can either stay in comfortable cottages or camp under the stars and pine boughs. Easy-to-follow trails lead to Central America's highest waterfall, several caves, and a small lake. A large section of the property constitutes the Hidden Valley Reserve and Institute for Environmental Studies, where biologists recently found a new toad species and a rare nesting pair of orange-breasted falcons. Tours—including river rafting and photo safaris—are arranged to Caracol, the Chiquibul rain forest, Tikal, and other area attractions. Hidden Valley's bungalows are plush, complete with fireplaces and bathtubs (both hard to find in Belize). The resort even grows its own coffee.

Lower-priced but highly recommended accommodations catering to nature-lovers include the Belizean-owned Crystal Paradise Resort, which offers horseback riding, nature treks, boat trips, bird-watching (binoculars provided), and Mayan ruin tours from a 100-acre parcel below the pine ridge along the Macal River, near the village of Cristo Rey. Members of the large and friendly Victor Tut family go out of their way to please guests and know the Cayo as only lifelong residents can. Check out their extensive natural history library and impressive collection of historic artifacts. The homegrown coffee and Teresa Tut's Creole cooking are delicious. Pickup by boat or van can be arranged. Some of the more unusual activities include stargazing (with a powerful telescope) and trips to Laguna Aguacate (a jungle lake near a Mennonite settlement), as well as Mayan ruins.

Located only a few hundred yards from downtown San Ignacio, moderately priced Mida's Resort offers thatch-roofed cabins on the banks of the Macal. Operated by a British-Belizean couple, Mike and Maria Preston, Mida's arranges canoeing, sightseeing, and nature treks. (Canoes can also be rented at the nearby Snooty Fox.) Inexpensive camping and a full range of meals are offered at Mida's. Further west, near Xunantunich, is a 400-acre working ranch called Nabintunich ("stone cottage"), with 11 cabins and lots of horses. Bridle trails extend through miles of dense bush. On a sharp bend in the Belize River, near Bullet Tree Falls, the Parrot's Nest accommodates visitors in rustic tree houses. German-born owner Fred Prost raises orchids commercially and is known to many returning visitors as the former manager of Belize City's Seaside Guest House. Here, as there, Prost has kept his lodge affordable for backpackers. Swimming and birding are excellent at Parrot's Nest; horseback tours are also offered to the nearby Mayan ruin of El Pilar and a jungle chicle camp.

Worthy of special mention is Ek'Tun ("black rock" in Mayan), where American expatriates Ken and Phyllis Dart have created a lovely two-cottage Macal River retreat on their 200 acres of pristine jungle. One of the most isolated lodges in the Cayo, it is worth the extra effort (four-wheel-drive Land Rover and boat) to get here. You'll feel like you're miles away from civilization: and indeed you are. Many guests have commented on the "spiritual energy" they feel at this place, which is built on the grounds of an ancient Mayan village. The Darts love to pamper their guests with personal, customized service, ranging from gourmet meals to canoe trips down the Macal and guided tours of unexcavated ruins. The beautiful Yucatán Mayan-style accommodations are handcrafted and elegantly appointed. Outside your door is the cathedral-like majesty of a high-canopy tropical forest, with the soothing sound of the river constantly in the background. Ek'Tun is heaven for bird-watchers, with more than 120 species observable in a random week. Sightings include the spectacled owl and orange-breasted falcon, along with jaguar, howler monkeys, tapirs, tayras, peccaries, and brocket deer. Mayan artifacts have been found in nearby caves, and there is even an ancient well. Committed environmentalists, the Darts spend part of their time growing mahogany, teak, and other highly valued trees that have become scarce through exploitation.

There are at least two dozen other lodges, campgrounds, and hotels in the Cayo to suit every taste and pocketbook. Check with travel agencies, the Belize Tourism Industry Association, or the Belize Tourist Board for a complete rundown. Bob Jones at Eva's Restaurant is also an excellent source of up-to-date information and can help budget-minded travelers find the best values. For those heading off the beaten path, we recommend The Divide Ltd. (tel. 92-3452). Those who wish to stay in town can't do better than the Belizean-owned San Ignacio Hotel, which has a very good restaurant (specializing in beef), comfortable rooms (some with satellite TV and direct-dial phones), a nature trail, gift shop, basketball court, and the best swimming pool in Cayo. There are budget-priced accommodations in San Ignacio as well, however we have received inconsistent reports about most of them. For those who wish to stay in a jungle setting close to Belmopan, we recommend the Carrs' Banana Bank Lodge. Much of their 4,000-acre property is old-growth subtropical forest, with over 200 species of birds and many other creatures identified. The lodge specializes in canoeing (up to 3 hours on the Belize River), horseback riding (select from among 25 saddle horses), and stargazing (with an 8-inch Meade telescope). Meals are provided.

Like Bob Jones at Eva's, Remo Montgomery of the Sandcastle Bar & Grill is a gold mine of travel information and even does river trips on area waterways. Also recommended is B&M Mountain Bike Hire, on Burns Ave., which rents and services bicycles, as well as dispensing helpful travel advice.

If You Go: The Cayo District is easily reached by private or rental car on the Western Highway, or by the same route via the low-cost Batty, Novelo, Piache, and Shaw bus lines. Check with local agents or innkeepers for schedules and fares. The drive from Belize City to San Ignacio takes just under 2 hours, the bus somewhat longer. There are taxi stands at Columbus Park (the traffic circle by the suspension bridge) in San Ignacio and Market Plaza in downtown Belmopan. Most resorts can arrange pickup at Belize's international airport for a fee of about $100.

Ix Chel Farm and Rainforest Medicine Trail

A few miles west of San Ignacio, a dirt side road follows a Macal River tributary called Chaa Creek, which has become one of the centers of laid-back Cayo tourism. The Chaa Creek Road first winds through a series of barren cattle pastures before bisecting verdant farmland: vast Mennonite plantations on one side, small Mayan fields on the other. About 4 miles from the Western Highway the road splits, with one branch heading toward DuPlooy's Resort and the other to Chaa Creek Cottages, both recommended for those seeking an authentic jungle experience with plenty of creature comforts.

Both lodges perch on cliffs above the swift Macal River and are surrounded by thick second-growth subtropical vegetation. The forest setting is tranquil and shady, a perfect setting for a slow canoe trip, unhurried horseback ride, or leisurely nature walk. A maze of pathways penetrate the foliage, including the remarkable Rainforest Medicine Trail. This unusual trail is located about 100 yards away from Chaa Creek Cottages on the grounds of Ix Chel Farm, a pioneering research facility specializing in the healing properties of plants.

During the summer rainy season, when visitors from other parts of Belize complain about bug bites, Ix Chel founder Rosita Arvigo walks out the back door of her farmhouse and snaps a small branch off a red gumbo-limbo tree. The bark, she informs them, produces a

Rosita Arvigo and jackass bitters (Photo by Richard Mahler)

natural insect repellent. It can also be made into a tonic for treating urinary tract infections and provides an antidote to the itchy rashes caused by contact with the poisonwood tree, which invariably grows nearby. Many other local trees, shrubs, and vines have proven equally useful.

A dedicated herbalist and botanical field practitioner from Chicago, Arvigo is in a race against time. She and her colleagues at this remote encampment are scouring the Central American forests in search of tropical plants that may help win the war against a number of deadly diseases. With her husband, Greg Shropshire, Arvigo works at the place where the timeless wisdom of venerable native healers intersects with the untested theories of Western medicine.

"Much of what I have learned is from Don Elijio Panti," she explains, referring to the traditional Mayan healer who began—albeit reluctantly at first—sharing his secrets (beginning at age 86) with

Arvigo. This local Mayan *yerbero*, or herbalist, has provided Arvigo's Ix Chel Tropical Research Center with vital information about hundreds of plants that have been used by Belizeans to treat everything from heart attacks to snakebites.

Arvigo has recently accomplished one important goal: to preserve the encyclopedic herbal lore Don Elijio has memorized during his long lifetime. Major progress has also been made in determining the healing properties of hundreds of other native plants that may never have been ingested by humans and thus have unknown biochemical effects.

"In 1987 the U.S. government's National Cancer Institute awarded a contract to the New York Botanical Garden's Institute of Economic Botany to survey the flowering and cone-bearing plants in the New World tropics for chemical compounds that could be used to treat diseases such as cancer and AIDS," explained Dr. Michael Balick, a director of the Institute of Economic Botany, New York Botanical Garden, in a 1995 interview. "Ix Chel Tropical Research Foundation is the collaborating center for this work in Belize." Drs. Balick, Arvigo, and Shropshire have—in collaboration with numerous Belizean traditional healers—collected hundreds of plants in support of the project. The effort underscores a deepening alliance between native healers and modern scientists in a bid to study potentially useful plants before they are wiped out by deforestation and industrialization.

The World Health Organization, among other international agencies, has studied plant samples from Ix Chel Farm. The materials are dried in a specially made oven in Arvigo's botanical workshop, then labeled and packaged before being sent to a laboratory for analysis. All this work is carried out in an isolated setting that has only solar electricity, minimal hot water, and no telephone.

The campaign is spurred by the knowledge that the world's forests have already yielded such medicines as quinine (an antimalarial), vinblastine (used to treat Hodgkin's disease), and taxol (a treatment for ovarian cancer). Many so-called miracle drugs are plant-derived compounds from tropical forests. Examples include tubocurarine (curare), used in operating rooms to relax muscles and prevent spasm, and pilocarpine, used in ophthalmology for the treatment of glaucoma. Scientists estimate that 25 percent of all prescription drugs were derived from the plant kingdom.

At Ix Chel Farm, the Rainforest Medicine Trail winds through a living display of arboreal and herbal remedies. Signs describe the plants, many bearing unusually descriptive names. The *tres puntas* plant—distinguished by its large three-pointed leaves and also known as "jackass bitters"—is used to treat and prevent a variety of parasitic ailments such as malaria, fungus, and ringworm. A few steps farther is skunk root, effective in treating alcoholism and ulcers, and wild grapevine, filled with an antiseptic used to wash newborn infants. Nearby grows the fiddlewood tree; its bark in an herbal bath kills the parasite known to cause a painful condition called leishmaniasis. Also present is the wild yam, a popular Belizean household remedy for urinary tract ailments and reliever of rheumatism and arthritis pains.

"We're teaching healthcare workers in village clinics how to use medicinal plants," says Arvigo, who welcomes between 3,000 and 5,000 visitors a year to Ix Chel Farm and sees patients privately for specialized forms of acupuncture, chiropractics, and other health treatments. Her husband is a homeopathic doctor with his own practice, as well.

The facilities at Ix Chel Farm have been expanded to accommodate conferences where Arvigo and Shropshire, residents of Belize since 1983, share their knowledge of natural healing practices. The couple sell a variety of teas and ointments directly to the public (mail orders carry a 15 percent surcharge). They also use an adjacent property to study the economic value of rain-forest plants, focusing on the sustainable harvest of various species. In 1993, the couple worked with the Belize Association of Traditional Healers in spearheading a campaign (believed to be the first of its kind in the world) to protect yet another tract of old-growth forest in western Belize for the specific purpose of growing and harvesting medicinal plants. The resulting 6,000-acre medicinal plant reserve, Terra Nova, is not currently accessible to tourists.

If You Go: Open during daylight hours every day but Monday, the Rainforest Medicine Trail and Ix Chel Farm are located at the end of Chaa Creek Road, next to Chaa Creek Cottages. The site can be reached by car (four-wheel-drive recommended during wet season) or taxi. Turn south off the Western Highway about 6 miles west of San Ignacio (watch for Chaa Creek signs). An alternative is to take a boat 5 miles upstream from the Hawkesworth Bridge and put in at the Chaa Creek Cottages dock. Call Eva's Restaurant in San Ignacio (tel. 9-22267) for more information, or write Ix Chel Farm, General Delivery, San Ignacio. The Ix Chel fax is 92-3870.

A self-guided tour of the mile-long Panti Medicinal Trail is $5 per person, including an explanatory booklet. Fresh fruit and spearmint tea are available on request. A guided 1-hour tour and lecture by an Ix Chel staffer is $30, if arranged in advance. There is an additional charge for meals and canoe trips.

Ix Chel Farm sells many herbal elixirs and potions, with names like Belly Be Good and Female Tonic; prices are around $10. Some of these items are also available in gift shops and groceries in other parts of the country; look for the Rainforest Remedies label, which is also marketed in the United States. Ten percent of all sales goes to traditional healers and educational programs in Belize.

Arvigo and Shropshire welcome tax-deductible donations to support their research, either sent directly to Ix Chel Farm or in care of Michael J. Balick, Director, Institute of Economic Botany, New York Botanical Garden, Bronx, NY 10458. Checks sent to Dr. Balick should be payable to the New York Botanical Garden, with an accompanying letter specifying use by the Belize Ethnobotany Project.

The Mountain Pine Ridge

A peculiar sight for many travelers is their first glimpse of stately pine forests carpeting the steep hillsides of the Cayo District's subtropical Maya Mountains. After winding through moist broadleaf jungle en route to this highland ecosystem, you are suddenly confronted with a landscape straight out of red-dirt Georgia. As far as the eye can see, tall pine trees reach to the deep blue sky. The sandy terrain is covered with rust-colored pine needles interspersed by maidenhair ferns, sparse grasses, and delicate wildflowers. In some areas, clusters of gnarled oaks and other hardwoods grip the thin topsoil.

The Mountain Pine Ridge—in Belize, the term "ridge" refers to a forest type and not a geographic formation—is an unusual natural phenomenon covering nearly 300 square miles.

The ancient Maya chose not to settle here, apparently concluding that seasonal droughts and shallow soils made the area unsuitable for farming. They did, however, extensively use the many caves along its limestone perimeter. Unpaved but well-maintained logging roads and nature trails cross the forest reserve, and the terrain is especially suited for hiking, mountain biking, and horseback riding. Birds and butterflies are numerous. Travelers will spy many unusual varieties of bromeliads, orchids, and other air plants among the boulders and branches.

Along the edges of the pine ridge are waterfalls, white-water rivers, and sharp escarpments with sweeping views. The almost total lack of human habitation means that much of this wilderness is virgin, although hurricanes and selective logging have occurred in some areas.

If You Go: The easiest way to see the Mountain Pine Ridge is by signing up for a minivan tour through a hotel or travel agency. This can be done easily through one of the lodges within the forest reserve or those located in the rest of the Cayo District. During the dry season, several vehicles a day explore the area, and overnight camping and equestrian trips can be arranged. Camping is allowed in certain areas with permission from the Department of Forestry (check with officials in Belmopan or the guard at the main entrance). There is no public transportation into the Mountain Pine Ridge except for taxis and rental cars. Drivers of their own vehicles are advised that the region's dirt roads are sometimes a challenge during rainy periods: four-wheel-drive is advised.

Hidden Valley (Thousand-Foot) Falls

Hidden Valley Falls, also known as Thousand-Foot Falls, is one of the Mountain Pine Ridge's primary attractions. This is believed to be the tallest waterfall in Central America, plunging almost one-quarter mile over a granite precipice into a deep jungle canyon. The distance is so great that the bottom of the waterfall becomes lost in mist and green foliage.

To see the falls, follow Baldy Beacon Road east of the forest reserve's main entrance for about 5 miles. Then proceed as directed by the well-marked signs for a couple of miles to an overlook area where a $1 admission fee will be collected by the resident caretaker. This is a good place to take photographs, savor a picnic, and observe bird life. The king vulture and rare orange-breasted falcon are sometimes seen riding the thermal air currents here—the latter predator nests near the waterfall. On a clear day, the capital buildings of Belmopan shimmer on the horizon.

Across from the caretaker's cabin is the Hidden Valley Institute for Environmental Studies, a privately funded research facility that conducts field work and develops much-needed conservation education materials for local schools. Wooden bungalows accommodate visiting naturalists and a small natural history museum. Immediately below the institute is a rugged 4-mile track to the base of the waterfall. The trail is not well maintained and should not be attempted without a guide. A round-trip hike may take all day.

Guests of the nearby Hidden Valley Lodge have access to three other magnificent falls: King Vulture, Tiger Creek, and Butterfly. Inquire at the resort about permission to visit them on your own.

Río On Pools

About 10 miles southwest of the Hidden Valley Falls overlook, the forest reserve's main road crosses the Río On, a cascading upland tributary of the Macal River. As it makes its way down from the Mountain Pine Ridge, the Río On swirls and splashes through a maze of granite boulders. The warm pools formed by these enormous rocks are as much as 15 feet deep and make delightful swimming holes, especially after a long day of hiking, biking, or horseback riding. The smooth stones make natural water slides, and many visitors like to stretch out and sunbathe on them in the tropical sun. There are outhouses (doubling as changing rooms) and picnic tables nearby, plus a freshwater tap. The parking lot accommodates a growing number of visitors, which may swell to several dozen on weekends and holidays, when Belizeans like to picnic here.

The Mountain Pine Ridge (Photo by Richard Mahler)

Río Frío Cave and Nature Trail

Not much farther south, a few miles past the village of Augustine and the forest reserve headquarters, visitors descend into subtropical vegetation and one of Belize's best-known cave districts. Look for a sign indicating the start of the Río Frío Nature Trail, which makes its way through dense forest to the largest and most spectacular cave in the group. (Río Frío Cave can also be easily reached by driving a mile or so down the same road to a picnic area outside the cavern's entrance.)

The nature trail takes about 45 minutes to negotiate and displays a wide variety of trees, each carefully labeled. The common names of many of these species are rather whimsical: they include the give-and-take palm, quamwood, boy job, poisonwood, and gumbo-limbo. There are even naturally occurring rubber, mahogany, and sapodilla trees (the latter is the source of chicle, a natural chewing-gum base). Birds and other wildlife in the area are abundant.

The Río Frío Cave extends about 300 yards through a solid limestone mountain. Centuries ago the tunnel was used as a ceremonial center by local Maya, but all artifacts have long since been removed or washed away. There are enormous arched entryways at either end of the cave, which narrows midway to a height and width of about 40 feet. Because the Río Frío cuts a broad channel through the underground passage, the cave is sometimes difficult to traverse during rainy months. Even in the dry season, visitors will probably find it necessary to at get least their feet wet. The interior of the cave is musty and cool but not entirely dark. Enough daylight filters through from either end to make flashlights unnecessary. Footholds can be slippery, however, and some rock climbing is required.

The cave displays unusual striations and colors that result from erosion and mineral deposits. Some rock surfaces have an odd, spongy texture; others resemble rice-paddy terraces or water fountains. Many stalactites hang from the ceiling and bats dwell in the darkest crevices.

The other, larger caves in the region—including the Domingo Ruíz, Blancaneaux, Skeleton Head, Barton Creek, and Chiquibul Caves—should not be visited without an experienced, knowledgeable guide. Guides can be engaged through hotels, travel agencies, or conservation organizations (see Inside Belize for suggestions). Recommended local guides include Richard, at Pine Ridge Lodge, and Mr. Bol, at Bol's Guiding Service, near the Mountain Pine Ridge Forest Reserve's main gate.

Augustine Village and Beyond

The headquarters for the Mountain Pine Ridge Forest Reserve is in a large wooden building in the settlement of Augustine, renamed Douglas DiSilva in 1990 after a politician's grandfather (who happened to be the area's first forest ranger). Only about 100 people—all forestry employees—live here, and the place has the look and feel of a run-down summer camp. Many of the houses are in disrepair, and others are being used to store pine seeds for reforestation projects. Worth visiting are the self-guided nature trail on the headquarters grounds and the small store (the only source of supplies for many miles around). Thatch-shaded tables are available to picnickers, but there is no restaurant or gas station. Inquire at the headquarters about camping and overnight rental of government-owned guesthouses. If you are continuing on to the Mayan ruin at Caracol (see description below), you will need to secure a permit from the Forestry Department officer on duty in Augustine. Permits are not granted when the road is judged to be in such poor condition that travel will be hazardous (both to visitors and the road surface itself). When the surface is dry, Caracol is about 45 minutes from here. Heading in the other direction, Georgeville and San Ignacio on the Western Highway are between 90 minutes and 2 hours away.

San Antonio Village

The more westerly of the two routes leading into the Mountain Pine Ridge—the Cristo Rey Road—passes through the small and mostly Maya Indian farming village of San Antonio, one of the few remaining communities in Belize where the Mopan dialect is spoken. (Note that there is another San Antonio, populated by Kekchí-speaking Maya, in the Toledo District near Punta Gorda.)

The Cayo's San Antonio village is situated in a picturesque valley where terraced fields of beans and corn have been carved out of the leafy jungle. Agriculture has persisted here for thousands of years. Recently, a few small shops, restaurants, and museums have been opened in an attempt to diversify the local economy.

Among the several attractions that are worth visiting in the San Antonio area are the García Sisters Museum, the Itzamna' (Magaña Family) Gallery and Gift Shop, and the Pacbitun archaeological site. For those wishing to spend some time here, the Blue Ridge Lodge provides basic cabins and meals. Horseback riding, cave trips, and tours of Pacbitun can also be arranged at Blue Ridge, located on the road to Pacbitun.

Pacbitun (meaning "stones set in the earth") is one of the oldest middle Pre-Classic Mayan ruins in the country, first occupied in 1000 B.C. and abandoned around A.D. 900. The location was known for many years by local residents but not registered by the Belize Department of Archaeology until 1971. Canada's Trent University excavated and partially reconstructed this ceremonial site during the

1980s. Findings include a number of Mayan altar stones and ball courts, as well as ancient musical instruments, such as ocarinas, fashioned out of carved and molded pottery. Pacbitun has at least 24 temple pyramids, the largest standing 60 feet tall. Two thousand years ago this was apparently a wealthy trading center with fancy homes, elevated walkways, a ball court, and raised irrigation causeways up to a half-mile long.

The Pacbitun site is on private farmland, but owner Fidencio Tzul welcomes visitors for a $1 fee. His family home is at the well-marked turnoff to Pacbitun one-half mile east of San Antonio. The ruins are about 3 miles farther down the side road. Mr. Tzul will be happy to give you a tour and answer any questions. There have been persistent rumors that the Belize government will some day purchase the Pacbitun site and relocate the Tzul family, so access may have changed by the time you read this.

Immediately north of San Antonio on the main road to Cristo Rey and Santa Elena is the García Sisters Museum—a combination crafts shop, herbal medicine pharmacy, and Mayan shrine. At least one of the five García sisters is always on hand, making and selling black-slate carvings that depict Maya-related masks, gods, and historic figures. Although this art form has been practiced by the modern Maya for years in neighboring Guatemala, only since the 1980s has this tradition been revived in Belize. At one end of the museum building is a round structure built in the shape of a traditional Mayan hut, where explanations of the various masks and symbols seen in the carvings can be found. There are also some large pieces of carved slate that emulate the sacred altar stones of ancient times. Be advised that the museum has a $5 admission charge and that the García sisters are aggressive salespersons.

Another group of local artisans, the Magaña family, also operates an art gallery and gift shop; they produce and sell wood and limestone carvings that incorporate traditional Mayan themes. Glyphs from the Mayan calendar are also hand-painted by family members on the same type of cloth supposedly used by ancient royalty. The Magaña enterprise is a few miles north of San Antonio on the Cristo Rey Road.

Vaca Falls and Che Chem Ha Cave

The upper stretches of the Macal River extend into a remote and seldom-seen area that drains the Vaca Plateau watershed and much of Chiquibul National Park. Access has improved in recent years through grading of a new road used in the construction of a Taiwanese-funded dam and hydroelectric plant, which was scheduled to flood part of the upper Macal basin above the confluence of the Mollejon River beginning in mid-1995.

A highly recommended destination is the privately owned Che Chem Ha Cave (sometimes called Vaca Cave), located near Vaca Falls, a scenic and rocky plunge on the Macal River. This location can be reached by a 1-hour boat trip from San Ignacio or a 2-hour hike from the hydroelectric project road. The Antonio Morales family provides bungalow-style accommodations and delicious meals as well as guided tours of Che Chem Ha, which means "poison vine water." This extensive, important Mayan ceremonial cave, discovered in the early 1990s by William Morales, is well worth seeing. It contains many pristine artifacts, including ancient pottery vessels, paintings, incense burners, and a circle of special carved stones where animals were sacrificed and prayers spoken to underworld gods. These items have been left undisturbed for at least 1,200 years, and iron grates now protect them from looters and vandals. The interior of these caves is dark, wet, and slippery: visitors should wear grip-tread shoes and bring a flashlight or diving light. Some fairly strenuous climbing is involved but the effort is well worth it.

The Morales compound may be reached by local VHF radio (try Bob Jones at Eva's Restaurant in San Ignacio) or through either Ek'Tun resort or Chaa Creek Cottages, which arrange tours. Visitors are asked not to enter Che Chem Ha Cave without a member of the Morales family. This is not only for safety, but also to protect the integrity of the cave's fragile artifacts, which have been left exactly where they were placed many centuries ago. The visit lasts roughly 90 minutes and costs about $10, with a minimum of three people on each tour. If you arrive in the late morning and place your order, the Moraleses will have lunch ready when you finish your cave tour and make the 30-minute hike back to the compound. Meals are about $6

Entrance to Che Chem Ha Cave, a sacred Mayan ceremonial site (Photo by Richard Mahler)

and overnight accommodations are about $80 (double occupancy, including three meals a day).

From the Morales home you can hike to Vaca Falls in about an hour, then trek onward to the previously described Ek'Tun resort, located a few miles downstream from the waterfall. (Guacamallo Ruins Campground lies a few miles along the Macal River in the other direction.) Ek'Tun and Che Cham Ha have a reciprocal agreement for those who wish to overnight in both places. Horses can be obtained at either location for rides into the jungle. Trails lead from here as far as San Antonio and Caracol. Note that the road to Che Chem Ha can be treacherous when wet; it's not unusual for cars to get stuck in the last 100 yards of steep road, just below the Morales residence. The turnoff to Che Chem Ha is 6 miles south on the Negroman Falls Road from Benque Viejo. Watch for the signs.

Chiquibul National Park
Rather than loop through the Mountain Pine Ridge in only a day or two, some travelers continue south beyond the Río Frío Cave into

some of the wildest areas of Belize. Only a handful of people live full-time in this area, mostly chicle tappers, illegal Guatemalan immigrants, poachers, and looters. In late 1991, the Government of Belize established more than 200,000 acres of this former forest reserve as a national park, currently Belize's single largest protected area.

Inside the Chiquibul National Park is the enormous Mayan ruin of Caracol, currently under excavation, located about 30 miles south-west of Augustine. Caracol is protected under a separate designation because of its archaeological significance. Chiquibul's broad tableland consists of hundreds of square miles of intact forest, the last strong-hold of many wildlife and plant species that are endangered elsewhere in Central America and southern Mexico. The plateau is crisscrossed by old logging and *chiclero* trails, but many have been reclaimed by the jungle. A detailed map may suggest that there are a number of villages in the area, but in reality these are abandoned lumbering camps established long ago, when mahogany and other hardwoods were being selectively harvested and skidded, then floated, downriver to Belize City. Travel in this area is now limited to horseback and high-clearance, four-wheel-drive vehicles. Overnight trips can be arranged through local operators to such spectacular destinations as Puente Natural, a high-arch cave similar to Río Frío, through which a small river flows. Highly recommended for such rugged adventures is Mountain Equestrian Trails; contact Neil Rogers or Jim Bevis for details.

Several other local tour operators, notably Chaa Creek Cottages and Maya Mountain Lodge, also run overnight or day-long mule/horse trips into this area. Destinations include remote Mayan ruins, caves, waterfalls, rivers, and chiclero camps. Because of the rough terrain and the absence of freshwater streams during the dry season, overland trips to the area are recommended only for travelers who are healthy and adventurous. The scenery, however, is some of the finest in Central America.

St. Herman's and Other Caves; Blue Hole and Five Blues Lake National Parks

For experienced spelunkers—the technical term for cave explorers—Belize can be a dream come true. Underlying most of the country (with the notable exception of the Maya Mountains) are the kinds of limestone platforms and uplifts that almost guarantee the formation of extensive cavern networks. Unlike the western rim of the Americas, which is part of the so-called Ring of Fire circling the Pacific Ocean, there is virtually no volcanic activity in Belize.

Because of their isolation, many Belizean caves have not been fully explored. It is likely that many entrances have not even been discovered. The Chiquibul complex of the Vaca Plateau, for example, is perhaps one of the largest underground labyrinths in Central America. No one knows for certain, since many branches have yet to be explored by modern cavers. In fact, no systematic scientific exploration occurred until the late 1970s. Since then, in some of the Vaca Plateau (Chiquibul) caves, researchers have found fossilized insects and crustaceans that have been extinct for many centuries. Many of the caves show signs of ceremonial usage by the ancient Maya, who considered such places to be sacred passages to the underworld. Pots and other artifacts are often found in dusty yet pristine condition.

According to Logan McNatt, a former Department of Archaeology employee who spent many years exploring Belizean caves, most of these sites are and should remain closed to the general public. "There are three main problems," McNatt told us. "First, most of the caves are important archaeological sites that have not yet been evaluated or protected. Second, many cave systems of Belize are subject to sudden, unexpected flooding that can make them very dangerous. Finally, few maps of the inner passageways exist."

McNatt points out that many of the caves are part of underground river courses that form a massive aquifer beneath Belize. A caver may descend under a clear blue sky, only to find a rapid surge in water elevation caused by a far-off thunderstorm. For these reasons, only experienced and well-equipped cavers should attempt to explore the wilder, lesser-known caves of Belize. Knowledgeable and experienced guides should also be engaged for every journey, except for such small and well-traveled caves as Río Frío, St. Herman's, and Ben Lomond. These latter caves have an eerie kind of beauty, punctuated as they often are by occasional streams of light from ceiling cracks and side entrances. Some of the underground chambers are 100 or more feet high, adorned with majestic stalactites and stalagmites. They provide an unusual habitat favored by bats, sightless fish, spiders, and other small creatures.

A well-marked sign guides visitors to the entrance trail of Blue Hole National Park, a federally protected area administered by the Belize Audubon Society and located 12 miles southeast of Belmopan on the Hummingbird Highway. (This Blue Hole is not to be confused with the offshore Blue Hole located near Half Moon Caye.) Although one of the smallest protected areas managed by Belize Audubon, Blue Hole National Park receives thousands of visitors each year.

In late 1993, Belize Audubon improved Blue Hole National Park by completing a first-ever management plan for the area. Another promising development for Blue Hole was initiated in late 1994 through an agreement involving the California-based Christian Environmental Association, Belize Audubon, and Caribbean Investment Limited. The Association is purchasing 4,000 acres of adjacent tropical forest to be overseen in accordance to guidelines established by the Blue Hole management plan.

The centerpiece of the park is an amazing sight: a deep pool of churning sapphire water formed by the collapse of an underground river channel. The Caves Branch Creek tributary wells up from an unseen source and travels for about 100 yards before plunging mysteriously down a siphon that carries it into yet another cave beneath the mountain. The dome-shaped chamber where the water is sucked underground creates an unusual echo-chamber effect as liquid swirls beneath it. This idyllic setting is a good spot for swimming, picnicking, and bird-watching. There are no overnight camping facilities. The sparkling pool is about 25 feet deep and moves fast, so bathers should be careful. Some foreigners swim nude here, although this practice offends the large percentage of Belizeans who are deeply religious.

The same Caves Branch Creek travels through nearby St. Herman's Cave and Mountain Cow Cave, which are accessible from the Blue Hole via a well-maintained forest pathway called the Nature Trail. Fauna recorded in this area include jaguar, ocelot, jaguarundi, tapir, peccary, anteater, gibnut, coatimundi, deer, and kinkajou. Once you arrive at the cave, a flashlight is handy for exploration, along with a good pair of waterproof boots, such as Wellingtons. A smaller cave in the area not connected to St. Herman's or Mountain Cow is Petroglyph Cave, named for its ancient rock drawings left by Indians many centuries ago. Permission from the Department of Archaeology must be obtained to enter either Mountain Cow or Petroglyph Cave, which are beyond the borders of Blue Hole National Park. The park itself is open from 8:00 a.m. to 4:00 p.m. daily. Warning: Numerous car break-ins have been reported at the Blue Hole parking area; take extra precautions if the park warden is not in the vicinity.

The hike to St. Herman's Cave from the Blue Hole is about 1.5 miles and takes about 45 minutes. An alternative route involves driving 1 mile north along the Hummingbird Highway, where it is possible to join the Nature Trail only 10 minutes from the cave's entrance. Look for the Blue Hole National Park sign next to a citrus orchard at about Mile 11 on the Hummingbird Highway. The trail to St. Herman's begins immediately behind the sign and curves to the right along a dirt road next to the citrus plantation.

St. Herman's was used by the Maya during the Classic period, A.D. 100 to 900, and the concrete steps leading into its mouth are laid over stone steps carved more than 1,000 years ago. Ancient pots used to collect "virgin water" from cave drippings, along with spears and torches, have been removed by archaeologists for study.

For those with a special interest in caves, we recommend a visit to Caves Branch Jungle River Camp, which offers camping, bunkhouses, and private cabañas on a 55,000-acre estate a few miles from Blue Hole National Park (14 miles south of Belmopan on the Hummingbird Highway). Ian Anderson uses the camp, owned by Caribbean Investments Ltd., as a base for daily adventure tours. The specialty of Anderson's Adventure Tours Belize is guided "tubing" through three flooded caves in the area. This involves floating gently along the slow-moving underground rivers on the inflated inner tube from a truck tire. Miles of floatable passageways allow visitors hours of looking at pristine Mayan artifacts and magnificent natural formations, including a "crystal room" where stalagmites sparkle like diamonds as they rise from below the river's surface. For the more adventurous traveler, Anderson leads expeditions that last up to six days and include treks through dense jungle. Horseback riding, bird-watching, wildlife searches (both day and night), swimming, and guided nature walks are other options available at Caves Branch Jungle River Camp. Accommodations are rustic and prices moderate; they include meals cooked by local Belizeans over an open hearth.

Besides caves and underground rivers, the area's attractions include a majestic hardwood forest full of ferns, orchids, bromeliads, vines, and shrubs, as well as an impressive number of birds (at least 100 species have been confirmed here) and spider monkeys. If you're traveling the Hummingbird Highway by private vehicle, food and drinks are available at the Oasis Bar and Restaurant, located at about the halfway point between Belmopan and Dangriga, next to a Texaco gas station.

Down the road from the Oasis is St. Margaret's Village, located near the crest of a ridge on the Belize and Stann Creek District borders. A small sign marks the turnoff (Mile 32 of the Hummingbird Highway) onto the unpaved road heading north several miles to Five Blues Lake National Park. The park's crown jewel is a small, 200-foot-deep lake surrounded by steep limestone hills. It is called Five Blues because of the various shades of blue reflected by the sky during the course of a typical day.

Five Blues Lake National Park is a remarkable testament to the conservation success in Belize: it represents the country's growing trend toward local involvement in the management of protected areas by residents of nearby villages. Largely through the efforts of the Association of Friends of Five Blues, a grassroots community group, the original 885-acre park has been expanded to include some 4,200 acres of pristine tropical forest and an extensive limestone cave complex.

The Friends of Five Blues, with support from the Natural Resource Management and Protection Project, have built a small visitor's center from which a park warden guides visitors on two main trails that wind through the jungle to an interesting cave. Near the visitor's center, accessible by an unpaved road, is Five Blues Lake itself. You can enjoy a picnic lunch, take a swim, or arrange for a serene boat ride across the water. With your guide, we also recommend a short trek past the lake into a Mayan cave complex located within the protected area. The ancient Maya also used the deep pools of the lake as sacrificial wells.

One main goal of the Friends of Five Blues is to establish enduring local participation in nature-oriented tourism so that residents of nearby St. Margaret's Village will see some economic benefit from protecting the park. The Friends group is also working to expand the park and create protected corridors linking Five Blues with the nearby Sibun watershed, Monkey Bay National Park, and Manatee Forest Reserve. This network could simultaneously address the need to protect biological diversity and wildlife movement through undisturbed lands. This protection, however, must come quickly in light of citrus encroachment and other development in the region.

Before you go to St. Margaret's Village and Five Blues Lake National Park, we suggest you contact the Friends of Five Blues at Box 111, Belmopan (tel. 81-2005). Park visitors are offered camping, horseback riding, hiking, caving, birding, overnight guided jungle trips, and Spanish language classes. There are several rustic overnight options in the Five Blues area: Palacio's Resort, Tamandua (a private 170-acre wildlife sanctuary and fruit farm, close to monkey troops and a "hurricane shelter" cave), and the Five Blues Bed & Breakfast Association (a Hopkins-style cooperative of 20 local women who maintain guest rooms in their homes and prepare meals for visitors).

Another fairly large cave that is open to the public but not as accessible as St. Herman's is Ben Lomond Cave, located in the limestone hills fringing Southern Lagoon, about 25 miles southwest of Belize City and not far from Five Blues Lake National Park. An excellent choice for a beginner, Ben Lomond is full of Mayan artifacts and its surroundings offer a perfect example of habitat transition from savanna to tropical forest. It can be reached only by taking a boat to the lagoon and then hiking through dense coastal bush. A stream flows from the cavern's wide mouth. We recommend hiring a local guide in Gales Point or Dangriga for the trip. Bardy Riverol of Jal's Travel in Belize City offers excellent tours to destinations in this area, including Ben Lomond Cave, as does the Pelican Beach Resort in Dangriga. The seldom-seen Manatee River Caves, located in the same limestone karst area, are considered dangerous and should be explored only by serious cavers.

Horseback riding in the Cayo District (Photo by Richard Mahler)

Belmopan

The capital city of Belize has yet to find its way onto the itinerary of most foreign visitors. This is not surprising, considering the community's meager attractions. Looking more like a second-rate college campus than a national seat of government, Belmopan's concrete and stucco buildings are spread over a wide expanse of weedy lawns and empty lots. The main complex is clustered around a central plaza that features a lively market, several unremarkable restaurants, and a noisy bus depot.

The architecture and layout are designed to evoke a Mayan feeling: the name Belmopan combines the "Bel" of Belize with the name of one of the country's indigenous tribes, the Mopan Maya. Despite warnings that another big hurricane could level Belize City, as Hattie did in 1961, only about 6,000 Belizeans have heeded the call to relocate to Belmopan.

The main attraction for travelers in Belmopan is the Archaeology Vault of the country's Department of Archaeology. While the vast majority of Belize's Mayan treasures have been hauled off to foreign museums and private collections, enough fine pieces remain to make a stop here worthwhile. Department staffers take reservations for tours (two days' notice required) at 8-22106. The vault—which is exactly that—is open from 1:30 to 4:00 p.m. on Mondays, Wednesdays, and Fridays. Permission from the Department of Archaeology is also required to visit Caracol and certain other Mayan ruins. Serious students of the culture may wish to schedule a conversation with Harriet Topsey, Archaeology Commissioner.

In early 1995, the Belize government commenced construction of a long-awaited national museum in Belmopan that will eventually house the Archaeology Vault collection, as well as many other historic and cultural artifacts. Projected to cost at least $3.5 million, the facility is expected to open in late 1996.

If You Go: Belmopan is located a short distance south of the intersection of the Western and Hummingbird highways, about 40 miles in either direction from San Ignacio and Belize City. Frequent, inexpensive bus service runs to Belmopan from Belize City, San Ignacio, and Dangriga. Buses run about once every hour between these communities from 8:00 a.m. to 5:00 p.m., less often on weekends and holidays.

Services in Belmopan include a bank, a post office, and several hotels and restaurants. Because most visitors are on expense accounts, most accommodations are pricey, although the Bull Frog Inn and Circle "A" Lodge, both on Halfmoon Ave., are more moderate. Be advised that the Bull Frog bar can be very noisy until the wee hours of the morning. The best budget hotel (and café) is the El Rey Inn, located on Moho Street in a residential area. Free overnight parking is available to recreational vehicles at The Oasis, near Guanacaste Park, which also has an inexpensive restaurant, restrooms, and a water tap.

Belmopan's restaurants are characterized by overpriced, undistiguished food and slow service. The best establishments are Yoli's Lounge (Belizean, Mexican, Italian and American food) and the Bull Frog Inn, although the Chinese restaurants serve cheap, acceptable meals, as they do throughout Belize. An important exception is Little

Dragon, near the Hummingbird Highway, where several travelers have reported intestinal distress.

Guanacaste National Park

On Earth Day (April 22) 1990, the Belizean government officially created 50-acre Guanacaste National Park in a lush parcel of forest alongside the Belize River. Located less than 2 miles from Belmopan, at the intersection of the Hummingbird and Western Highways, the park is named after a huge guanacaste tree growing near the reserve's southwestern boundary. Also known as the tubroos or monkey's ear tree, the guanacaste is a highly prized hardwood known for its resistance to insects and decay. Guanacaste lumber is the material of choice for construction of dugout canoes, feeding troughs, and rice-hulling mortars. Cattle and monkeys love to nibble on guanacaste fruit, which appear during the dry season as shiny brown pods after an explosion of small white flowers.

This particular giant (the species is one of the largest in Central America) towers more than 120 feet above the forest floor and was spared the woodcutter's ax only because naturally occurring splits in its massive trunk make it unusable as timber (all other guanacaste trees in the park have been harvested). The tree's broad, sky-seeking branches support hundreds of epiphytes, including many brilliant species of orchid and bromeliad.

A short trail leads through the forest to the guanacaste tree from a visitors' center operated by the Belize Audubon Society. Known as the Guanacaste Education Center, this facility was dedicated to the U.S. Peace Corps as Audubon's way of honoring the Corps' many contributions to conservation and education in Belize.

Other large trees seen along the trail to the guanacaste tree include the mammee apple, bookut, ramon, quamwood, silk cotton, and raintree. Several mahogany trees have been planted near the park's visitor center as part of a reforestation program. You can hike a self-guided interpretive loop trail and view a display of native orchids at the visitors' center.

Despite Guanacaste's diminutive size, it harbors abundant wildlife. Species observed here include jaguarundi, kinkajou, paca, armadillo, iguana, deer, and opossum. Resident birds include the blue-crowned motmot, black-faced ant thrush, smoky-brown woodpecker, red-lored parrot, black-headed trogon, and squirrel cuckoo, among more than 50 confirmed species.

Guanacaste National Park is easily accessible by bus, taxi, private car, or package tour. Restrooms, drinking water, and picnic facilities are available. Cooking and camping, however, are not permitted. The well-maintained trail network throughout the park follows a graceful curve of the Belize River at its confluence with Roaring Creek.

Río Bravo Conservation and Management Area

A nonprofit group called Programme for Belize has, since its formation in 1988, achieved remarkable success in protecting a major portion of the northwest corner of Belize as pristine lowland jungle. Thanks to their intervention, this forest remains one of the largest tracts of undisturbed subtropical habitat in the region. From its inception, the sponsoring group's primary objectives have been to create a model of appropriate economic development and to provide funding for conservation, education, and scientific and management training throughout the country for the lasting preservation of Belize's natural heritage and biological diversity.

In the early 1990s, Programme for Belize acquired a key area of land covering 26,892 acres in the Río Bravo area. This acquisition connects two blocks of land that, together with other acquisitions, comprise the Río Bravo Conservation and Management Area. The Programme has thus converted 229,000 acres into a single unit that facilitates management; assures the future for an extensive, wildlife-rich tract of tropical forest; and secures a vital habitat corridor along a site known as Irish Creek.

As early as 1989, Programme for Belize, then administered by the Massachusetts Audubon Society, began purchasing 110,000 acres of tropical forest in Belize's northwest corner. High-quality forest tracts totaling over 90,000 acres have reportedly been donated by the Coca-Cola Company. With help from other friends, Programme for Belize has raised several million dollars to purchase and administer these wildlife-rich lands.

The government-approved management plan for the Río Bravo Conservation Area allows for the development of low-impact agriculture, forest product harvesting, and tourism based on archaeology and natural history. A fundamental long-term goal for the Río Bravo area is to pay for its conservation through sales revenues derived from its renewable natural resources. Programme for Belize believes lessons learned at Río Bravo will serve as a model for the region.

Private contributors continue to be key to the success of this large-scale conservation project. Through the Massachusetts Audubon Society, contributors are invited to donate $50 to protect an acre of tropical forest, something many schoolchildren have done as class projects throughout the United States and Europe. The Society sends a certificate to donors indicating how many acres the individual or group has helped protect.

Most of the Río Bravo area is a nearly untouched subtropical haven where howler monkeys, spider monkeys, king vultures, gray foxes, more than 80 species of bats, and 110 species of orchids now enjoy a permanent refuge. Some 200 species of trees have been identified here along with all five Belizean species of cat: margay, jaguarundi, jaguar, puma, and ocelot. Nearly 400 species of birds have been identified as either year-round residents or migrants that frequent the area. A late 1994 identification of a gray-breasted crake—a small bird that resembles a black rail—was confirmed by Carolyn Miller, one of Belize's leading naturalists. This sighting is believed to be only the third record of this species in Belize.

The Río Bravo Conservation and Management Area covers the northeastern part of the Petén wilderness, a large, biogeographically distinct expanse that extends into southeastern Mexico and northern Guatemala. Río Bravo is now mostly undisturbed by human activities; although much of the area was occupied by the ancient Maya.

Nick Brokaw and Elizabeth Mallory, arguably two of the most qualified scientists currently working in Belize, have identified more than a dozen floristically distinct vegetation types in Río Bravo, including upland forest, palm forest, swamp forest, riparian forest, and second growth. A research facility has been constructed by Belizeans deep within the forest, strategically located for easy access to these distinct habitat types. It provides training in archaeology, forest management, and ecology while concurrently monitoring the reserve's biological diversity.

Although the Programme is difficult for some environmentalists to embrace, the authors believe it is taking a realistic approach to conservation and sustainable development. Saving wildlife and the forest is a primary objective at Río Bravo, but the Programme also recognizes that preservation must generate income and cannot simply lock up resources forever. The larger goal is for people to benefit from the land without destroying it.

Visitors wishing to see Programme for Belize lands are best off staying in Chan Chich Lodge, located near the settlement of Gallon Jug. This is a luxurious and expensive group of elegant cabañas set in the middle of a Classic-period Mayan ruin. The accommodations were constructed for Belizean businessman Barry Bowen (the lodge's owner) by Tom and Josie Harding, who now manage Chan Chich. Ancient Mayan monuments border the resort's grounds on all sides, giving the impression that the cabañas are original Mayan homes. Their plush interiors, however, give a different impression. Polished and oiled woodwork, colorful drapes, a full bar, and gourmet dining combine to make Chan Chich one of Belize's finest lodges. Indeed, it has received a top ranking in at least one world survey of jungle accommodations.

By prior arrangement with Programme for Belize, tourists can visit the nearby La Milpa archaeological site. (Details follow later in this chapter.) Other activities around Chan Chich and the Río Bravo wilderness include superb bird-watching (Chan Chich means "little bird" in Mayan), jungle walks, canoeing, horseback riding, guided nature/archaeology tours, and simply relaxing.

If You Go: Book a stay at Chan Chich Lodge well in advance, as rooms fill up quickly. In Belize, call 2-75634 (fax 2-76961); in the United States, call (800) 343-8009. Unless the weather has been dry, it is best to fly to Gallon Jug rather than attempt the rough dirt roads into the area. Javier's Flying Service, Ltd. (tel. 2-45332) is one of the

Cabañas at Chan Chich Jungle Lodge (Photo by Kevin Schafer)

best charter companies and flies frequently to the area, charging at least $175 round-trip from Belize City. Expect to pay about $120 per person each night for accommodations.

It is possible to drive to Gallon Jug by turning north at Orange Walk Village (not to be confused with Orange Walk Town) near Belmopan and following the Iguana Creek Bridge road or by turning south from just west of Blue Creek Village near the Mexican border. The Blue Creek road is shorter (about 4 hours from Belize City) and better maintained than the Iguana Creek route. Be sure to inquire locally about road conditions, especially when the ground is wet. A four-wheel-drive vehicle is recommended during any season.

Excellent educational resources for visitors to this area include cassette tapes of bird songs and calls made by Wildlife Conservation Society research fellow Bruce Miller. Miller and his wife, Carolyn, also a WCS field scientist, wrote *Exploring the Rainforest*, a 64-page trail and natural history guide to the Chan Chich area that includes an exhaustive flora and fauna checklist for all of Belize. The Millers live in Gallon Jug and guide occasional (and highly recommended) tours through the Río Bravo lands.

Tapir Mountain Nature Reserve

Wedged between Roaring Creek and Upper Barton Creek in the northern foothills of the Mountain Pine Ridge, not far from the capital city of Belmopan, the 6,741-acre Tapir Mountain (formerly Society Hall) Nature Reserve is an intact block of tropical forest, home to all manner of flora and fauna. It has been kept this way because of the determination and foresight of its conservation-minded landowner.

Svea Dietrich-Ward had for many years sought a way to permanently save this area. Finally, in 1986, the German-born conservationist (now a dual citizen of the U.S. and Belize who raises Arabian horses near San Ignacio) entered a long-term lease agreement with the Belize government on the condition that the property's natural resources be protected. Soon after, officials proclaimed it a "nature reserve." (In Belize, this designation is a subcategory of the National Parks System Act, specifying that such lands be preserved only for scientific research and education.)

The nature reserve label means that Tapir Mountain is not a destination for the casual tourist: the only legally allowed visitors are researchers with specific scientific objectives or groups of students with competent leaders, all with prior permission. A separate permit is required from the Belize Audubon Society, since that organization manages Tapir Mountain.

Perhaps the greatest threat to Tapir Mountain is encroachment into the reserve by farmers engaged in slash-and-burn agriculture. A growing number of Guatemalan and Salvadoran refugees are practicing this traditional form of agriculture in the area; there have been reports of this forest-destroying practice actually occurring within Tapir Mountain's borders, farmers apparently taking advantage of the fact that the area is so remote. This is compounded by the lack of access for land managers to monitor and prevent such deforestation.

At Dietrich-Ward's requests, the conservation flying group Light-Hawk has monitored and shown law enforcement officers these incursions from the air.

The Tapir Mountain area consists of undulating limestone karst topography dotted with sinkholes, exposed rock outcrops, small streams, and bubbling springs. Middens—the garbage heaps of the Maya, consisting mostly of shells, pot shards, and bones—are concealed by a dense forest of climbing vines, cohune palms, and scores of other tree species. In some of the valleys and low-lying portions of this reserve, the forest canopy crests at nearly 100 feet. Massive brown termite nests envelop tree trunks here and there, while leaf-cutter ants march past brilliant red and yellow giant heliconias, methodically going about the rigorous business of collecting and transporting food for their vast colonies. Collected leaves are masticated and regurgitated by the ants, who later eat the fungus-covered results.

In 1994 a preliminary biological survey of the reserve began generaating baseline data and setting the stage for possible development of a tropical research and training facility at Tapir Mountain. However, like other protected areas the Belize Autobon Society manages, Tapir Mountain needs financial support to help protect it over the long haul.

If You Go: Because of its protected status, access to the Tapir Mountain Nature Reserve is limited to scientists and other researchers. Contact the Belize Audubon Society in Belize City for specific information. Not far from Tapir Mountain is the Slate Creek Preserve, a private, community-based reserve spearheaded by Jim Bevis, president of the Belize Ecotourism Association. Contact Bevis at Mountain Equestrian Trails for information on access to this 3,500-acre wilderness.

Cockscomb Basin Wildlife Sanctuary

Standing at the entrance to the Cockscomb Basin Wildlife Sanctuary, with its modest sign wired to the pendulum gate and lush tropical forest as a backdrop, visitors may sense that beyond them lies an exotic domain rich in history and wildlife. And as they enter, this intuition will unquestionably be proven correct.

This huge tract of Stann Creek District wilderness—locally referred to as "the Cockscomb"—encompasses a sweeping mountainside basin about 25 miles southwest of Dangriga. This is the world's first-ever reserve established to protect the jaguar, one of the largest and most endangered felines in the Americas. It is also steeped in a dynamic evolution of nature's wonders, scientific research, and conservation prowess.

The Cockscomb Basin Wildlife Sanctuary is highly recommended as a rewarding destination for the traveler who wants to actively support Belizean conservation while simultaneously reaping its benefits. This is one of the least expensive and most impressive locales for exploring Belize's lush tropical forest. Wildlife and plant life are abundant, and the patient visitor will likely see some truly exotic creatures.

From the combination registration hut and craft shop in the village of Maya Center (a mandatory check-in stop), located immediately west of the Southern Highway, travel about 7 miles on a rough dirt road to reach the Cockscomb visitor's center, campground, and guest huts. Stay alert as you proceed up this road. You may be fortunate enough to see a tayra, a small weasel-like animal common in the region. A turkey-sized crested guan or a flock of toucans may also catch your eye in the forest canopy.

There is a small parking lot at the sanctuary's headquarters, located at the site of an abandoned lumber camp littered with some of the iron cages used by zoologist Alan Rabinowitz during his pioneering studies of the jaguar here in the mid-1980s. Nearby are a campground and rustic cabins available for overnight travelers. From the visitor's center and museum, you can take self-guided tours along a number of well-maintained forest trails. Brochures, maps, and signposts help identify the various tree and plant species seen along the way, which include colorful orchids and naturally buttressed hardwoods. The pathways vary considerably in their length and ruggedness, so check with the resident manager before heading out. There are some fine swimming holes near the visitor's center where you can cool off after a strenuous trek.

Within minutes of arrival, you realize why the Cockscomb Basin has a reputation as a bird-watcher's paradise. At least 290 species have been recorded here, including the endangered scarlet macaw, chestnut-brown Montezuma oropendola (distinguished by its bright yellow tail), Agami heron, collared aracari, keel-billed toucan, and king vulture. In 1994 the park director and a warden recorded a flock of 10 scarlet macaws flying over Maya Center, at the Cockscomb's entrance. Another group of macaws was spotted by a warden a few days later within the sanctuary.

The basin provides habitat for many amphibians, lizards, and snakes. Observations by a team of Belizean conservation leaders and scientists identified over 35 species that included 9 snakes, 12 lizards, 14 amphibians, and a frog known as *Smilisca phaeota*, not previously recorded in Belize. The red-eyed tree frog was also identified, and one of its major breeding areas located. The team estimated that the Cockscomb provides habitat for roughly 70 percent of Belize's non-marine reptiles.

Among the main attractions for any visitor, of course, are the cats of Cockscomb. Because of their mostly nocturnal habits, however, the odds are that you will not actually see one. Still, your chances are better here than perhaps anyplace else. Besides embracing one of the highest concentrations of jaguars anywhere in the world, the sanctuary is home to many ocelots, margays, jaguarundis, and pumas. Best bets for a sighting are along the roads and riverbanks of the Cockscomb, where the felines like to hunt.

The Cockscomb Basin's human history dates back to the ancient Maya, who left a Classic-era ceremonial site called Chucil Baalum deep within the forest. Pockets of fertile soil helped support their milpa agriculture for many generations. The last of these Indians were relocated during the late 1980s in the interest of wildlife habitat preservation.

The Cockscomb's powers of forest regeneration are among its most intriguing qualities. The area's lushness is particularly amazing when you consider the hurricane damage inflicted on many of its tall trees and the collective insults of slash-and-burn agriculture and timber-cutting over long periods of time. If you hike along the entrance road, you will need an experienced local guide to distinguish what is left of an airstrip that was last used in 1984 to facilitate radio tracking during Rabinowitz's jaguar studies. In a few short years, the tropical forest has almost completely taken over what was once a bare piece of land. At one end of the runway a narrow trail leads to a crash site, where a small plane still hangs from the forest canopy. The passengers (Rabinowitz, a pilot, and a cameraman) were only slightly injured.

Back at the visitor's center, you can see Victoria Peak jutting up from the back of the basin. At 3,675 feet, this is Belize's most spectacular mountain. Sheathed in verdant forest, the rocky summit is capped by dark quartzite. At 4 million years of age, Victoria Peak may be part of the oldest geologic formation in Central America. The tall peak—easily seen from the barrier reef—has been a sailors' landmarks for centuries.

The most recent—and perhaps the most relevant—sequence of human involvement in the Cockscomb Basin is the effort to protect it. This campaign initially focused on preserving the jaguar, an "indicator species" that can serve as a good index of an ecosystem's health. Where there are large predators like the jaguar, there are likely to be hundreds of smaller animals.

The chain of events leading up to the designation of this area as a permanent wildlife sanctuary began in 1983 with a two-year jaguar study sponsored by Wildlife Conservation Society, a division of the New York Zoological Society. Living in what is now a restricted-access warden's building, Rabinowitz carried out an intensive field study of the jaguar's range, diet, habits, and general ecology. The U.S. scientist trapped several jaguars, recorded their vital statistics, and fitted them with radio collars. This enabled him to track the felines and thus determine the size and location of their territorial ranges. Rabinowitz lived among the local Maya, employed several of them during his studies, and chronicled his many adventures—with certain embellishments—in an entertaining book entitled *Jaguar*.

With strong backing from Wildlife Conservation Society and important in-country political assistance from the Belize Audubon Society, Rabinowitz recommended that the area be set aside for official protection of the jaguar. In late 1984, the Cockscomb Basin was declared a national forest reserve with a "no hunting" clause to protect the cat. The World Wildlife Fund then provided crucial financial assistance to support the basin's status as a protected area. In 1986, after much deliberation about the trade-offs involved, the government declared 3,000 acres of the 108,000-acre area as the Cockscomb Basin Wildlife Sanctuary/Forest Reserve. This made Belize the first country to protect an area specifically for jaguars.

Several Mayan families were required to move to Maya Center, where they have shifted from milpa agriculture to craftwork. Their cooperative sells the work of local artisans at the Maya Center visitors' registration booth. Some of the men transplanted from the sanctuary are employed there as managers, caretakers, and guides. The Maya-descended Belizean now in charge of the reserve, Ernesto Saqui, is one of the best-trained and most knowledgeable nature reserve managers in Central America.

In November 1990, the Cockscomb Basin Wildlife Sanctuary was expanded to include 102,000 acres of the Cockscomb Basin. This feat was accomplished through the joint efforts of the Belizean government, Belize Audubon, World Wildlife Fund, and other groups. Management by Belize Audubon has enabled the Cockscomb to emerge as a successful model of ecosystem conservation that integrates low-impact tourism with science. Wildlife habitat and ecosystem field work, such as a 1990 expedition sponsored by the Belize Center for Environmental Studies, is crucial to continued success in Cockscomb management.

During the early 1990s, an exciting and historic collaborative effort succeeded in reintroducing black howler monkeys into their former range within the Cockscomb. Primate scientist Rob Horwich and the Belize Audubon Society report that hunting, logging, a yellow-fever epidemic in the 1950s, and devastation by Hurricane Hattie in 1961 are all factors that probably accounted for local extinction of howlers. According to Horwich and his affiliated organization, Community Conservation Consultants/Howlers Forever, a total of 63 howler monkeys were relocated into Cockscomb from other parts of Belize from 1992 to 1994. Hermelindo Saqui of Maya Center, a Cockscomb warden, diligently tracked the new howler populations for two years, with the help of radio telemetry, to provide crucial progress and distribution information. The survival rate for the relocated howlers was as high as 90 percent.

Although the howler monkeys are a delight to behold, the most royal creatures of today's Cockscomb Basin are its jaguars. This cat is the third largest of its genus in the world and the most powerful land predator in Central and South America. The jaguar is called "tiger" by many Belizeans, *tigre* by local Spanish-speakers, and *balum* by the Maya. Its diet includes white-lipped peccaries, armadillos, agoutis, Virginia opossums, iguanas, coatis, and kinkajous. Even if they cannot see the cats, Cockscomb visitors sometimes swear they can feel the presence of these elegant and graceful creatures. This is particularly true when you take a nighttime walk along the sanctuary's main road, as the croaking of thousands of frogs in the shallow ponds reaches a crescendo.

In case you're wondering, jaguars are not known to attack humans, except when provoked. It's not as if they are incapable of succeeding in such a foray, however. They are believed to sometimes prey on the Baird's tapir, an endangered relative of the horse (locally called the "mountain cow") that may attain 650 pounds when fully grown. You can sometimes see the tapir's tracks in the muddy banks of South Stann Creek. Like the jaguar, the tapir is very shy, so this may be your closest encounter.

During hikes through the Cockscomb, you may also come across the Central American river otter, a playful mammal that epitomizes an exuberant *carpe diem* lifestyle. Seeing one frolic or fish in the clear waters of Cockscomb's rivers is a real thrill.

Since Rabinowitz's pioneering studies of the jaguar, several other scientists have also used the Cockscomb as a research base. One often-overlooked researcher is Michael J. Konecny, who lived in the Cockscomb from 1984 to 1986 and studied other carnivores that inhabit the sanctuary. Konecny was affiliated with the University of Florida, and supported by the National Geographic Society and the National Wildlife Federation.

Like Rabinowitz, Konecny trapped the animals he was studying and affixed them with radio collars. This allowed him to determine their ranges and habits as he monitored their movements from aircraft. During his 18 months of fieldwork, Konecny collected an enormous amount of data. He confirmed, for instance, that the jaguarundi and tayra are active during the day, while the ocelot and margay are largely nocturnal.

This was the first attempt at field studies of some of these species. Although the density of margay in the Cockscomb appeared rather low at the time, Konecny was able to gather some fascinating facts about the arboreal feline, known to jump more than 8 feet straight up into an overhanging branch. The scientist's study of several captured ocelots suggested that these graceful creatures were having trouble reproducing fast enough to keep up with losses to human hunters and deforestation.

Konecny also shed early light on the ecology of the relatively unknown tayra, a weasel-like species whose hind legs are longer than its front legs, giving it an advantage for climbing. Called "bushdog" by Creoles and *cabeza de viejo* ("old man's head") by Spanish-speakers, the tayra is a fierce-looking omnivore that thrives on fruit, insects, and small vertebrates. Konecny encountered this creature on 15 separate occasions, suggesting it may be one of the easiest of Cockscomb's mammals to see. On his first trip to the sanctuary, one of this book's authors saw a tayra cross the entrance road.

Visitors interested in the many animals roaming the Cockscomb Basin Wildlife Sanctuary owe much to the work of Michael Konecny, Alan Rabinowitz, Ben Nottingham (Rabinowitz's partner), and others who have turned the basin into a living laboratory. Much more work, however, remains to be done; for example, none of the carnivore studies gathered data about the puma (or mountain lion). Although they are suspected to inhabit the area, the puma's place in the field community remains a mystery.

As you make your way along the Cockscomb's pathways, keep your eyes open for the area's resident creatures. Even fleeting sightings of discreet animals like the puma (which should be reported immediately to the sanctuary manager) are valued by the scientific community. And nowhere else in Belize will you find such an organized system of well-maintained trails. They are quite wide, and most are short and level enough that they do not involve difficult hiking. A complete trail map is posted in front of the visitor's center and guest huts.

The Ben's Bluff Trail takes the more ambitious walker, willing to endure a short but strenuous trek, to a ridgetop from which a good part of the entire Cockscomb Basin is visible. This high point has been frequently used to track jaguar via radiotelemetry. Picture a researcher slowly sweeping the antennae back and forth across the dense jungle that stretches for miles before her. Or envision the wily cat, resting in the shade of a tall tropical hardwood (probably one you are unwittingly staring at), or stalking its prey along the bank of a rushing stream.

An easier trail takes you to a bank of South Stann Creek for a refreshing plunge into clear, swift water. This swimming hole also has a picnic area beneath a shady tree. Yet another easy path heads in a westerly direction from the visitor's center, past the camping area and in the direction of Victoria's Peak. It is cut through a bamboo grove that is a remarkable sight for visitors who have never encountered such a dense and sticky thicket. A side trail on the left, past the bamboo thicket, takes you well into the forest, over a picturesque suspension bridge, and past a swampy area that is a fascinating observation ground for the Cockscomb's many amphibians (bring repellent to ward off mosquitoes).

If You Go: The only road in and out of the Cockscomb Basin is well marked and intersects the Southern Highway at the village of Maya Center, about 25 miles south of Dangriga. The Cockscomb's headquarters are about 7 miles up the dirt road. Walking there from the Southern Highway is possible, but no services exist en route, and it can get very hot and dusty. The road has been improved in recent years but is sometimes impassable during very wet weather, even for those on foot.

All tourists must register at the visitors' booth in Maya Center before heading into the Cockscomb. Cold drinks and Mayan crafts are sold here.

Rustic, dorm-style cabins (about $8 a night) and campsites ($2) are for rent near the Cockscomb reserve manager's headquarters. Reservations are strongly recommended, especially from November through April; contact the Belize Audubon Society office in Belize City or Pelican Beach Resort in Dangriga. There is fresh water, but you must bring your own food and other provisions (a stove is available). Those who do not wish to spend the night can easily find accommodations in Dangriga, Placencia, Sittee River, and Big Creek. Tours can be arranged from these locations, or you can be dropped off by one of the public buses that pass the entrance (ask to be let off at Maya Center) and walk in. Trail maps are available at the headquarters, and guides can be hired on-site.

There are fine swimming holes in the Cockscomb along South Stann Creek, so you may wish to bring a swimsuit and towel. Long-sleeved cotton shirts, trousers, sunscreen, and hats are advisable. Tuck your pants legs into your socks to repel chiggers. Without such preparations, including insect repellent, a visit can become uncomfortable.

Bladen Nature Reserve

The 1990 designation of the Bladen Branch (of the Monkey River) watershed area as a nature reserve set a significant benchmark in the race to protect the earth's most biologically diverse ecosystems —tropical forests—before humans destroy them. Protection of this 97,000-acre Toledo District wilderness, sprawling across the Maya Mountains' rugged foothills, helped set the stage for an even bolder action in which Bladen became part of a vast protected area that includes Chiquibul National Park and the nearby Cockscomb sanctuary; together it encompasses some 450,000 acres of tropical forest.

The Bladen Nature Reserve provides refuge for at least 194 bird species and at least 300 plant species, in addition to such creatures as the Baird's tapir, white-lipped peccary, mountain lion, iguana, jaguar, southern river otter, greater bulldog bat, white-tailed deer, brocket deer, and Central American spider monkey. The Bladen's important birds include the king vulture, mealy parrot, slaty-breasted tinamou, ornate hawk eagle, Philadelphia vireo, and rufous-capped warbler. The area contains uninvestigated Maya ruins, steep granite mountains, conical limestone outcrops, sinkholes, caves, underground streams, and waterfalls. Within the reserve's boundaries is Richardson Peak, the second-highest mountain in Belize.

Local conservation leaders such as Dora Weyer had long recognized Bladen's significance as an unspoiled, remote haven for wildlife. As early as 1984, the upper Bladen watershed appeared at the top of a "wish list" of proposed protected areas. The Belize Country Environmental Profile characterized the upper Bladen Branch as almost completely undisturbed by humans. It collects water from a series of almost parallel creeks that drain the main divide of the Maya Mountains over approximately 135 square miles. The lower watershed is subtropical wet forest, while higher areas include subtropical lower montane wet forest, with cloud elfin forest on the higher peaks. Reports from the few early expeditions to the upper Bladen include sightings of tapirs, spider monkeys, great curassow, and crested guan.

A 1987 biological survey of the upper Bladen Branch watershed by scientists from the Manomet Bird Observatory and the Missouri Botanical Garden (sponsored by the Brehm Fund of West Germany) yielded a special report that is one of the most in-depth biological analyses of the Bladen's flora and fauna. At this juncture the conservation group LightHawk joined with Victor Gonzalez (then Belize Audubon's president, now the permanent secretary for the Ministry of Tourism and Environment) to convince Belize authorities to protect the Bladen permanently. Over a period of three years, LightHawk flew government leaders over the Bladen, providing many with their first look at the rugged watershed. Early proposals to allow logging were thus thwarted, and the value of preserving this vast freshwater catchment became clear.

With the help of the World Parks Endowment and a financial commitment from the Weeden Foundation, the Bladen Nature Reserve was finally created in 1990. As a nature reserve, it allows only educational activities and scientific research within its boundaries. Like the Tapir Mountain Nature Reserve, special permission is required for scientists and educators to visit the Bladen. The primary motivation is to protect the integrity of the watershed and the abundant wildlife that inhabits it. The Bladen Nature Reserve was not set aside for the benefit of tourists, although low-impact tourism may be considered in the future as a means of generating income for residents of the area.

The upper Bladen Branch watershed shows traces of the past presence of ancient Maya. In the early 1990s, surveys by archaeologist Peter Dunham and a team from Cleveland State University turned up four previously unknown Mayan sites. These settlements provide new evidence for a thousand-year-old trading network in the Bladen. According to Dunham, up to 7,000 people may have inhabited the Bladen valley. A flood plain in the area called Quebrada de Oro ("the passageway of gold") contains other Mayan ruins that archaeologists have never excavated. Participants in the Manomet field study found 18 roughly rectangular mounds here, now overgrown by vegetation. An abundance of breadfruit trees suggests that the Maya cultivated this species at Quebrada de Oro, as they did at Tikal. There appeared to be some looting of the Quebrada ruins and at another more western site in the Bladen. In addition, just prior to the Dunham expedition, looting at one of the four newly discovered ruins resulted in the destruction of an ancient structure at this site. Unregulated visitation remains one of the biggest problems facing the reserve's managers and others concerned with protecting these and other Mayan sites throughout Belize.

Specialists on the Manomet expedition identified about 90 tree species in the Bladen, including cramtree, copal, white gumbo-limbo, banak, ironwood, breadnut, and mammee apple. The most abundant woody plant is the spiny understory palm. This species, much shorter than trees reaching the forest's canopy, commands even greater respect than the forest giants. The unfortunate person who runs into its long sturdy spines is treated to a painful ordeal not soon forgotten. Less common trees identified by the Manomet team included the bullhoof, ceiba, hogplum, mapola, mylady, ormiga, red gumbo-limbo, waika chewstick, mahogany, and Spanish cedar.

Using a technique called "mist netting," scientists visiting the Bladen catch birds in fine mesh nets stretched between trees. Birds are then banded and recorded by age, sex, wing length, weight, breeding condition, and other features. Thirty species of migrants, most of which nest far to the north in the temperate zone, have been seen in the Bladen. The barred forest-falcon, vermiculated screech owl, white-necked jacobin, keel-billed motmot, barred antshrike, eye-ringed flatbill, royal flycatcher, rose-throated becard, prothonotary warbler, yellow-throated euphonia, blue grosbeak, and yellow-billed cacique are among birds seen less frequently here. Birds that remain in the canopy or feed on the wing—such as parrots, toucans, hawks, and swifts—are not generally caught in the mist nets and are identified through a censusing technique wherein researchers fan out at given times and locations to seek them out specifically. Such strategies have yielded two species found elsewhere in Central America but not previously recorded in the Maya Mountains: the magnificent hummingbird and Audubon's oriole. Additionally, a 1994 Nature Conservancy ecological assessment team recorded 123 bird species, nine of which had not previously been recorded in the Bladen. This assessment also yielded records of three plants (two tree species and a bromeliad) that may prove to be previously unknown to science.

One of Dunham's teams made a stunning ornithological discovery in 1994 in the Bladen: they watched a rare harpy eagle for 40 minutes as it perched in fig trees as close as 20 meters from its onlookers. This huge flying predator, which feeds on monkeys and sloths, had not been seen in Belize for twenty to thirty years prior to this date.

As of mid-1995, there was still a pressing need for on-the-ground management of the Bladen Nature Reserve. Illegal hunting, looting of archaeological resources, and unregulated visitation have created an urgent demand for full-time reserve wardens.

The Bladen may someday become the core of a much larger protected area through its possible designation as a United Nations (UNESCO) Biosphere Reserve. The government has considered protective declarations linking the Chiquibul National Park east to the Maya Mountain Divide. This new reserve would include the rugged Trio watershed that is sandwiched between the Bladen and the Cockscomb Basin Wildlife Sanctuary. If interconnected as a Biosphere Reserve, this Chiquibul-Bladen-Trio-Cockscomb combination would certainly form one of the most biologically diverse and significant natural areas under protective designation in Central America. These vast, biologically diverse habitat corridors can continue to support viable populations of large predators like the jaguar. Whatever the outcome, one thing is certain: the Belize government has set an international standard in protecting the existing pristine watershed. As one Belizean put it, "The Bladen is a little gem, and it shines."

If You Go: Access to the Bladen Nature Reserve is strictly limited to qualified scientists, archaeologists, and other designated researchers. Permission must be obtained in advance from the Belize Audubon Society, which manages the Bladen, as well as appropriate government officials.

Mayan Ruins

Neither archaeologists nor government officials know exactly how many ancient Mayan sites there are in Belize, but certainly the number is in the thousands. The remnants of Mayan occupation—ranging from microscopic vegetable pollen found in the dust of potsherds to sky-scraping temples poking through the forest canopy—are found from border to border. Such artifacts are even commonplace on the offshore islands. It is now widely conceded that Belize was once at the very heart of lowland Maya civilization. Experts speculate that this relatively small territory may have easily supported as many as 1 million or more Maya, several times the present population.

Yet despite their clear domination of the area for hundreds of years, precious little is known about these early residents. Formal excavation of the largest ruins is relatively recent, and much of the early archaeological work is now regarded as amateurish and slipshod. Many important sites have remained virtually untouched and others have received only cursory field research. Even Caracol, the country's biggest Mayan complex, saw no serious investigation until the mid-1980s.

Although many foreign agencies and universities are now helping the Belizeans study and preserve their Mayan relics, many precious artifacts have already been lost to looters, farmers, adventurers, collectors, and the vagaries of nature. A great threat continues to exist, as

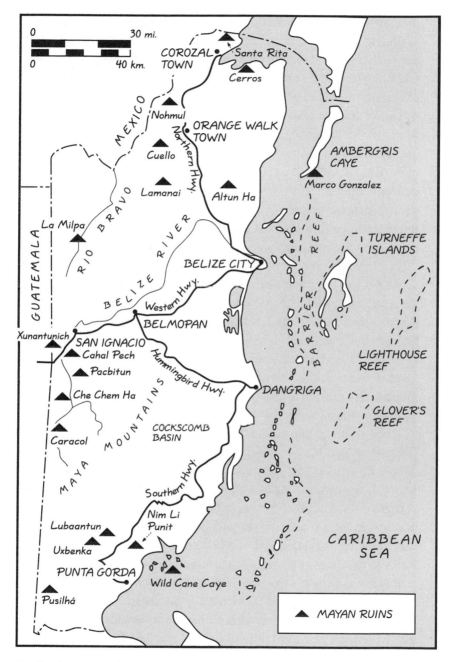

Belize's Major Mayan Sites

impoverished and/or unscrupulous people plunder sites in the hope of finding valuables that can be sold for starting prices of about $300 per pot. In some areas, the limestone ruins are still being carted away piece by piece, to be ground up by local residents for the ingredients of cement or used as building blocks.

Unlike Mexico and Guatemala, Belize has lacked sufficient funds to restore its ancient Mayan cities, and only a handful of caretakers are looking after them. Informed guides are rare; literature on the individual sites is hard to come by. Access to many locations is difficult and only improving slowly. In some cases, the ruins are on private property. Even during the peak tourist season, it is not uncommon to find yourself entirely alone at one of these Mayan ruins, or in the company of a single resident manager.

For travelers with an interest in the Mayan history of Belize, we suggest some background reading before setting out (see Appendix for suggested books). Once you are in-country, by far the best local guidebook is *Warlords and Maize Men: A Guide to the Maya Sites of Belize*, which contains detailed travel instructions and maps, plus photographs and archaeological histories for each location. Another good resource is *The Belizean Bullet*, an infrequent publication of the Department of Archaeology that provides detailed information about ongoing research.

Keep in mind that under Belize law, all "ancient monuments" (structures over 100 years old) and "antiquities" (man-made articles crafted more than 150 years ago) are the property of the state. Their removal, destruction, or possession is expressly forbidden without the permission of federal authorities. The collecting, buying, and selling of such artifacts is also illegal, and anyone engaged in such activity should be reported at once. Looting continues to be the single biggest threat to the integrity of Belize's Mayan sites.

Beware also that a thriving business exists in imitation artifacts, and many travelers spend good money on cheap fakes. Trading in these items is not illegal, but without proper documentation the items may be seized by customs officials when departing the country.

Because of the sites' varying degrees of isolation, it is best to visit during the drier months (February through May). Remember, however, that it can rain at any time and place, and waterproof boots or shoes are advisable. Lightweight, comfortable clothing should be worn, and a hat or raincoat may be useful. It is also a good idea to bring along insect repellent, sunscreen, and drinking water.

Few of the Mayan sites allow overnight visits, and only a handful have sanitation facilities. Admission fees are about $1.50 per person, although not always collected. Children under 12 are admitted free, as are all Belizean nationals on Sundays. For further information, contact the Department of Archaeology in Belmopan at 8-2106.

Note that all of Belize's major Mayan sites are described in this section except Altun Ha, which is included as a day trip from Belize City in Chapter 5, and Pacbitun, discussed earlier in this chapter.

A handful of U.S.-based tour companies specialize in trips to Mayan ruins. Our favorite is Far Horizons, operated by archaeologist and conservationist Mary Dell Lucas, who has lived in Belize and helped excavate several sites. Trips organized by Far Horizons are led by well-informed archaeologists and deliberately kept small to minimize disruption of research teams and rural communities. Part of each trip fee is turned over to local archaeology projects. Based in Albuquerque, N. Mex., Far Horizons can be reached at (800) 552-4575 or (505) 343-9400.

Caracol (Cayo District)

Until 1992, this largest Mayan site in Belize was one of the most difficult to reach. Located in the Cayo District's rugged backcountry, Caracol is in the middle of the remote Chiquibul National Park, only 7 miles east of the Guatemalan border. The complex—which covers at least 55 square miles—is a bumpy 2- to 3-hour journey (in good weather) by four-wheel-drive vehicle from San Ignacio via the Mountain Pine Ridge village of Augustine (now called Douglas DiSilva), about 30 miles distant.

The most extensive known Mayan ceremonial center in the country, Caracol's central core covers 30 square miles of thick, high-canopy forest and comprises a Classic-period complex that includes many pyramids, five plazas, and an astronomical observatory. The main plaza is linked by causeways to a number of outlier ruins.

Overall, the network of structures is at least three times denser and 85 percent larger than nearby Tikal. Although estimates of Caracol's size are being revised upward every year, in 1995 it was estimated that 180,000 or more people lived in this area at the city-state's peak, around A.D. 700. The site has ruins of an estimated 35,000 buildings, with more discovered each year.

Remarkably, Caracol (Spanish for "snail"; a reference to the numerous land-snail shells found here) remained unknown to the outside world until the early 1930s, when a local woodcutter stumbled upon its mysterious mounds while searching for mahogany and chicle. Loggers subsequently cut timber in the area over the next two decades—crushing many valuable artifacts in the process—and it was not until 1950 that archaeologists began mapping it. The ruin was mistakenly considered a small site and left to loggers, looters, and army patrols for some time. It began receiving considerable academic attention in 1985, after husband-and-wife archaeologists Diane and Arlen Chase began making annual research pilgrimages from the University of Central Florida.

In 1986, while planting a plot of corn at the site, Caracol caretaker and guide Benjamin Panti made a major discovery. He chanced upon a well-preserved stone ball-court marker that contains a startling carved hieroglyphic record of a military victory by an underdog Mayan leader known as Lord Water of Caracol over the mighty warlords of Tikal, some 60 miles to the northwest. This A.D. 562 conquest was the culmination of many years of fierce fighting between the two powers. The carving was significant because it documented Caracol's domination of the area throughout most of the so-called Middle Classic Hiatus, a period between A.D. 534 and 690 when Tikal built no carved monuments, used inferior construction techniques, and buried even its holiest priests in tombs more suited to impoverished peasants. Caracol did its best to humiliate the royalty of Tikal and the neighboring city-state of Naranjo (conquered by Caracol in A.D. 631) during Caracol's 140 years of domination, possibly even sacrificing its high-ranking captives in demeaning public executions.

Excavations at Mayan ruin of Caracol (Photo by Kevin Schafer)

The glyphic record shows a change in warfare strategies that spared the conquered city-states but shattered the ruling elites' power. This allowed Caracol, much smaller than Tikal at the time of its victory, to divert the larger community's resources (and perhaps many of its citizens as slaves) to expand its own boundaries and wealth.

Excavations at the outskirts of Caracol suggest that the ancient Maya were not divided exclusively into elite and peasant classes, as previously believed. By studying ancient garbage, archaeologists believe that the city's sizable middle class apparently had access to jade, polychrome pottery, ritual vessels, and even fancy burial tombs. Experts conclude that Caracol grew rapidly for quite a while before suffering a period of decline, possibly caused in part by an equalization in social power that destroyed the influence of Mayan royalty.

Clues contained in the hieroglyphics of several circular stone altars now unearthed at Caracol may eventually help the Chases determine why the Maya fled. "We know that when they finally left, they left fast," Diane Chase told an Associated Press reporter in 1993, noting that buildings were burned and the body of a child was abandoned on the floor of a palace.

Another riddle not yet solved is why a city as large as Caracol was built on a plateau that has almost no reliable water supply during the four or five months of dry weather each spring. Mayan engineers managed to overcome the limitations of nature by painstakingly building effective reservoirs, aqueducts, and gardening terraces that optimized use of rainfall. Nevertheless, their ingenuity does not explain the reason for locating such a large population here in the first place. It is speculated that Caracol may have been a good location for trading with other Mayan communities spread throughout present-day Guatemala, Honduras, and Mexico, or that prized plants such as cacao grew here. Even today, 2,000 years after Caracol's founding, visitors are advised to bring with them all the water they will need during their stay. (A Mayan reservoir fulfills the needs of the research team during its February-to-June encampment.)

Another major discovery at Caracol was the bones of a woman in a royal tomb at the top of the highest pyramid. The find suggests that, in the absence of a male heir, females may have periodically ruled Mayan city-states, although this skeleton also could be that of a ruler's wife or close relative.

The most visually striking structure at the site is Caana ("sky palace"), a temple towering 140 feet above the plaza floor. It is 2 meters higher than El Castillo at Xunantunich, previously regarded as the tallest man-made structure in Belize. (Several modern hotels in Belize City now compete for this honor.) Visitors can climb to the summit of Caana and enjoy a sweeping view of the Vaca Plateau's tall deciduous and evergreen hardwood forests, which extend for as far as the eye can see. Looking west and southwest from the temple, dozens of unevaluated building mounds up to 70 feet in height are evident all the way to the horizon.

Much of Caracol is still to be excavated, although in recent years as many as 100 people at a time have worked here—clearing, digging, mapping, measuring, photographing, cataloging, and analyzing. Laser technology is applied to eroded hieroglyphics taken from underground tombs, and experts are brought in to read them on-site. A solar system has been donated by a Florida firm in order to produce electricity, and a sophisticated subsurface radar unit is used to find the most promising areas for excavation.

In the first four years of digging, Caracol yielded 54 burial tombs, twice as many as have been found in all the decades of searching at Tikal. The project's directors estimate there are as many as 4,500 structures at the core of Caracol, compared to 2,300 mapped in the center of Tikal. The archaeological richness of this site, one of the five largest Mayan cities anywhere, is expected eventually to result in a much better understanding of the civilization, particularly since many of Caracol's tombs and monuments clearly indicate the year of their initial construction.

The Belizean government has expanded the Caracol Archaeology Reserve to the borders of the surrounding, much larger Chiquibul National Park. The region's high-canopy forest, much of it in pristine condition, is an important habitat for several species of cat and the endangered howler monkey, plus such rare birds as the keel-billed motmot, thought to be extinct in Guatemala, Mexico, and Honduras. Endangered ocellated turkeys and other large birds fly among the ruins with impunity, though they have completely vanished from most of the rest of Belize. A wide variety of orchids, vines, and trees (many as tall as 120 feet) are found in the area. One enormous ceiba tree, at least 700 years old, towers above the epicenter of Caracol. The Maya considered ceiba trees sacred because they connected the underworld, the earth, and the sky.

The vast Chiquibul cavern system (believed to be the longest in Central America and one of the longest in the world) begins about 8 miles south of Caracol, although access is restricted. The three largest caves in the complex measure a total of at least 20 miles in length and have yielded several invertebrates that were new to science. A chamber in one Chiquibul cave is said to be the fourth-largest on earth. Many important Mayan artifacts have been found in these caves, which were also considered sacred.

En route to Caracol, visitors pass through the abandoned logging camp of San Luis and cross the Guacamallo Bridge (*guacamallo* is the local name for the scarlet macaw) spanning the upper Macal River. If you have some spare time, this is an excellent place to observe flora and fauna. The contrast between pine forest and subtropical hardwoods is like night and day here, owing to sharp alignments in geology. Farther along the road to the ruins are one or more chicle camps that have been revived in recent years as Japanese companies buy more of this natural chewing-gum base from Belizean tappers. Most *chicleros* speak only Spanish.

Following Guatemala's example with its famous Tikal National Park, Belize is eager to turn Caracol into a major tourism attraction some day, in a manner that will preserve present-day natural beauty as well as ancient history. In a 1990 interview, the Chases told a *Smithsonian* magazine reporter that they are looking forward to Caracol's ultimate status as an important archaeological park. "But," Diane Chase cautioned, "it will take years [of excavation] to get to the point where visitors can get a sense of what it once was."

If You Go: Permission must be obtained in person from the Forestry Department's western division in Augustine prior to any visits to Caracol. As of mid-1995, there was no fee for the permit, although this could change. In the past a second permit has been required from the Department of Archaeology, but this procedure has been relaxed. A verbal okay by telephone is now considered sufficient, and tour operators usually handle this formality. A proposed

Detail of carved limestone ball-court market at Caracol (Photo by Richard Mahler)

check-in gate on the road to the park may eventually modify the permit system still further.

Forestry officials grant access based on road conditions, since the last 30 miles between Augustine and Caracol are rough—especially during or after wet weather. High-clearance four-wheel-drive vehicles are recommended. The nearest gas station and mechanic are in San Ignacio, about 65 miles away. There is no public transportation to Caracol, and few taxis will make the trip. Rather than attempting a visit on your own, we recommend checking with local resorts for guided tours to the site. Chaa Creek, Maya Mountain Lodge, and Mountain Equestrian Trails are among the recommended operators. Since road improvements were made in 1992, tour companies no longer schedule regular horseback trips to Caracol, although these can be arranged. During the wet season this may be the only access.

There are no overnight accommodations at Caracol, and camping is allowed only with special permission from the Department of Archaeology. The nearest campground is in Augustine and the nearest lodges are in the Mountain Pine Ridge. Remember to bring your own food and water. A solar-powered telephone is available for emergency use only.

The $1.50 visitor's fee is payable upon registration at an open-air kitchen used by Caracol's Mayan caretakers. These workers are fairly knowledgeable about the archaeology and wildlife of the area—some, like Benjamin Panti, have worked here for many years—and they will provide guided tours when archaeologists are not available. Fluency in Spanish is helpful. When researchers are encamped, archaeologist-led tours are given only at specified times. Check with tour operators or hotel managers for the current schedule.

Xunantunich (Cayo District)

In contrast to Caracol, Xunantunich (the Mayan "x" is pronounced like a cross between an English "s" and "z") is one of the most accessible ancient Mayan sites in Belize. The ruins are located near the confluence of the Belize and Mopan rivers, on a naturally occurring limestone bluff above the Western Highway.

This is a Late Classic period ceremonial center of impressive height but relatively small size. It is just across the Mopan River from the Mayan village of San José Succotz and only a few miles east of the Guatemalan border. The temple complex, occupied from about A.D. 700 until at least A.D. 1000, is surrounded by thick bush that is gradually being whittled away by local farmers.

Because of its commanding presence and proximity to populated areas, Xunantunich has been visited by a lengthy parade of archaeologists stretching back to 1894. Sadly, several of these investigators botched their work and in one instance lost an irreplaceable set of altar hieroglyphics. Other inept researchers freely dispersed the burial goods and ceremonial offerings to museums in England and Germany. No serious archaeological work was done until 1938, and the tallest structures were not stabilized until 1960.

In 1959, it was determined that the site had been partially destroyed in an earthquake during the Late Classic era. Some experts feel this incident may have shaken the faith Mayans had in their leaders, who claimed an intimate relationship with the gods.

Dominating the entire topography of Xunantunich (variously translated from the Mayan as "stone woman" or "maiden of the rock") is a spectacular 135-foot monolith known as El Castillo (The Castle). In typical Mayan fashion, the corbel-vaulted temple at the summit is actually built on the rubble of several earlier temples constructed one atop the other over the centuries. Visitors can climb nearly to the top of this impressive tower, which affords a wonderful view of the steamy green jungle and overlooks the three adjacent plazas and various corbel-arched buildings that surround them.

Visible on the east side of El Castillo's lower temple is an unusual stucco frieze, restored in 1972, showing symbols of the sun, moon, Venus, and days of the week. Also included is a headless man, apparently decapitated for some long-forgotten transgression against the royal rulers. Originally the frieze continued all the way around the structure, and its highest point was probably topped by a roof comb. An excavated stairway continues to a small chamber in the upper temple of El Castillo. Near the structure's base is a wide terrace that once supported several smaller temples.

The grass-covered mounds surrounding the three primary plazas

Astronomical frieze at Mayan ruin of Xunantunich (Photo by Kevin Schafer)

are the remains of ancient residential buildings that might have been something like modern condominiums. On the west side, near the restrooms, is a flat, narrow rectangle believed to be a ball court, used in a complicated and deadly form of basketball developed by the Mayan hierarchy. Also visible is a room with a built-in stone bench and some walls bearing Mayan graffiti.

Judging from the jewelry, tools, semiprecious stones, and weaving materials found here, archaeologists believe this was once an important and well-ordered city. No one is sure why it was abandoned, or why it flourished so late in the Mayan epoch.

In the early 1990s, the University of California, Los Angeles, began its eight-year Xunantunich Archaeological Project field study here; you may encounter project archaeologists and researchers during your visit. On the west side of El Castillo, the team has uncovered a spectacular plaster frieze, one of the largest man-made structures in Belize. Thirty feet long, the frieze was made between A.D. 800 and 900, a time when most other Mayan cities were collapsing. Archaeologists are also uncovering small homesites and farms along the length of a *sacbé*, a 1,000-year-old Mayan road.

The $1.50 admission fee is collected by resident caretaker Elfego Panti, himself of Mayan descent and very knowledgeable about the history of Xunantunich. He is happy to point out structures of interest and is familiar with local wildlife and plants. Drinking water is also available near his office. Xunantunich was the first Mayan site in Belize to open to the public (in 1954), and it is now among the best maintained in the country.

If You Go: Heading west about 10 minutes from San Ignacio on the Western Highway, the tower of El Castillo is suddenly visible on the western horizon. As you enter the village of San José Succotz, look for a sign and bus shelter marking the turnoff on the right-hand side of the highway. You will cross the Mopan River on a tiny, hand-cranked ferry (that handles two cars at a time) secured to a steel cable. There is no charge, as this is a public right-of-way. Follow the dirt road for about one-half mile up the hill to a small parking lot, then walk into the site. The road can be very slippery when wet. If you decide to go on foot, it takes about 40 minutes to walk up the hill from the ferry.

Besides passenger cars and package tours, visitors can take taxis to the Xunantunich ruins from Benque Viejo or San Ignacio for about $5. An alternative is to take a bus from either town and ask the driver to stop at the river crossing. Xunantunich is an easy trip—usually less than 2 hours—from the many resorts of the Cayo District or the hotels of Benque Viejo, San José Succotz, and San Ignacio.

About a mile from the site, on the Mopan River, is a stretch of surging rapids that some travelers enjoy running in canoes, kayaks, rubber rafts, or inner-tubes. There are also several fine swimming holes in the area, and bird-watching is excellent. Several area operators arrange excursions down the Mopan and other nearby rivers (see Inside Belize).

Lamanai (Orange Walk District)

While the towering temples of Xunantunich and Caracol are impressive by any measure, a different kind of beauty awaits visitors making the scenic journey to Lamanai, which is variously translated as "the submerged crocodile" or "the drowned insect." These intriguing ruins are about 70 miles northwest of Belize City, on a patch of high

Mound and structure enclosing excavated stelae at Xunantunich (Photo by Richard Mahler)

ground that looms over the west bank of the picturesque New River Lagoon.

Lamanai is unusual in that it was occupied longer than almost any other known Mayan site, from about 1500 B.C. (or earlier) until at least A.D. 1650 and for varying intervals to the present day. An important trading center and ceremonial site, its history extends from the formative years of the civilization until well after Franciscan friars arrived from Spain in the 1540s to convert Lamanai's "heathen" residents. The city enjoyed its greatest strength during the Pre-Classic era of A.D. 200 to 900, and Lamanai's major pyramid—referred to as the Southern Temple or N10-43—was completed around 100 B.C., then modified several times before A.D. 600.

Some of Lamanai's ruins are among the oldest surviving buildings from the Pre-Classic period, dating back to 700 B.C. Pollen samples show that corn was being cultivated here at least eight hundred years earlier. There are 700 buildings in the complex, which is believed to have supported at least 35,000 people when its population peaked. Only about 5 percent of the known structures have been excavated.

Thanks to records kept by early Catholic missionaries, we know that Lamanai is a Spanish corruption of Lamanain, the original Mayan name for this place (most other sites were named by their European discoverers). The term is fitting, since the lagoon nearby was—and is—perfect crocodile habitat. Many representations of the reptile have been found here, including ceramic decorations and plaster masks, some of which may be seen in the excellent on-site museum. A figure wearing a crocodile headdress, found in many forms throughout the area, is thought to represent one of Lamanai's important rulers.

Although it is possible to drive here (in about 2 hours from Belize City), many visitors prefer to come to Lamanai by boat up the New River, as the ancient Maya did. After navigating through miles of constantly dividing tributaries and closed-in landscape (teeming with waterbirds and their predators), the pyramid-shaped temple looming 112 feet above the New River Lagoon and main plaza is an awesome sight. When the temple's crown was placed in about 100 B.C., this may well have been the tallest building in the Mayan world.

Beyond the highest pyramid, known as N10-43, thick forest has taken over many of the unrestored limestone mounds where thousands of Maya once made their homes. At the apex of its considerable power, this well-situated city-state is said to have had a trading influence that extended over much of present-day Mexico, Guatemala, and Honduras, plus all of Belize.

The site's central core covers about one square mile, with residential structures and smaller buildings spread over more than 1,000 acres. The overgrown vegetation makes it difficult to get an adequate perspective on the ground, so a hike to the summit of one of the temples is a good idea: three are over 100 feet tall.

In one section, accessible by a short path, are a few crumbling walls that remain from a couple of 16th-century Catholic missions, one of the few reminders of Spanish occupation extant in all Belize. Conversions of the Maya to Christianity began here in 1544. The Spanish remained until 1641, when the Indians rebelled and burned their church to the ground as part of a regional uprising that included Lamanai's sister city of Tipú, on the Macal River (destroyed not long ago when a citrus plantation was put in). A second chapel was later built at Lamanai using stones from one of the Maya's most sacred temples, which contributed to the friction between Europeans and Indians. In fact, a Mayan stela (still visible) was erected in front of this church after its destruction, containing a written message firmly disavowing any allegiance to Christianity. A figurine found in the ruins of the second church has gaping jaws at either end with a god coming out of one of these mouths. It is thought to be the Maya's way of saying, "This could happen to you!"

After the missionaries were eradicated, Lamanai was apparently devastated by successive epidemics of malaria, smallpox, and yellow fever. Virtually no one lived here when the British loggers arrived with their Jamaican slaves in the 18th century to extract mahogany and other trees. Chinese and East Indian laborers were imported about ninety years later to work in the local sugarcane fields, but they did not react well to the demanding climate and debilitating diseases; most of the plantations were soon abandoned. The ruin of a 19th-century sugar mill, complete with ficus-entangled flywheel and boiler, is still visible. It was built in 1866, then burned by the Maya (along with other European constructions) the following year. When the mill's manager succumbed to fever a short time later, the settlement was taken over by local Indians. A corroded molasses storage chamber, now home to bats, lies a short distance from the abandoned mill.

Many Guatemalan and a few Salvadoran refugees now live in the area as subsistence farmers. Some were relocated to the nearby village of Indian Church after they homesteaded within the park's boundaries.

Because of the ruin's protected status as an archaeological reserve, the number of black howler monkeys and other endangered mammals has been on the rise. In 1993, researcher Hal Markowitz of San Francisco State University began a long-term study of the behavioral ecology of howler monkeys here. Volunteers may work alongside the primate experts through Oceanic Society Expeditions (OSE) tours (see Inside Belize). Participants help in all aspects of noninvasive data collection and live in double-occupancy cabañas at the site. OSE also offers Lamanai trips in which participants help researchers identify and record birds. The goal is to collect as many tropical birdsongs as possible for laboratory study.

Vegetation here is lush. Common trees at Lamanai include the guanacaste, mahogany, rubber, cohune palm, poisonwood, and ficus (strangler fig). The adjacent lagoon, fed by a maze of underwater springs and aquifers, is teeming with fish and virtually unpolluted; many waterbirds make this their home. On the western bank stretch miles of savannas that are an important habitat for jaguars and other cats.

Although most of Lamanai is still uncleared and unreconstructed, it has received much more serious archaeological attention than many Mayan sites in Belize. Minor excavation and mapping were carried out in 1917 and again during the 1930s and 1960s. An extensive, long-term project began in 1974 under the direction of Canada's Royal Ontario Muscum and was largely completed in 1992. Among noteworthy findings by the Canadian research team were a tenth-century ball-court marker and a cache of bones of humans who may have been sacrificed here during certain religious ceremonies.

The wide array of artifacts found suggests that Lamanai's residents were enthusiastic and successful merchants. One ancient pottery vessel contained several small offerings floating in pools of liquid mercury, their purpose a complete mystery. Other oddities include an unusually small Mayan ball court and an extraordinarily preserved carved offering stone that now lies under a protective palm thatch. It is believed that this carving escaped destruction because it apparently fell face-forward to the ground during a Mayan fire ceremony and was therefore left unmolested for fear the event itself portended evil. The stone's outstanding depiction of the Lamanai priest-king Lord Smoking Shell (whose reign began about A.D. 608) clearly shows his open-mouthed-serpent headdress and other accoutrements. He holds a ceremonial bar in his arms, symbolizing his royal authority.

The small but impressive museum at Lamanai contains incense burners (censers), burial urns, and chalices discovered here, along with eccentric flint carvings, tools, and many ceramic objects. If you are fortunate enough to visit while the well-informed Mayan archaeologist and curator Nasario Coo is in, you can obtain a thorough account of Lamanai's fascinating history. Coo will provide a guided tour if his schedule allows.

If You Go: Lamanai is off the beaten track. Public transportation is limited to taxis (from Orange Walk Town), rental cars, supply trucks, and hired boats. A dirt road, occasionally impassable during the wet season, extends to the site from Orange Walk Town via the village of San Felipe. Watch for the signs directing you to Indian Church Village and/or Lamanai.

Most visitors arrange a boat trip through local hotels, travel agencies, or package tour operators. We recommend Jungle River Tours, which offers a fine New River/Lamanai archaeological tour. Another approach is to drive as far as Tower Bridge, Guinea Grass, or the Mennonite community of Shipyard, then head up the New River by locally hired boat. (There is no public transportation to Guinea Grass or Shipyard.) Boats can usually be rented on the spur of the moment in any of these riverside villages or can be arranged in advance through large hotels, such as the D'Victoria in Orange Walk Town, or the Maruba in Maskall.

The boat trip is very pleasant, affording opportunities for swimming and other water sports along the way. Many orchids and other flowering plants are visible in the trees overhead. Hollowed-out trunks along the riverbank provide a daytime home to a small, fish-eating bat. Many kinds of birds and animals live along the banks of the lagoon and are easily glimpsed en route to Lamanai. Crooked Tree Lagoon (described in Chapter 5) is only 8 miles to the east, and many species are present in both locations. Jabiru stork, snail kite, northern jacana, squirrel cuckoo, blue-crowned motmot, limpkin, cormorant, and night heron, along with huge flocks of parrots, are among the birds recorded near Lamanai. You also may see crocodiles, although the noise of powerboats tends to scare them away.

The accommodations closest to the ruins are ½-mile away in Indian Church, at the highly recommended Lamanai Outpost Lodge. Rooms are also available in Orange Walk Town, about 20 miles to the northeast. Several operators now schedule Lamanai as a day trip from Belize City or San Pedro.

Camping is not allowed at Lamanai, and no food or drink is sold here. The site has restrooms, a picnic area, and several trails cut through the forest. Besides curator Nasario Coo, the resident caretakers can answer basic questions about the site. The structures are not well marked, however, and no literature is available. Bring your own guide or a map and guidebook, as well as the usual sunscreen and insect repellent. A swimsuit is also a good idea; New Lagoon is one of the best swimming holes in Belize.

Cuello (Orange Walk District)

Cuello is located on private land, and permission is needed to visit this ancient site, a minor ceremonial center and settlement area about 4 miles southwest of Orange Walk Town on Yo Creek Road. Arrangements can be made by calling the Cuello Rum Distillery, the site's owner, during business hours at 3-22141. Tours of the distillery, which bottles sugarcane spirits under the "Caribbean" label, can also be scheduled. Permission can usually be obtained by simply showing up; the facility is open Monday through Saturday. Ask to speak with Hilberto or Oswaldo Cuello. Their biggest concern is that visitors not disturb their cattle, who are pastured near the ruins.

Although not well developed for visitors, Cuello is one of the most exciting discoveries in the Mayan world. Before the exploration of this site in 1973 by Cambridge University (and later Boston University), most experts believed the Mayan civilization had its start around 600 B.C., which was the earliest date of any previously known settlement. Applying state-of-the-art carbon dating techniques to ancient maize fragments and wooden posts, it was determined that occupation by the Maya began here around 1000 B.C., possibly even earlier. Thus, the "start date" of the civilization was pushed back substantially. Subsequent findings at the Colha and Pulltrouser Swamp sites in northern Belize have set that date back to as early as 2500 B.C.

It was also once believed that the initial development of a distinct Mayan culture was spurred by contact with other ethnic groups, such as Mexico's early Olmec people. Trade artifacts found at Cuello suggest that the sophisticated social and religious institutions of Mayan life may have developed independently or through contact with still-unknown cultures. The jade and obsidian found here do not naturally occur in Belize and were probably traded for parrot feathers and animal skins collected from the nearby jungle.

Other findings at Cuello raise more unanswered questions. Why did a mass slaughter of at least 32 individuals take place here about 400 B.C.? Why were earthenware pots placed over the heads of the deceased in some of Cuello's burial chambers? Did the Maya originate their pyramid-plaza architectural style here, as many have suggested?

One certainty is Cuello's continuous occupation for thousands of years, until as recently as A.D. 1500. The site has yielded evidence that the Maya may have been able to build the strength of their city-state empire partly through the development of more productive strains of corn, their principal crop. Some of the earliest known ceramics and masonry buildings in Belize have also been found here.

Actually, there is not a lot for the casual visitor to see at Cuello, which lies in a forested compound of the distillery. Norman Hammond and his Cambridge research team continue to conduct research at the ruin, but they fill in excavated areas after completing their studies. Still, this is an important historical site for any serious student of the Maya.

If You Go: Cuello can easily be reached by taxi ($6) or private car via Yo Creek Road, which begins in Orange Walk Town as Baker's Street. No information or guides will be found at the site, although the Department of Archaeology can provide background materials in Belmopan.

About 25 miles down the same road are traditional and modern Mennonite farms and settlements that fan out from Blue Creek Village (see Chapter 7). By heading through August Pine Ridge and San Felipe, you will eventually reach the Mexican border crossing (pedestrians only) at La Unión. This is also the preferred route for those driving to Chan Chich Lodge, the Programme for Belize lands, and the Río Bravo Conservation Area, described earlier in this chapter.

Cerros (Corozal District)

About 20 miles northeast of Cuello, on an uninhabited stretch of Caribbean coastline overlooking Corozal Bay, are the ruins of

Cerros (also known as Cerro Maya, or Mayan Hill). During the dry season, the site can be reached by a dirt road via Chunox, Progreso, and Copper Banks, but it is more commonly visited by boat from either Corozal Town or Consejo Shores. On a clear day, especially at sunset, the profile of the ruins is clearly visible from the opposite side of the bay.

Cerros is a late Pre-Classic era (350 B.C. to A.D. 250) complex with virtually no construction after A.D. 100. Experts believe it was an important center of maritime commerce, probably handling much of the seagoing trade headed up the nearby New River to Lamanai and the Río Hondo to the Yucatán. Its early demise may have been caused by a gradual Early Classic period shift in Mayan trading patterns in favor of overland routes between the lowland and highland city-states. During this time, inland population centers such as Tikal and Caracol became established.

Although the archaeological reserve is small (53 acres), it includes three large structures that loom above several plazas and a few pyramid-like buildings. The tallest temple is 72 feet and provides a sweeping view across the water. Cerros probably reached its peak around the time of Christ's birth. During this period it appears to have shifted from an economy dependent on fishing, hunting, and farming to one reliant on the importation of pottery, salt, jade, and obsidian by dugout canoe. It was almost certainly linked by trade to the many smaller trading sites on the Belizean cayes and atolls farther south.

Ancient ball courts, quasi-religious tombs, elegant residences, farming terraces, and boat canals have been found at Cerros, indicating that its social structure was once highly developed. Surrounding the site is a man-made drainage canal that was nearly a mile long, 20 feet wide, and 6 feet deep. The immediate area has been uninhabited for some time, and part of the original complex is now underwater as a result of a rise in sea level over the last 2,000 years.

Some of the buildings at Cerros display large painted stucco masks, up to 13 feet high, that depict images of humans and animals. Unfortunately, because the sea air speeds erosion and no money is available for restoration, most of the masks have been plastered over to prevent further decay. The pyramid known as 5C, however, still has four masks: two identified as the sun and Venus, the others unknown. Some feel that the presence of these large friezes demonstrates that the divine Mayan elite were in power by the end of the Pre-Classic era, or about A.D. 250.

Although long recognized as an archaeological site, Cerros received almost no formal excavation or consolidation until 1973, when a team from Southern Methodist University (SMU) conducted preliminary field studies. The last SMU researcher departed in 1983, and no further archaeological work has been carried out since.

If You Go: Largely unrestored, much of Cerros appears to the casual visitor as little more than a series of low mounds, with only the tallest ceremonial structures hinting at past grandeur. Cerros remains without accommodations or services. Camping is not allowed. A resident caretaker will collect the $1.50 entrance fee.

The roundabout road from Corozal Town visits some idyllic lagoons and relaxed mestizo fishing villages, but this route cannot be recommended during wet weather.

By easily chartered private boat at the Corozal Town public pier, Cerros is about 5 miles (20 minutes) across Corozal Bay. Corozal's Caribbean Village Resort can also arrange transport. Expect to pay at least $75 for the trip. Because of the ruin's close proximity to the mouth of the New River and adjacent wetlands, insect repellent and long-sleeved clothing are necessary.

Santa Rita (Corozal District)

Amateur archaeologist Thomas Gann, a turn-of-the-century British physician living in Corozal, was perhaps the first European to recognize Santa Rita and Cerros as ancient Mayan sites. Located directly across the bay from the latter ruin and northeast of the Corozal Town center (now encircled by private homes and businesses), Santa Rita flourished off and on from at least 1800 B.C. until the arrival of the Spanish in the 1530s. Some might convincingly argue that since part of the present-day town is built atop Santa Rita, human habitation has continued here without interruption since at least 18 centuries before the birth of Christ!

Gann theorized that Santa Rita was one of an important series of coastal towns strategically located so that signal fires could be used to send messages up and down the Yucatán peninsula. Although this theory has never been conclusively proven, there is plenty of evidence that Santa Rita was in fact one of the region's most powerful Mayan communities and even regained some of its prominence after the disintegration of the civilization as a whole. Its strategic placement within a few miles of the Río Hondo and New River trade routes was one key to its long survival.

Santa Rita's location, on a limestone plateau overlooking the Chetumal and Corozal bays, immediately attracted the attention of Spanish conquistadors, who seized the city-state under the leadership of Alfonso Davila in 1531 from the Mayan warlord Nachacan. Although they were eventually routed by the Indians, the Spanish simply relocated farther north (at what is now the Mexican city of Chetumal) and managed to sever the remaining trade routes that fueled Santa Rita's prosperity. Within a few years the community was almost completely abandoned. The modern town of Corozal was subsequently established on the ruins' foundations in 1858 by survivors of the famous massacre at Bacalar, Mexico.

Despite its long and impressive history, only one visible structure remains at Santa Rita: a 55-foot-high, partially restored pyramid-shaped tomb, where two important burials were excavated. This site includes several chambers and an offertory niche. One of the rulers found buried here wore a kind of gold earring reserved only for the highest noblemen, another hint of Santa Rita's importance not only as a city, but as a terminus for trade with other rich communities. Not incidentally, the discovery of gold objects here is believed to have prompted the first attack by the Spanish.

Like nearby Cerros, Santa Rita appears to have been an agricultural center long before the seagoing trade boom hit. Once its boats got under way, however, Santa Rita found eager markets for the prized commodities gathered or cultivated nearby, including cacao, vanilla, honey, and spices. Unlike Cerros, Santa Rita thrived through the Classic period and was still stockpiling turquoise and gold from the Aztecs long after more-distant Mayan cities had collapsed. Relics from Santa Rita's tombs even include pottery made in the Andes mountains of far-off Peru.

Gann uncovered several burial sites, along with sculptured friezes and stuccoed murals. Much of this material has subsequently been lost—Indians deliberately destroyed six murals in 1900 before Gann could copy them—but some of the doctor's meticulous notes and drawings survive.

It was not until 1979 that a more thorough series of excavations was undertaken at Santa Rita, in a project led by Diane and Arlen Chase, the same archaeologists responsible for the ongoing study of Caracol. Among important discoveries made here over a seven-year period was a skeleton adorned with jade and mica ornaments. Many of these findings are now held in the Archaeology Vault in Belmopan.

Sadly, since the founding of Corozal Town some 150 years ago, a good part of Santa Rita has been looted, paved over, or built on. Hundreds of ancient structures and artifacts have been lost forever as a result.

If You Go: The last ancient building at Santa Rita, known as Structure 7, is an easy walk or car ride from the plaza of Corozal Town. Local residents will be happy to point you in the right direction: turn left at the Hilltop Bar and follow the road to the Coca-Cola bottling plant. No services are available at the site, although Pedro, the caretaker (who once lived in one of the tombs), is very helpful and knowledgeable. He collects a $1.50 fee during Santa Rita's hours of admission, 8:00 a.m. to 5:00 p.m. daily, except Sunday. Menzies Travel Agency, on the south side of Corozal Town, is a recommended contact for excursions to Santa Rita and other Mayan ruins in the district. Be sure to lock your car when you go to Santa Rita, as some visitors have reported thefts during their visit.

Lubaantun (Toledo District)

Lubaantun is modern Mayan for "place of the fallen rocks," which aptly describes this Late Classic ceremonial center, noted for an unusual style of construction that is unique to southern Belize. The large pyramids and residences observed here are made of crystalline limestone blocks with no visible mortar binding them together, not unlike constructions by the Inca civilization in the high Andes of Peru and Ecuador. This means that every hand-cut stone was carefully measured and shaped to fit together with the adjoining stone. (Remember, the Maya had no stone tools and used the wheel only in toys.) The effect of their masterful dressed stonework looks a bit like marble. Unlike most other Mayan ceremonial sites, the buildings that were then placed on top of these pyramids were made from perishable materials, such as tree limbs and palm fronds, and obviously no longer remain. We can only guess at what they looked like.

The austerity of this site—Lubaantun is now essentially a single stone acropolis—is reminiscent of Quiriguá, located about 100 miles away in southeast Guatemala, and there may have been close contact between the two city-states. Curiously, Lubaantun has impressive stone architecture, but virtually no carved stone stelae. Yet nearby Nim Li Punit and Uxbenka have plenty of sculpted rock monuments but no large masonry structures. This suggests to some authorities that a diverse social organization once prevailed in this area and that each site served a distinct purpose.

At Lubaantun, 11 large pyramid-platform structures are built around five main plazas and three ball courts. The tallest of these rises 45 feet above the jungle. The Caribbean Sea (about 20 miles distant) is visible from its summit. There are 13 smaller plazas and a number of other structures, but the entire complex is badly eroded.

It is believed that carvings and other types of building decorations commonly fashioned out of stone at other Mayan sites were made out of wood at Lubaantun, located in one of the most rain-soaked and densely forested corners of Belize. One theory persists that Lubaantun was an important religious, administrative, political, and commercial center, but only for a brief time—a couple of centuries at most, but perhaps as few as twenty years. No one knows what led to abandonment around A.D. 850, or why the hilltop site was not leveled before construction began, in the traditional Mayan manner. Instead, workers simply filled in gaps with stones and mortar.

Colonial officials began surveying Lubaantun with the help of

Thomas Gann in 1903, and the British Museum started serious excavation work in 1926, joined the following year by the renowned Mayan authority J. E. S. Thompson. Some of the most impressive artifacts these teams unearthed were taken to museums in London and the United States. Archaeologists abandoned Lubaantun from 1929 until 1970, when Norman Hammond returned with a team of Cambridge University researchers.

It is thought that the greatest wealth of Lubaantun came from the production and trading of wild cacao—the modern source of chocolate—which was so highly prized by the Maya that they used it as a form of currency. Even today the area is considered prime cacao-growing country, and the 1970 discovery of a ceramic musician wearing a cacao-pod pendant lends credence to the notion that the prized beans were grown here in the eighth century. Cacao, used to make a drink prized by Mayan royalty, was probably exchanged for jade and obsidian.

The best-known discovery at Lubaantun is the remarkable Crystal Skull, supposedly unearthed in 1926 by Anna Mitchell-Hedges (daughter of archaeologist F. A. Mitchell-Hedges) on her 17th birthday. This artifact demonstrates superb artistry and workmanship; it is perfectly carved from an 8-inch-cube of pure rock crystal and shows virtually no tool marks. The item appears to have been modeled after a specific human head, but the identity of that individual—and the Crystal Skull's significance—remains unknown. Some believe the skull was brought from somewhere else for a "staged" discovery at Lubaantun; others are convinced it is linked to the lost continent of Atlantis. Archaeologist Norman Hammond believes the skull is not a Mayan creation. As of mid-1995, the relic still remained in Canada, although the Belize government has been negotiating for its return from an Ontario museum.

If You Go: Lubaantun, the largest archaeological site in southern Belize, is on a high limestone ridge just north of the Columbia River, about 1 mile by unshaded dirt road past the village of San Pedro Columbia (turn right at the public water well). The Monday/Wednesday/Friday/Saturday public bus to San Miguel will drop you off near the entrance to the Lubaantun site. The ruins are then a short walk from the San Pedro Columbia/San Miguel Road by a steep but well-marked trail. An even steeper pathway leads to Lubaantun from the banks of the Columbia River.

Less than a half-mile walk behind the ruins is the Belize Agroforestry Research Center (BARC), a farm engaged in alternative forms of agriculture and permaculture, including pre-Columbian Mayan farming methods. It is operated by several expatriate Americans—all environmental activists—through the Tropical Conservation Foundation (14 N. Court St., Athens, OH 45701). BARC sponsors permaculture design courses catering to North Americans. Drop-in overnight guests are welcome at $5 a night, with an additional fee for meals. There are considerable flora and fauna on the BARC grounds, as well as many ruins of Lubaantun outliers.

Accommodations and services are also available among the present-day Maya in San Pedro Columbia as part of the "indigenous experience" home-stay service offered by Dem Dats Doin, located less than a mile from the village. The operators of Dem Dats Doin, Alfredo and Yvonne Villoria, can also accommodate a small number of overnight guests on their permaculture farm by advance arrangement. Yet another option is to overnight in Punta Gorda (21 miles away) or San Antonio Village (5 miles distant). Camping at the ruin is not allowed.

Several hotels and travel agencies in the Toledo and Stann Creek districts arrange tours to Lubaantun and other nearby Mayan ruins. There are restrooms and a picnic area here but no drinking water, food, literature, or trained guides. The setting is peaceful and birds abound. A resident Mayan caretaker, Santiago Coc, answers questions and sometimes waives the $1.50 entrance fee.

Nim Li Punit (Toledo District)

Located about 25 miles north of Punta Gorda off the Southern Highway, this Late Classic ceremonial center remained hidden from outsiders until oilworkers stumbled upon it in 1976. Since then, excavations have revealed 25 stelae, at least eight of which are carved, including the tallest (at 31 feet) carved stone monument in Belize. The site's name is Mayan for "big hat" and refers to a headdress-adorned figure on the tallest stela.

Archaeologists believe Nim Li Punit may have been affiliated with nearby Lubaantun, which flourished around the same time and is architecturally similar. Digging did not start here until 1983, after the site had been badly looted. Nevertheless, an impressive stela and royal tomb were uncovered in 1986. UCLA archaeologist Richard Leventhal continues to oversee excavations.

There are several tall structures (up to 40 feet high) around two plazas and the remains of a fairly large settlement. More than two dozen monuments have been identified at Nim Li Punit, many of an unusually long and low design. One building, for example, is only 9 feet high but 215 feet long. It is believed that the site may have been a funerary cult center that acted as a kind of service community to the local elite, who were probably headquartered in Lubaantun. The true function of Nim Li Punit and its relation to other Mayan centers remains unclear.

Although it is small, Nim Li Punit has interesting hieroglyphics and many interesting carvings on its ceremonial stones. As is the case at many Mayan sites, there is an enormous ceiba tree (next to the caretaker's hut) and many flowering plants. The friendly resident caretaker, Placido Pec, will answer questions, direct you to sign the guest registry, and collect the $1.50 entrance fee.

If You Go: Nim Li Punit is about ½-mile off the Southern Highway at Mile 75 near the Mayan village of Indian Creek. It is not directly accessible by public transportation, although daily Z-Line buses pass by on their way to and from Punta Gorda and Dangriga.

A well-marked track leads visitors to the site from the highway in about 20 minutes. The trailhead is not far from Whitney's Grocery Store (if you pass Whitney's Lumber Mill, heading south, you've gone too far). The nearest accommodations are in Silver Creek and Big Falls. We recommend Rav's Guest House, next to one of the only hot springs in Belize. You can also stay in Punta Gorda (25 miles south), San Antonio (10 miles south), or one of the Mayan villages participating in the previously-described guesthouse or home-stay program. Several hotels and tour operators in the region make trips here, often in combination with Lubaantun.

The ruins overlook a mixture of second-growth jungle and milpa garden plots. Local Mayans use the nearby streams to bathe and are friendly to tourists, sometimes approaching them with handicrafts for sale. Except for a small sun/rain shelter, there are no facilities at Nim Li Punit. Only the southernmost cluster of buildings is open to visitors.

Uxbenka (Toledo District)

Local Maya have known about Uxbenka—"the old place" in their local dialect, also spelled "Uxbenton"—for many years. But the outside world only learned of the site's existence in 1984, when reports of looting filtered back to Belmopan. On further investigation,   officials learned that indeed this was a very ancient settlement and, yes, parts of it were being carted off for private sale. One of the seven carved stelae found here dates from the Early Classic period, the earliest archaeological date yet recorded in southern Belize, but most of the sculpted stones are too badly eroded to read. An additional 13 uncarved stelae have been unearthed at Uxbenka, which also features a couple of unexcavated pyramids and a small plaza, plus some overgrown structural mounds. There's been virtually no restoration work here.

The site, which is not extensive, perches on a lovely ridge overlooking the foothills and valleys of the Maya Mountains. The nearby hillsides have been faced with cut terrace stones, a form of agricultural masonry not found outside the Toledo District. The Uxbenka caretaker lives nearby in Santa Cruz Village and may or may not be present when you visit. A map of the ruins was produced with help of the British Army, but you'll have to ask around in order to find a copy.

If You Go: Uxbenka is on the outskirts of Santa Cruz Village, about 3 miles west of San Antonio, 20 miles from Punta Gorda, and 9 miles east of the Guatemala border. Besides private four-wheel-drive vehicle, you can get here on the Wednesday/Saturday bus that shuttles between Punta Gorda and Pueblo Viejo, or take the P.G. bus to San Antonio and hitch a ride (or walk) the rest of the way. Other transportation for visitors is through arranged tours from Punta Gorda or via the supply trucks that come through the area once or twice a week. There is a guesthouse in San Antonio and overnight accommodations can probably be arranged with a Mayan family in Santa Cruz. Camping is not permitted.

Be sure to check out the soothing waterfall and swimming hole just east of Santa Cruz. Several caves are also worth visiting in the hills to the north, near San José Village. A local guide is helpful in finding these destinations.

Nohmul (Orange Walk District)

Nohmul is a major ceremonial center spread among privately owned sugarcane fields near the village of San Pablo, about 7 miles north of Orange Walk Town. Permission from the property owner is required before visiting. The site—located on a limestone ridge and dominated by a massive acropolis atop which a pyramid has been built—consists of two groups of buildings incorporating ten plazas and connected by a raised causeway.

Nohmul (Mayan for "great mound") was occupied first during the Pre-Classic era (350 B.C. to A.D. 250) and again during the Late Classic period (A.D. 600 to 900). At its height, the community was the seat of government for an area encompassing 8 square miles and including the nearby settlements now known as San Esteban and San Luis.

The dominant ceremonial structure at Nohmul, a large limestone-block rectangle, was built during the late Pre-Classic era with several modifications in subsequent years. Interestingly, this acropolis seems to have lost its religious significance over time and to have been converted into residential quarters by the end of Nohmul's Mayan occupation.

Thomas Gann first recorded the large mound as a Mayan site in 1897 and conducted digs here over the next 39 years. He and his wife found jade, seashells, flint, obsidian, pottery, and human bones. Much of this material was removed from burial tombs and sent to the British Museum in London. Neglect, looting, and the use of ancient buildings as road construction material took their toll on Nohmul before full-scale excavation could begin in 1982.

If You Go: Nohmul is about 1 mile west of the village of San Pablo, which straddles the Northern Highway midway between Orange Walk Town and Corozal Town, both about 8 miles distant. The site's owner, Esteban Itzab, should be contacted before proceeding to the ruin.

He lives in the house directly across the street from the community water tower.

There are no facilities or services. Buses pass through the village hourly en route to Orange Walk Town or Corozal Town. Nohmul can also be easily reached by private car or taxi from either of these communities in about 20 minutes. Part of the ruin can be seen from the Northern Highway.

Cahal Pech (Cayo District)

The ridgetop ruin of Cahal Pech, practically within the town limits of San Ignacio, underwent extensive excavation and restoration during the early 1990s by San Diego State University, the University of Oregon, Canada's Trent University, and the Belize Department of Archaeology. Some visitors may be surprised—and even put off—by the overlay of limestone plaster on much of these ruins, but supervising archaeologists insist that such restoration is historically accurate. We are not used to seeing these smooth plaster surfaces on ancient Mayan buildings, the experts point out, because it has almost entirely eroded over the years.

Cahal Pech derives its Mopan Mayan name, "place of the tick," from the large number of bovine parasites found here when the area was used as a cattle pasture. Local residents acknowledged the site's presence, but the ruins were not mapped until 1950 and were periodically looted until a complete survey was made in 1988.

This ceremonial complex of what was once a medium-size Mayan settlement and political center consists of 34 structures spread across several acres. There are seven courtyards, plus a number of ball courts, stelae, and temple pyramids. The tallest building is 77 feet. The site functioned as a kind of royal castle, standing guard over the nearby confluence of the Mopan and Macal rivers. Cahal Pech is believed to have been closely associated with nearby Buena Vista and Xunantunich, both dating from the same era.

Preliminary analysis indicates that Cahal Pech was occupied during the Late Classic period from at least 900 B.C. to about A.D. 1100, reaching its greatest strength around A.D. 600. At that time it may have been the primary Mayan center in the central Belize River watershed. Notable findings here include an altar, a mosaic mask, and what appears to have been a sweat lodge. Research supports the theory that the famous Classic Maya "collapse" of the ninth century came neither swiftly nor easily, at least to Cahal Pech. Based on new evidence of lingering squalor and decay, it appears that the break-down of the civilization dragged on for as many as 100 years, until the early tenth century.

If You Go: Visitors are welcome at Cahal Pech, which is a pleasant 20-minute walk (or short drive) west of downtown San Ignacio a few blocks off the Western Highway. Look for a sign where the highway makes a sweeping turn as it goes up a hill outside San Ignacio. The site is on the south side of the road, out of view in a cluster of trees.

A worthwhile museum and visitor's center are at the entrance to the site, open daily from 8:00 a.m. to 4:00 p.m. A very informative free pamphlet about Cahal Pech is distributed here, and the admis-sion fee of $1.50 is collected. A hardback book about the site, pub-lished not long ago by San Diego State University, is sold at the museum and various bookstores around Belize.

On top of a hill a few hundred yards from the ruin is the Cahael Pech Tavern, a popular bar and dance hall that is worth a visit. The place gets loud, and sometimes rowdy, on weekend nights.

La Milpa (Orange Walk District)

A fairly large but unrestored site, these ruins are located on property within the protected Río Bravo Conservation and Management Area in northwest Belize. Located near a biological field station in the mid-dle of the 250,000-acre Río Bravo tract, La Milpa comprises about 40 structures scattered throughout thick forest. At least twenty court-yard groups have been counted, plus an elaborate system of reservoirs and causeways. Three pyramids rise to about 100 feet, and a "great plaza" here has been judged to be one of the ancient civilization's biggest. In fact, archaeologists now believe that La Milpa may be the third-largest Mayan complex in Belize, after Caracol and Lamanai, although precious little is known about it.

Stelae and other artifacts indicate major occupation during the Early and Late Classic periods. Extensive mapping did not get under way here until 1990, and very few structures have been excavated or evaluated. With the establishment of a nearby research center, a better picture of La Milpa is gradually emerging.

If You Go: La Milpa (wrongly spelled Las Milpas on some maps) is located in a remote area that is inaccessible by road during wetter months. Most visitors arrive by private plane via the Gallon Jug airstrip and stay at Chan Chich Lodge, located in the plaza of yet another Mayan ruin. Lodge bookings and archaeological tours are arranged through Programme for Belize offices in Belize City and the United States (see Inside Belize). Arrangements should be made as far in advance as possible. Casual visitors who have obtained a permit from Programme for Belize can drive to the site in about 4 hours from Belize City during dry weather, via Blue Creek Village in the Orange Walk District. Bungalows for tourists may have been built by the time you read this, otherwise overnight visitors are housed (with advance permission only) in the dormitory of the Río Bravo Project's field station. Meals and guiding services can also be arranged here.

Other Ancient Mayan Sites

The following ruins have been documented by the Belize government and are in varying stages of study or excavation. In some cases, no work has been done beyond the most basic forms of mapping and cataloging. All are accessible to the public, although permission must be obtained from private landowners in some instances. There are, of course, many other Mayan sites in Belize, but in an attempt to discourage looting, the authorities prefer not to discuss locations that have not yet been evaluated. The Colha site is located on the Rancho Creek Farm, about 7 miles north of Maskall on the (old) Northern Highway, roughly 40 miles northwest of Belize City in the Belize District. Permission of the landowner is required to see this small ceremonial site. Colha shows occupation as early as 2400 B.C., making it one of the oldest Mayan sites. It is under excavation by the University of Texas, which is also exploring the nearby Blue Creek site.

El Pilar is a Classic era ceremonial center being excavated by researchers from the University of California, Santa Barbara. At 50 acres, it is one of the largest unconsolidated Mayan ruins in the country, located in a cultivated part of the Cayo District near the Belize River and about 16 miles directly north of Xunantunich. Archaeologists are especially intrigued by an unexplained causeway that extends from the site across the Guatemalan border into the dense Petén jungle. There are 15 plaza groups built over many centuries. El Pilar can be reached by high-clearance private car, taxi, or horseback. Drive to the village of Bullet Tree Falls and ask area residents for directions to the ruins. Fred Prost of Parrot's Nest Riverside Treehouses is also a good resource and leads guided tours of the area regularly. From San Ignacio, the trip takes about an hour. Parrot's Nest also runs trips to chicle camps in the nearby jungle.

Buena Vista is located on a private cattle ranch, Nabuntunich, about 3 miles west of San Ignacio on the east bank of the Mopan River. The Cayo District site is fairly large but mostly unexcavated. Prior permission from the landowner is required to visit.

Floral Park and Baking Pot are two small but potentially significant sites on the south bank of the Belize River near Central Farm and Georgeville, respectively. The ruins are currently being excavated and evaluated. Some of the vegetation-covered mounds of these sites are easily visible from the Western Highway.

Marco Gonzalez is a late Pre-Classic era (A.D. 1100 to 1300) residential and sea-trading center that was active for hundreds of years. Located in the thick mangrove swamp at the south end of Ambergris Caye, its ruins have been studied by the Royal Ontario Museum, which found no intact structures. It's believed that most buildings were constructed of seashells, particularly conch. Pottery, obsidian, and jade, as well as basalt grinding tools, stelae, and temple mounds, were unearthed here. Access to Marco Gonzalez, which has been heavily looted, is by foot trail from the town of San Pedro.

San Juan, excavated by a Texas archaeological team, is at the north end of Ambergris Caye and dates from the Pre-Classic period. It is one of about a dozen Mayan sites pinpointed on the island, all largely abandoned by A.D. 1000, as trading patterns shifted to overland routes. Many of the other cayes and atolls have similar sites and middens, the equivalent of Mayan trash heaps.

Pusilha is on the Moho River in the Toledo District, about 1 mile east of the Guatemala border. The ruins, built on top of a hill above the river, can be reached only by boat. The plaza contains about two dozen carved stelae.

Other lesser-known Mayan ruins include K'axob, an agricultural site in northern Belize near Pulltrouser Swamp that dates to 2500 B.C., under excavation by Boston University and Florida State University; Shipstern, located south of Sarteneja Village in the Corozal District; El Posito, about 4 miles west of Guinea Grass in the Orange Walk District; Actun Balam, near Caracol in the Cayo District; Blackman Eddy, on the Macal River about 10 miles southwest of San Ignacio; Tzmin Kax, also in the Cayo wilderness; and Dolores Estate, an unexcavated Early Classic site near the Toledo District village of Dolores. An even smaller ruin in the Toledo District is Naheb, just west of the Southern Highway near Indian Creek Village. Four large Mayan ruins, yet unnamed, were found during 1994 in the Bladen Branch area of the Toledo District's Monkey River. Not yet open to the public, the sites are significant because it was previously assumed that few Maya lived in this area during ancient times.

Tikal

The famous Mayan ruin of Tikal is located about 50 miles (2 to 3 hours) northwest of the Belize border in Guatemala. Set in an incredible high-canopy jungle, the site encompasses at least 3,000 buildings, including a handful of impressively tall temples that loom about the forest. At its peak some 1,500 years ago, Tikal was home to an estimated 100,000 Maya. Yet this city-state was virtually forgotten by the outside world until its rediscovery in 1848. Because it is so close to Belize, many travelers make a side trip to Tikal, which is one of the most impressive in the entire Mayan world. For a detailed discussion of Tikal and other nearby ruins, see Richard Mahler's *Guatemala: A Natural Destination*, (Santa Fe, N. Mex.: John Muir Publications).

If traveling to Tikal on your own, you can now obtain Guatemalan visas and/or tourist cards in Belize, and formalities at the border are straightforward. (If you travel from Belize to Tikal in a package tour, paperwork and fees are usually taken care of by the operator.) The border is open daily from 8:00 a.m. to noon and 2:00 p.m. to 6:00 p.m.; crossing during off-hours is sometimes possible for an extra fee.

Guatemalan tourist cards and, less reliably, visas are issued at the frontier, which runs along the east bank of Mopan River between the towns of Melchor de Mencos, Guatemala, and Benque Viejo, Belize. Both documents require a $5 fee. If you are driving a vehicle, be sure to have your registration and insurance papers in order, and expect to pay a few dollars to have the car fumigated with insecticide on the Guatemalan side (this is required by law and is one reason almost no Belizean companies allow their rental cars to enter Guatemala).

Bus passengers usually have to stop on the Belize side of the crossing and walk or take a taxi a few hundred yards into Melchor de Mencos, where Guatemalan buses pick up westbound passengers. The same thing happens going the opposite direction. Belizean taxi drivers often intercept passengers as they descend from buses on the Guatemala side and take them all the way to San Ignacio, for a fee of about $7 each. If you simply want a quick glimpse of Guatemalan life, Melchor de Mencos is the place to find it. There is a colorful market where handicrafts are sold at fair prices, and a bank where Belize dollars can be exchanged for quetzales (moneychangers at the border offer slightly lower rates). The hotels are inexpensive, and several offer reasonably priced tours to local Mayan ruins, including Tikal. Try the Hotel Melchor Palace on the Mopan River, which has a restaurant, a travel service, and a car rental agency. The operator, Marco Gross, also owns the Arts & Crafts of Central America store in San Ignacio (tel. 9-22823), where reservations for the Melchor Palace can be made.

The entrance to Tikal National Park is northwest of Melchor de Mencos via 2 hours of poor road, then a half-hour of paved surface to the ruins themselves. The $6 admission fee to Tikal National Park is good for the date of entry only. Because the site is so large, a good guidebook and/or map greatly enhances the experience. Well-informed, English-speaking Guatemalan guides can be hired at the site (Belizean guides are not allowed to escort visitors through the ruins). You'll need several days to take in the majority of structures here, but the highlights can be seen in a few hours. Be sure to spend some time in Tikal's Silvanus G. Morley Archaeological Museum ($3 admission), where many artifacts recovered by researchers are on permanent display, including relics from a ruler's tomb.

En route to the park, you may be stopped by the Guatemalan military and asked to show your passport or other identification. These spot checks are ordinarily uneventful, but make sure you do not photograph any soldiers or military installations. If you do so without permission, you may be detained for questioning and your film may be destroyed. The political situation in Guatemala is gradually improving, but parts of the Petén wilderness are still controlled by anti-government guerrillas and outlaws. There are reports of tourists being robbed by gunmen en route to Tikal from Belize, therefore you should take only as much money as you expect to need during your visit.

As tourism has increased in Belize, the number of alternative ways for getting to Tikal has also increased. Several scheduled flights each week between Belize City and Flores/Santa Elena (about 40 miles south of the ruins) are offered by Tropic Air, Aerovías, and Aviateca. Expect to pay about $130 round-trip. Charters can also be arranged from Belize City and San Pedro for about $200 and up. From the Flores airport there are frequent minibuses to Tikal, or a car can be rented for the 50-minute drive.

Both Novelo's and Batty's bus services carry passengers from Belize City to Melchor de Mencos, dropping passengers there for connections to Tikal and/or Flores. If you are heading directly to Tikal you will need to get off at El Cruce, an intersection about 20 miles south of the ruins. From there you can take a public bus or hitch the rest of the way, but there is a risk of getting stranded. Bus schedules being what they are, you will probably need to spend a night in Flores or Santa Elena to catch the early morning public bus or a private minibus to the ruins.

The most popular, and in many respects the easiest, way to visit Tikal from Belize is as part of a package tour. Most of the Cayo lodges arrange such trips (by van or airplane) on a weekly or even daily basis, often including the services of a knowledgeable guide. Similar tours can be arranged from Belize City, San Pedro, and other towns. Prices for package tours of Tikal vary, depending on the number of persons traveling and the duration of the trip. Expect to pay at least $50 per person, however, depending on the size of your group.

Bear in mind that a one-day overland round-trip means being inside a vehicle for 5 hours or more.

Overnight visits require lodging and meals in Flores, Santa Elena, or Tikal National Park. Popular hotels in greater Flores include the Petén, Posada Tayasal, San Juan, and Itzá. Some of these places are very picturesque, situated beside the large lake that dominates this Spanish colonial town, built on the site of an ancient Mayan city. Also recommended is the modern and luxurious (but environmentally friendly) Hotel Camino Real, located about 25 minutes (15 miles) west of Tikal on the eastern shore of Lake Petén Itzá. This resort has many amenities, including a gift shop and pool.

There are three basic guesthouses at Tikal National Park: the Jaguar Inn, the Jungle Lodge, and the Tikal Inn. The latter is highly recommended because of the conservation orientation of its owners, the Ortíz family. (Ask Mike Ortíz for directions to Tikal's various nature trails.) Rates start at about $35 a night. There is also one campground, which charges about $6 a night for tent, hammock space, or overnight parking. Water is scarce, so bring your own. Several undistinguished restaurants and overpriced gift shops are also near the Tikal ruins. There is a post office, but no telephone. An overnight visit to the park is highly recommended because of the tremendous amount of wildlife, including monkeys, deer, foxes, agoutis, and cats. Birders will be particularly rewarded. Because the area has been protected since the mid-1950s, many of the animals show little or no fear of humans.

7

Special Interests

For enthusiasts of diving, snorkeling, fishing, identifying wild creatures, or simply taking it easy, a trip to Belize presents almost unlimited opportunities. The detailed information below will help those with special interests in such pursuits. For specific details on individuals and services catering to these and other special interests, please see the Inside Belize section that follows this chapter.

Diving and Underwater Sports

In 1989, *Skin Diver* magazine described Belize as "one of the western Caribbean's premier dive destinations," praising its unspoiled waters and easy access. Today, many of the publication's readers might argue that Belize has since become the most highly regarded diving spot in all the Caribbean, and probably one of the top five in the Western Hemisphere.

With all those coastal waterways—along with literally thousands of little-known reefs, sand bores, islands, and marine formations—to choose from, there is something here for every specialty and level of ability. Belize's waters are consistently calm, warm (averaging 80 degrees), shallow enough to make long dives pleasurable, and also amazingly clear: up to 200 feet visibility is common in outlying waters. And when you and your companion get tired of scuba, there is always swimming, snorkeling, fishing, sailing, sea kayaking, windsurfing, and sunbathing. Most of the major hotels, especially those on Ambergris Caye, offer one or more of these activities, plus whatever related equipment may be required. The Ramada Royal Reef Hotel in Belize City, Belize Yacht Club on Ambergris Caye, Belize River Lodge on Moho Caye, Turneffe Island Lodge on Caye Bokel, and Blue Marlin Lodge on South Water Caye are also good places to inquire about diving trips and other water-related sports.

For the beginner, diving around San Pedro, Caye Caulker, Placencia, and the Hol Chan Marine Reserve will likely provide more than enough variation in underwater scenery and marine life. Night dives at Hol Chan, for example, often include glimpses of black-tip shark, lemon shark, squid, eels, and octopus. The more experienced diver or snorkeler will probably want to go even father afield, exploring areas that have not suffered as much habitat damage at the hands of commercial fishermen and tourists. Many small species of fish, crustacean, sponge, fan, and coral inhabit the more well-traveled areas, but such larger and more timid creatures as turtles and grouper are notably absent. (San Pedro and Caye Caulker are good places to find boats, guides, and instructors, however.)

In order to experience fully the best of what Belize has to offer—such as viewing deep-water gorgonians, black-coral forests, and the most exotic tropical fish—underwater explorers have three basic options. First, they may head for one of the more remote island hotels or resorts. Good choices include one of the several tourist operations on the Turneffe Islands, Glover's Reef, Lighthouse Reef, Spanish Lookout Caye, Placencia, or South Water Caye. Second, they may sign on with one of the several live-aboard dive boats shuttling among Belize's many uninhabited islands and isolated reef structures. And third, they may charter a boat, individually or as part of a larger group, so as to have maximum flexibility in destination and schedule. Any of these choices can be easily accomplished with the help of a local travel agent, dive shop, or large hotel.

Obviously, trade-offs are inherent in each selection. The less-accessible lodges are relatively expensive and usually require a minimum stay of six days or more. Some of these also close during the hot, insect-plagued months of July, August, and September. Live-aboard dive boats are also somewhat costly, with fixed schedules and routes that generally exclude the Belize interior. The expenses involved in chartering a private boat can also add up quickly, and the trip may be limited by the abilities of craft and crew.

The Inside Belize section contains a comprehensive roster of specialists involved in the three types of diving vacations just described. For further details, we suggest you contact these sources directly for advice on the most appropriate option. Keep in mind that many dive resorts also cater to anglers, so it is feasible to combine both pleasures in a single Belizean vacation. Examples include the Belize River Lodge, Blue Marlin Lodge, Ramon's Village, Blackbird Caye Resort, Wippari Caye Lodge, Ranguana Reef Lodge, and Manta Reef Resort. Such operators usually have special rates for nondiving and nonfishing travelers, or for off-season visitors.

Night diving and cave diving are increasing in popularity in Belize, and the major dive specialists can provide necessary guides, maps, lights, and other gear. You will see different species of animals at night, and the marine caverns here are some of the largest in the world. Belize Diving Services on Caye Caulker; Bottom Time Dive Shop, Tortuga Dive Center, and Reef Divers Limited on Ambergris Caye; Turneffe Lodge on Caye Bokel; Blue Planet Divers off Blackbird Caye; and Kitty's Place or the Rum Point Inn in the Placencia area are all highly recommended. Favored dive spots include Socorri-to Point and Mexico Rocks, both near Ambergris Caye, and The Elbow, off the southern tip of the Turneffe Islands. Glover's Reef and Lighthouse Reef also are full of excellent dive spots, especially in waters where the current stirs up plenty of oxygen and food sources for fish. There are a number of shipwrecks suited for diving at these outer atolls as well.

A variation on the live-aboard approach to diving and snorkeling is an overnight cruise from San Pedro via the *Reef Roamer II*, a converted shrimp boat that is booked through local hotels. The 50-foot craft makes 2- and 3-night trips to dive the Blue Hole, Turneffe Islands, and Lighthouse Reef. From Caye Caulker, an outfit called Sea-Ing Is Belizing offers excursions that last up to 8 days and include the outer

Sailboats in Belize City harbor (Photo by Kevin Schafer)

atolls and reef structures. Your live-aboard vessel is a 28-foot sailboat. Other popular live-aboard boats include *La Strega, Greet Reef, Belize Aggressor,* and *Coral Bay,* all operating out of Belize City. These vessels are equipped with diving platforms, tank racks, freshwater rinses, and other services.

For photo processing, try Wade Bevier (specializing in E-6 processing) at Placencia's Rum Point Inn, or James Beveridge on Caye Caulker. For diving instruction, excellent courses are offered by Blue Planet Divers, based in Belize City and on Blackbird Caye in the Turneffe Islands. We have also heard positive reports about the Blue Marlin Lodge on South Water Caye.

Although most dive boats and diving resorts happily accommodate snorkelers and can easily supply any necessary equipment, it may be both easier and cheaper to arrange personalized day trips and hire your own boat operator. This is most easily done at hotels that have their own marinas, such as the Ft. George, Bellevue, Ramada Reef, Sea Breeze (Ambergris Caye), and Pyramid Island (Caye Chapel). Local fishermen and guides are often willing to drop off snorkelers and swimmers in good locations, then pick them up a few hours later. Small sandy cayes—notably, Congrejo, Goff's, Rosario, Montego, English, and Rendezvous—are especially recommended. Even on the more active islands of Ambergris, Caulker, Chapel, and St. George's, plenty of reef—away from populated areas and traffic lanes—offers an astonishing array of marine life.

Rental of a full complement of scuba gear generally starts at about $45 a day, with an additional $75 and up for two tanks worth of diving. Full certification instruction costs $325 or more. Bring your certification card with you; reputable operators will not accommodate your scuba requests without it. Dive trips to Lighthouse Reef and other popular dive sites start at about $200 per day per person. For day trips to Lighthouse, Ambergris-based Out Island Divers has been recommended by experienced divers. Overnight trips on snorkel-only boats start at about $125 per person, with charters about $20 higher, based on a two-person minimum. Day trips start at around $40. The 45-foot catamaran *Stingray,* based at the Ramada Reef Hotel marina, has been recommended by experienced snorkelers. Contact owner/operators

Michael and Donna Hill through the Ramada. Another snorkel boat is operated by Ecosummer Expeditions.

One cautionary note: some individuals have occasionally reported finding rental water sports equipment to be substandard in Belize. Whenever practical, it's best to bring your own mask, snorkel, fins, and other paraphernalia to ensure reliability. The situation has improved greatly in recent years, but it is still a good idea to thoroughly examine any rental equipment before heading offshore. You should also ask around before hiring a diving instructor, since the level of expertise varies considerably. And do not let anyone try to rent you a surfboard in Belize. Except during hurricanes, surf is nonexistent here.

If you do decide to bring your own underwater gear to Belize, ask your airline about special size and weight allowances. They are accustomed to bulky baggage on the Belize City run and can usually accommodate all manner of equipment for little or no extra charge. The same is true for kayaks, windsurfboards, bicycles, and fishing gear.

Before departure, we also recommend that the serious water sports enthusiast check one or more of the specialty magazines and guidebooks that profile Belize on a regular basis. These are often available at large dive shops, sporting goods stores, or newsstands.

Once you arrive in Belize, several factors may influence your choice of diving and snorkeling spots. Clarity of Inner Channel waters, for example, is reduced near the outlets of jungle rivers and urban areas such as Dangriga and Belize City. The mainland side of the reef routinely has visibility of 50 to 100 feet. Conditions improve on the Caribbean side of the barrier reef and the farther south you go, with 150-foot visibility common. The most crystalline water is found around the three atolls, where visibility is often in excess of 200 feet along walls.

Water temperatures range from about 74 degrees in winter to 86 degrees in summer. A bodysuit is adequate much of the year, and you never need more than an eighth-inch wetsuit for thermal insulation. Your body temperature is 98.6 degrees, however, and low-grade hypothermia can set in if you stay in the water long enough without a break or some kind of protection.

Telephone service to the Belize mainland and the developed areas of Ambergris Caye and Caye Caulker is very good. Most of the outlying islands can be reached only by VHF marine-band radio. As in the United States, channels 16 and 68 are the standard hailing frequencies. Live-aboard boats and charter craft also stand by on channel 78. Many resorts now have two-way radio telephones.

Once in Belize, divers and snorkelers should not enter the water before identifying its possible hazards. Besides living coral polyps, which should not be touched or stepped on for reasons of ecology as well as health, there are the usual urchins, anemones, jellyfish, and stingrays to look out for. Fire worms (also called bristle worms) and certain types of sponges can cause a burning sensation if brushed against, and the aptly named scorpion fish will sting if stepped on. The sinister-looking barracuda and nurse shark cruise Belize's reefs by the hundreds but will not attack unless deliberately provoked or drawn by the scent of fresh food or blood (i.e., from spearfishing). Definitely don't pull the nurse shark's tail. Dolphins, also, generally prefer not to be touched, especially on certain sensitive spots. In general, it is best not to feed fish underwater. Every species is hungry, and some, such as the moray eel, have teeth sharp enough to remove a finger or two. A good pair of booties, fins, or Patagonia Reef Walkers will help reduce the risk of foot injuries. As a rule, it's not a good idea to dive or snorkel alone, or to dive or snorkel after drinking alcohol.

Medical experts recommend that beginning or infrequent divers over age 35 get a physical exam before diving, preferably from a physician who is familiar with the sport. Among older divers, one out of every four fatalities involves cardiovascular problems. Other conditions that should preclude diving, at any age, are severe asthma, seizure disorders, insulin-dependent diabetes, and any disease that could result in a loss of consciousness.

Divers should always be aware of the risks of decompression sickness, or "the bends," caused by entrapment of nitrogen bubbles in the bloodstream. It is treatable by oxygen therapy or by spending time in a decompression chamber, however decompression chamber treatments typically run $400 an hour, and only one unit is available in Belize (on Ambergris Caye). Because aircraft cabins are pressurized to the equivalent of about 8,000 feet, it is strongly recommended that scuba divers not fly less than 12 hours, preferably 24 hours, after a dive.

Sportfishing

All the joys of the ocean are found in the waters of Belize. Great fishing—spin, fly, or troll—can be enjoyed year-round, and the abundance of fish guarantees excellent sport. Some anglers insist that it is virtually impossible to go fishing in Belize and not catch something. A distinct advantage here for non-Spanish-speaking fishermen (and women) is that virtually all guides and boatmen speak English.

The estuaries and mouths of jungle rivers of Belize are best known for their tarpon, black snapper, jack-revalle, cubera, and snook; lagoons and coral flats for their bonefish, permit, triggerfish, and barracuda; reef formations for their king mackerel, kingfish, jackfish, grouper, barracuda, and snapper; and the deeper waters off the outer reefs and atolls for amberjack, sailfish, shark, wahoo, pompano, blackfin tuna, yellowfin tuna, bonito, dolphinfish (mahi-mahi), and marlin. Species availability varies considerably, depending on the depth and clarity of water, proximity to reefs and rivers, and time of year.

Many resorts, boat operators, lodges, and guides serve the needs of sportfishermen (see Inside Belize for a complete list of names and addresses). Almost any hotel near the water can easily provide you with a fishing guide, a boat, and tackle—for rent by the hour, day, or week. Flies, as well as extra tackle items, are available for sale to guests who need them. Many dive shops, dive resorts, and diving boats also welcome fishing enthusiasts.

Many saltwater fly-fishermen come to Belize to stalk the elusive bonefish, an almost transparent fish known for its feisty spirit and crafty ways. (As the name implies, the creature is too bony to make a decent meal.) Although the bonefish is relatively small—averaging 2 to 6 pounds—ounce for ounce it is considered perhaps the toughest fighter in the sea. This predator is often found in knee-deep, crystal-clear coral flats, particularly from November through April, where it

Fisherman and his catch on Laughingbird Caye (Photo by Kevin Schafer)

attacks smaller fish with lightning speed. The bonefish is taken on both fly and lure. Fishing resorts that specialize in guided bonefish excursions include Turneffe Flats, Turneffe Island Lodge, Belize River Lodge, and Wippari Caye Lodge.

The same marine habitats also teem with the wily permit, especially on coral flats at incoming tides. Many fishing lodges claim Belize is the "permit capital of the world," with specimens weighing in at 30 or more pounds. The largest concentrations of this elusive species are in the southern coastal waters of Belize. For those determined to snag a permit, we recommend the outfitters listed above for bonefishing, along with the Blue Marlin Lodge on South Water Caye.

Torpedo-shaped tarpon, sharp-eyed barracuda, and cubera snapper are equally plentiful near Belizean reefs. Forty-pound or larger tarpon are fairly common from February to June, and good-sized snook are reported all winter, both in rivers and estuaries. These two species can be found around coral flats and mangrove cayes the rest of the year. The aggressive barracuda are notorious for breaking leaders in the water or, once landed, snapping at fishermen's feet. Mutton snapper and jack also frequent the coral flats, along with the occasional grouper and red snapper. Fishing outfitters specializing in snook and tarpon include the Belize River Lodge and El Pescador, on Ambergris Caye.

The much deeper, ocean side of the barrier reef yields king and Spanish mackerel, grouper, snapper, bonito, blackfin tuna, and wahoo, along with sailfish (March to May) and marlin (November to May). You will also encounter many shark, porpoise, and dolphin. The warmest months offer the best chance to hook grouper, mutton snapper, and mangrove snapper. For a sight not soon forgotten, head for Glory Caye during the night of January's full moon and watch the spawning of thousands of Nassau grouper.

Lobster season is July 14 to March 15, but most of these spiny crustaceans (lacking the large claws of the cold-water species off the Maine coast) are taken by local fishermen, who also commercially harvest conch, shrimp, snapper, and other species.

Saltwater fly-fishing is best in the southern part of Belize, where the presence of divers, snorkelers, and Belizean fishermen has been felt the least. Anything south of Dangriga is likely to be especially promising. It's not unusual to go for days at a time without seeing another rod or line.

If fishing is the primary purpose of your trip, you'll want to spend as little time as possible in Belize City. There is no beach here, and the waters are foul. Luckily, with some advance planning, you can easily transfer to a better base of operations on the day you arrive. Many fishing lodges have airport pickup service and often arrange overnight accommodations in Belize City, departing the next morning on chartered boats. Scheduled domestic airline service is also easily arranged from Belize City's municipal airport to Ambergris, Caulker, and Chapel Cayes, as well as the outlying coastal towns of Placencia, Dangriga, Corozal, and Punta Gorda. The only other island with an airstrip is Northern Two Caye, at Lighthouse Reef. There are a few seaplanes in Belize, but they seem to get very little use.

Because of their years of experience, many private fishing boat operators are also excellent guides. Some resorts hire locals whose only job is to help you find and catch the fish of your choice. With hundreds of varieties to choose from, simply making a selection may be a daunting task. Native Belizean "consultants" are sometimes included in the price of package tours, especially the week-long excursions to outer islands. The services of such guides can also be engaged for about $200 a day, including boat, tackle, and fuel. Week-long fishing packages begin at around $1,100 for six days of actual fishing. These Belize-born experts are considered some of the best fly-fishermen in the world. Local guides such as Charles Leslie, of Placencia's Kingfisher Belize Adventures, specialize in fly-fishing guiding, spin fishing, and offshore fishing. Other recommended guides include Richard Young Jr. of Belize City; Cagey Eiley, Eddie Leslie, and Kevin Madera of Placencia; and the Cabral family at Wippari Caye Guiding on Wippari Caye (10 miles east of Placencia). On Calabash Caye in the Turneffe Islands, David Young has an excellent reputation as a fishing guide. The investment in a good "consultant" is worth it: during guided visits to nearly virgin Belizean waters, anglers regularly complete a "grand slam" by landing at least one tarpon, snook, bonefish, and permit within a 24-hour period.

On Ambergris Caye, the El Pescador lodge is recommended as a well-equipped base of operations for saltwater anglers. The resort, which has its own sportfishing boats, guides, and marina, was built by a German-American couple with the help of local Mennonite carpenters. The flats between here and the Belizean mainland are renowned for their tarpon (also called silver kings), recorded at up to about 100 pounds. Although they are not considered good eating, a large tarpon can easily take 90 minutes to subdue with a 10-weight fly rod. Prime time is considered April through August.

Although foreigners are allowed to take as much as 20 pounds of fish with them when they leave Belize, the more common practice is to measure the creature and throw it back for the next customer. An alternative is to share the game fish with your guide, boatman, and fellow fisherfolk as a supper entrée. Some fishing lodges, such as Blackbird Caye Resort, require catch-and-release for ecological reasons.

Although some fishing equipment can be rented from local hotels and outfitters in Belize, the selection is limited (but it is improving over time). Live bait, for example, is sometimes hard to come by. Fortunately, you can usually make do with frozen shrimp or wriggling fingerlings plucked from the sea.

Indispensable for Inner Channel fishing (between the barrier reef and the mainland) are a good 9-foot fly rod, a sturdy reel, and an 8-weight floating saltwater tapered fly line. Experienced sportsmen often bring along one each of a light and medium spinning or fly rod, along with a heavier fly, spinning, or bait-casting rod and a deep-running lure.

Major resorts that specialize in sportfishing, such as the Paradise Hotel or Victoria House on Ambergris Caye, or Pyramid Island on Caye Chapel, can make exact recommendations on tackle, line strength, lures, rods, and reels, depending on what the angler is after and the time of the year. In general, equipment will vary considerably for the following conditions: coral flats, mainland shoreline, mangrove lagoons, river-mouth casting, and deep-water jigging or trolling.

When fishing in tropical Belize, remember that reels in particular need daily cleaning in fresh water and regular lubrication. Other accessories often useful here include tennis shoes or Patagonia Reef

Walkers for wading in coral flats and shoals, lightweight ripstop nylon pants, and polarized sunglasses with side shields. The sun is so intense at these latitudes that a severe burn can occur after less than an hour of exposure. For that reason, we recommend that you bring long-sleeved shirts, cotton pants, wide-brimmed hats, bandannas, lip balm, and, of course, waterproof sunscreen (SPF 15 or higher).

Because of the unique conditions and high quality of the country's offshore waters, freshwater fishing in the interior receives scant attention from visitors. Conditions are excellent in many streams, however, and you should inquire locally about when and where to go.

For a comprehensive list of reputable fishing guides, outfitters, and sportfishing resorts, see Inside Belize.

River Trips, Kayaking, and Sailing

Although Belize is a relatively small and low-lying country, it gets plenty of rainfall and boasts 20 major river systems, plus innumerable perennial streams. These sources supply the nation's domestic water needs and the demands of local agriculture.

For travelers seeking white-water adventure, however, Belize may be a disappointment. Because of dramatic fluctuations in water levels and the long-term impact of dredging, there are few consistently reliable white-water flows suitable for rafting, kayaking, or canoeing. Some rivers in the upland areas (especially of the Cayo District) have navigable white water during certain periods of the year, but it is best to check with tour operators who specialize in such sport for expert advice on where and when to go. The Mopan, Macal, and their tributaries are your best bet. See Inside Belize for local operators specializing in river trips. In San Ignacio, we recommend Remo Montgomery of Float Belize (he also owns the Sandcastle Restaurant), and in nearby Cristo Rey, Victor or Jeronie Tut of Crystal Palace Resort.

Historically, rafts and canoes have always been common modes of transportation on Belizean waterways, and such vessels can be rented through most major hotels and travel agencies. The cottage resorts of the Cayo District, for example, often supply rafts, canoes, and occasional kayaks to their guests or even casual visitors. The area's Macal, Mopan, and Belize rivers are particularly well suited to these craft during the drier months, beginning in about January. Small boats can be rented for as little as one-half hour or as long as two weeks. Some operators arrange trips by raft or canoe all the way from the Guatemalan border to Belize City. This sort of journey is an excellent way to observe birds, plants, animals, and people along the riverbanks. Such travel is problematic during the rainy season, for obvious reasons. Lowland river trips can be arranged at Banana Bank Lodge, the Toledo Adventure Club, Paradise Inn, and Jungle Drift Lodge, among others.

Popular destinations by boat include the offshore islands, the Crooked Tree Wildlife Sanctuary, the Community Baboon Sanctuary, and the Mayan ruins of Cerros, Lamanai, and Xunantunich. A trip up the New River from Orange Walk to Lamanai is a must for bird-watchers, and the New River Lagoon is arguably the loveliest body of fresh water in the country. Boat trips are also recommended to the Northern and Southern lagoons, Gales Point, Placencia, Sittee River, Monkey River Town, and the Temash River.

Sea kayaking and windsurfing are rapidly increasing in popularity. The calm and relatively shallow waters of the Inner Channel (that portion of the Caribbean between the barrier reef and the mainland) are ideal locations for enjoying these activities, and the islands' larger resorts can arrange equipment rental and instruction. Some of these hotels also rent small sailboats on a daily or weekly basis. On a recent visit, one of this book's authors watched as a couple of windsurfers—strapped into their harnesses—enjoyed the long reach from Caye Caulker to Caye Chapel.

Areas favored by sea kayakers include the waters of Chetumal Bay, Ambergris Caye, Caye Caulker, the Hol Chan Channel, and offshore atolls. Experienced kayakers can also follow the entire length of the barrier reef, camping along the way on such small islands as Bluefield Range, Spanish Bay, Colson Caye, Half Moon Caye, and Northeast Caye. Windsurfers report the best conditions are on the leeward sides of the cayes, especially in the shallow waters west of Ambergris Caye.

Sailboards, Sunfish, and Hobie Cats are available for rent at some of the hotels on Ambergris Caye and Caye Caulker. More sailing equipment is being added at outlying resorts, so be sure to inquire in advance if this is a pastime of interest. Some of the larger resorts now offer complimentary windsurfing, Sunfish sailing, and pier fishing in their vacation packages. Even small guesthouses often have dories and canoes available for use by visitors. Be aware that currents and winds on the reef can be tricky, especially in the afternoon.

Waterskiing and windsurfing are most popular off the waters of Ambergris Caye. Check with Victoria Collins at the *San Pedro Sun* (tel. 26-2070) or Amigo Travel (tel. 26-2180) for suggestions. The Sunbreeze Hotel, Ramon's Village, and Journey's End Caribbean Club on Ambergris all rent waterskiing and windsurfing equipment. Slickrock Adventures has combination windsurfing/kayaking trips in the waters off Glover's Reef from December through April, and Eco-summer Expeditions runs kayaking trips during the same period around Lighthouse Reef. Kayaking equipment is also available in Placencia and on Ranguana Caye from the Ranguana Reef Lodge and Resort through their association with Reef-Link Kayaking.

The best book by far on kayaking in Belize is *Belize By Kayak*, self-published by Kirk Barrett. To buy a copy, call him at (515) 279-6699, or write 3806 Cottage Grove, Des Moines, IA 50311.

Flora and Fauna

Belize has several of the world's richest habitats. No fewer than 4,000 different species of native flowering plants are found within its borders, along with about 700 species of trees and several hundred species of other plants. Scientists are only now beginning to perform an exhaustive inventory of Belize's plants. The task is daunting: more than 70 percent of the country is under some kind of forest cover, and almost half of Belize's primary forest is still standing. (Happily, a major part of this forest enjoys some degree of government protection.)

In the animal kingdom, the numbers are even more staggering. Literally thousands of varieties of insects are native to the five major ecosystems of Belize, along with hundreds of mammals, reptiles, amphibians, and fish. Some of the rare or endangered species found here in relatively abundant numbers are the tapir, howler monkey, anteater, king vulture, Morelet's crocodile, sea turtle, manatee, and jaguar, the hemisphere's largest cat. The pamphlet entitled "Checklist of the Birds of Belize" (Carnegie Museum of Natural History) lists over 530 species that have been sighted here, including more than 200 migratory birds from North America who winter in the tropics. In many parts of the inland forest, it is not unusual to see as many as 120 different birds over a period of as little as four or five days. Of the world's more than 90,000 butterfly species, a very large percentage are found here.

Part of this species diversity is a result of Belize's relatively small population and the pristine quality of its wilderness. Another reason for the incredible assemblages of flora and fauna found here is the variation in habitat zones. There are five basic ecological regions: northern hardwood, southern hardwood, mountain pine ridge, coastal savanna and pine ridge, and mangroves and beaches. Within these categories, distinctions can be drawn based on rainfall amounts (varying widely from north to south), altitude (from sea level to nearly 4,000 feet), and soil types (from very poor to very fertile).

Scientists are still finding plants and animals in Belize which are completely new to science or previously unrecorded in Belize. One expedition into the Maya Mountains, for example, sighted a bird in the latter category dubbed the scaly-throated foliage gleaner. Several new species of amphibians and flowering plants have been found during the 1990s.

Rather than attempt an exhaustive discussion of Belizean ecosystems and their native inhabitants in this limited space, we will simply provide a few thumbnail sketches of some of Belize's most intriguing flora and fauna.

Jabiru Stork

The jabiru is the largest flying bird in the Western Hemisphere, standing up to 5 feet tall and with a wingspan reaching 10 feet. It is also one of the rarest birds in Central America. Besides its size, the jabiru can be identified by its massive black bill that turns up slightly and its bare black head, which has a wide, inflatable crimson band at the base of the neck.

In Belize, where the jabiru is fully protected, a population of about 30 storks nest during winter months along swamp edges and roadside pools, as well as wet savannas and lowland pine ridges. Considered "rare" in Belize and "imperiled" in other parts of its range, Belize's jabirus return from Mexico around November to make their nests, usually at the tops of tall, secluded trees. Breeding continues until early April, when the birds begin migrating back to Mexico for the summer. Crooked Tree Wildlife Sanctuary is a favorite breeding ground of this enormous bird.

Parrots

Seven species of parrots, one species of parakeet, and one species of macaw make Belize their home. Parrots have few enemies in the jungle except for larger predators, who tend to eliminate the weakest or most vulnerable birds. A far bigger threat is posed by humans, who continue to destroy the parrot's forest habitat, capture the animal for commercial purposes, or even kill it for food.

The capture of young parrots usually does considerable damage to the environment, since nesting trees are often cut down in the hope that chicks will somehow survive the fall. The species captured in greatest numbers here is the yellow-headed parrot, prized in North America as a fluent and easily trained "talker." Other vocal members of the same family are the Aztec (or olive-throated) parakeet and mealy (or blue-crowned) parrot. The latter mates for life and almost always flies in a two-by-two formation with its partner. These species are quite social and like to live near others of their kind.

The common names of parrots are inspired by easily identifiable head markings ("lore" refers to the area between eyes and beak, "crown" is the top of the head, and "front" is the forehead, while "hood" and "head" are self-explanatory). The less gregarious parrots found in Belize are the brown-hooded, red-lored, yellow-lored, yellow-headed, white-fronted, and white-crowned. Only sharp-eyed birders are usually able to tell the latter two species apart.

Like many tropical animals (and people), parrots usually nap

Red-lored Amazon parrot (Photo by Kevin Schafer)

during the heat of the day and are most often seen during later afternoon and early morning feeding periods. The birds roost overnight.

Scarlet Macaw

One of the rarest birds in Belize is the scarlet macaw, the third-largest of the world's 16 surviving macaw species. It is one of eight such species in danger of extinction throughout much of its range, which extends from subtropical Mexico south to Bolivia.

A macaw sighting is an unforgettable experience. Mature birds, locally referred to as parrots, are over 2 feet tall and adorned with brilliant plumage, particularly bright red wing feathers speckled with dabs of yellow, orange, and blue.

The greatest threat to this magnificent bird is the destruction of its forest habitat, nest-robbing for the wild bird trade, and killing for meat and feathers. The first (and only) systematic study of scarlet macaws in Belize was carried out by the Center for the Study of Tropical Birds. It concluded that the bird has a relatively confined range in the dense central forests of the country, extending from the Maya Mountain divide north to the Mountain Pine Ridge. A few individuals and small flocks have been seen in other areas from time to time. In recent years, however, no more than 30 birds have ever been seen at any given time or location.

"It is certain that the status of the scarlet macaw in Belize is precarious," concluded the final report of the Center for the Study of Tropical Birds. "Not only are there the persistent threats of habitat destruction . . . logging operations, plant collectors, etc., but the threat of wild birds being caught for the pet trade continues," despite the latter's illegality.

Blue-Crowned Motmot

This beautiful and relatively large bird is sometimes called Good Cook, because its deep-throated call (usually heard at dawn or dusk) resembles those two words. It is also distinguished by its indigo head feathers and long tail. The latter acquires an oddly pointed shape through removal of central feathers by preening and wear. While the blue-crowned motmot is fairly common, its cousin, the keel-billed

Blue-crowned motmot (Photo by Kevin Schafer)

motmot, is one of the rarest birds in Central America, and only a few sightings have been documented. The bird is believed to be extinct in Mexico. There have been only two known sightings in Guatemala, and until mid-summer of 1994, the keel-billed motmot had not been seen in Belize for more than eight years. A recent sighting was made at the Tapir Mountain Nature Reserve.

Jaguar

The jaguar was among the most revered animals of the ancient Maya, and even today this jungle cat commands great respect among Belizeans, who often refer to it as a tiger, or *el tigre*. Up to 6 feet long and weighing as much as 250 pounds, its likeness turns up on modern T-shirts as well as eroded Mayan ornaments. Originally found from the southwestern United States to Argentina, the jaguar (largest cat in the Western Hemisphere) has become extinct or endangered throughout its range. In Mesoamerica, only a few hundred jaguar are believed to remain. In Belize, however, the animal is still seen in many areas, even within a half-hour drive of Belize City. This nocturnal predator feeds primarily on peccary, paca, fish, or deer, along with an occasional bird, lizard, or turtle.

Contrary to local belief, jaguars will not attack humans unless provoked and usually do not kill livestock unless their natural habitat has been destroyed and their natural prey replaced by cattle. The respected *Neotropical Rainforest Mammals* field guide recommends never trying to run from a jaguar, since fleeing may give it cause to chase. Human encroachment continues to limit the cats' territory, and hunters, operating illegally, occasionally kill perfectly healthy animals in Belize for their hides.

Jaguars are very territorial, ranging over vast areas of forest and savanna. The male, a solitary creature who partners with one female at a time, marks the boundaries of his kingdom with tree scratches and ground scrapings. The other four native cats of Belize are the puma, ocelot, margay, and jaguarundi.

Baird's Tapir

Called a "mountain cow" by locals, this largely nocturnal species is the national animal of Belize. Still fairly plentiful here, the Baird's tapir has almost disappeared from the rest of its native Central America and Mexico, earning it a place on the endangered species list. It spends almost 90 percent of its waking hours feeding on fruits, browse, and grasses. Despite the fact that tapirs have thick hides and a disagreeable flavor, their ranks have been thinned by native hunters, many of whom mistakenly believe these docile vegetarians will attack and kill their domestic animals. The tapir is adaptable to almost any Belizean environment, but today it is most plentiful in mountain forests where there is water nearby. Although it can weigh up to 650 pounds, the Baird's tapir is surprisingly agile and has splayed feet for navigating mudholes. The herbivore's long, flexible upper lip and strong molars are well suited for foraging and swallowing twigs, nuts, and other tough plant tissues. The tapir has an excellent sense of smell and hearing, although its eyesight is weak. The docile beasts are usually solitary and tend to avoid confrontation by steering clear of other large animals. Perhaps the best-known Baird's tapir is named April and lives in the Belize Zoo, where she has become both a favorite of visiting schoolchildren and a kind of national mascot.

Hickatee

The Central American river turtle is making one of its last stands along the waterways of Belize. Locally referred to as the hickatee, it can be found only here and in the most isolated parts of southern Mexico and northern Guatemala. Prized as a food source, this turtle spends almost its entire life in the water, except when it lays its eggs in rotting vegetation along the riverbanks, where the eggs incubate themselves. The hickatee is brown or olive drab on its back, with a cream-colored underbelly. Large males weigh as much as 50 pounds. Unfortunately, the animal seeks out fish and aquatic plants by night, then sleeps or floats much of the day, making it an easy target for human hunters.

Sea Turtles

Three of the world's eight species of sea turtles are known to nest in Belize: the green, loggerhead, and hawksbill. Although the situation is changing, many are still taken for their flesh, eggs, and shells. Increasingly, turtles are being kept from their traditional nesting areas by fences, buildings, people, pets, bright lights, and loud noises. For these reasons, all three species found in Belize have been declared endangered. Visitors are urged to respect the nesting season (June 1 to August 31), refrain from buying turtle meat or products, and avoid throwing into the sea plastic bags in which turtles can become entangled.

No one knows how the female loggerhead turtle, called *lagra* in Belize, finds her way back to nesting beaches as many as fifty years after the same animal left that same stretch of sand to spend her life in the sea. Yet that is exactly what happens when this large turtle (up to 300 pounds) returns to Belize to lay up to 100 leathery eggs at a time. After a two-month incubation, tiny babies emerge from the shells and make a mad dash for the water. Most are caught en route by birds, crabs, lizards, and humans. Less than 5 percent typically survive to reproduce.

The green turtle is an even larger species, measuring up to 4 feet in length and weighing up to 600 pounds. Because its greenish meat and tender eggs are considered delicacies, this turtle has been hunted extensively. It also sometimes gets caught in shrimp nets while surfacing from the sea grass beds where it feeds.

One of the smaller sea turtles is the hawksbill, which gets its name from its sharp, hooked beak. The animal's top shell is covered with multicolored scales that have long been popular for use in combs, eyeglass frames, hair clips, and jewelry. The hawksbill is often killed before it reaches maturity, which has had a devastating effect on the species' ability to reproduce.

Dolphins

Bottlenose dolphins are common off the coast of Belize, and research is now being done on these marine mammals at Blackbird Caye on the Turneffe atoll. Thanks to the media exploits of Flipper, the bottlenose is the most well-known dolphin species in the world. Individuals may be gray or whitish in color and can grow up to 10 feet long. These very social animals can often be seen riding the bow wake of powerboats. They breathe air and give birth to live young, which they subsequently nurse. The complexity of the social interactions among dolphins, scientists believe, may help explain the evolution of their large brains. The creatures emit a variety of complex buzzing, whistling, and clicking sounds that bounce off objects like sonar echoes and enable dolphins to "see" those objects. This process is called "echolocation." The sound beams can apparently even penetrate living tissue, which seems to allow male dolphins to "see" when a female is approaching fertility.

Basilisks and Iguanas

Once you've seen a basilisk in action, you'll know why Belizeans have labeled it "the Jesus Christ lizard." The prehistoric-looking animal moves with such great speed—often on its hind legs—through its riverside habitat that it seems to be able to skim right across the surface of a creek or river without sinking, disappearing into foliage on the opposite bank. The basilisk is virtually impossible to catch; extra flaps of skin across the toes of its enlarged rear feet make this water-walking trick possible. While these omnivorous reptiles appear fierce—like miniature *Tyrannosaurus rex*—they prefer to munch on leaves, flowers, and fruit in their favorite trees (often a giant ficus), in addition to the occasional insect and bird. They can be distinguished by their ridged backs, ranging in color from yellow-brown to muted gray, and (among males) reddish throat sacs. Local people love to eat the raw eggs of the female basilisk, and the creatures are becoming scarce in areas where pesticides are used. Predatory birds are another enemy. The dominant males are quite territorial and can be seen perched on high tree limbs from which they can survey their domains along inland waterways.

Two iguanid species also live in Belize: the green iguana or "bush-chicken" and the black or land iguana, locally called a "wish-willy." These creatures spend most of the day sunbathing and are very territorial, responding to trespassers with repeated patterns of head-bobbing. Iguanas (and their eggs) are easy prey for hungry villagers, as well as for birds, snakes, and coati. Wish-willies are commonly encountered on the offshore cayes of Belize, where they frequent vegetation near beaches and mangrove forests.

Fer-de-lance

Variously known as the yellow-jaw tommygoff, *barba amarilla,* and *tres minutos,* the fer-de-lance is a nocturnal pit viper related to the water moccasin and tropical rattlesnake. Because of its fast-acting venom, the fer-de-lance is considered to be among the world's deadliest snakes. There are many reliable reports in Belize of individuals who have died soon after stumbling on the animal in the bush. However, unless it's provoked or you are very unlucky, the vipers will generally avoid you and stick to smaller game, such as birds, rats, and other small mammals. The fer-de-lance is at home in any part of Belize, including cities, and can be vicious if it does decide to attack. Adults can reach 8 feet in length, enabling them to strike from a coiled position. Their two retractable fangs are the largest of any snake, in proportion to size. Keen awareness of smell and temperature enables the fer-de-lance to accurately pinpoint warm bodies in the dark, when it is most likely to be active. It is easily identified by its arrow-shaped head, diamond-patterned back, and thick-set body. If you are bitten, seek medical help at once. The best prevention is wearing boots, however, since most fer-de-lance bites are in the feet and ankles.

Palm Trees

The cohune palm, widespread throughout Belize, is one of the forest community's most useful members. Its fronds are used as thatch in roofs, and a valuable oil can be extracted from its fruit. Husks from the tree's palm nuts make excellent fuel, and the nut meat can be pounded into a flour that will store many weeks without spoiling. The cohune was highly regarded by the ancient Maya, who considered it a symbol of fertility. Because of the palm's many practical uses, it is almost always spared when forests are cut down for subsistence agriculture.

Dominant in low-lying marshes and along riverbanks are palmetto palms, which can grow to great heights and provide fronds used in traditional house construction.

Mangroves

Almost the entire coastline of Belize, including the fringes of its many cayes, are covered by dense stands of black, white, and red mangrove, with the latter species dominating. Different types of mangroves are adapted to varying degrees of salinity, and you will notice them changing as you go away from sources of salt water. While 90 percent of the world's original mangrove forests have been destroyed, Belize can boast that 90 percent of its mangrove habitat remains intact. The ancient Maya made extensive use of the mangrove wetlands, as evidenced by the use of crocodile and manatee images in their artwork. Mangroves as tall as 100 feet or more can be seen along some waterways, such as the Toledo District's Temash River within the Temash/Sarstoon Nature Reserve. A more accessible protected area in which to celebrate and visit mangroves is the Burdon Canal Nature Reserve, just west of Belize City. Although these tangled saltwater thickets have traditionally been despised by settlers, who often cleared them as quickly as possible, they protect shorelines from erosion during storms and provide an irreplaceable nursery for small fish and crustaceans. Snorkeling near mangrove roots often is more rewarding, in terms of marine life, than swimming in open water or near coral reefs. Above the waterline, visitors can see egrets, herons, ibises, spoonbills, pelicans, frigate birds, raptors, and boobies amid the tangled roots and branches. Coatimundis, crocodiles, anteaters, tapirs, jaguars, raccoons, and boa constrictors are also found in these wetland areas.

Bicycling

Bicycling opportunities in Belize are limited, and until recently the sport of mountain biking was virtually unknown. Nevertheless, a growing number of tour operators, resorts, and lodges are now catering to the needs of bicycle enthusiasts, and an infrastructure is gradually developing. Check the list of tour operators in Inside Belize for specialists in this sport. Four of the best are Bike Belize in Belize City, Red Rooster Bicycle Tours and B&M Bike Rental in San Ignacio, and Paradise Bicycle Tours in Evergreen, Colorado. Several lodges, including a growing number in the Cayo District, now have bicycles available for free or low-cost use by their guests.

The biggest problem bikers will encounter in Belize is the limited network of roads in the country and an even smaller number of trails suitable for bicycle transportation. Belizean roads are notoriously bad, characterized by an unusual number of potholes, mud bogs, sharp rocks, and sand traps. Even the best thoroughfares, such as the Western Highway from Belize City to Benque Viejo, typically have narrow traffic lanes, few service stations, and virtually no shoulders.

Due to the rainy climate and lush vegetation, trails are often difficult to negotiate, even for those on foot. Bicyclists should be aware that unstable, slick, and mucky surfaces and narrow passageways are the norm off-road, not the exception. Trails are frequently blocked by fallen trees and branches, including those of many plants whose burrs, thorns, and nettles can lead to painful rashes and puncture wounds. Some very common varieties, such as the aptly named "give-and-take" palm and "sticky" bamboo, cause cuts that can become easily infected.

A different set of obstacles confronts bikers setting out on the crowded streets of Belize City and other big towns. Roads are sometimes very narrow and congested, crammed with jostling people, cars, trucks, and other bicycles. In addition, your bike may be much coveted by an impoverished Belizean, so make sure it is secured when unattended. Better yet, bring it indoors whenever possible.

On the cayes, sandy lanes that pass for modest thoroughfares may jam gears and swallow up narrow-tired bicycles. Ambergris Caye has the most navigable trails, and Amigo Travel in San Pedro (among others) rents bikes for a reasonable fee. The proprietors can direct visitors to scenic areas north and south of the town.

Currently the most accessible and rewarding area of Belize for bicyclists is the Cayo District, especially the Mountain Pine Ridge forest reserve. Mountain biking is increasingly popular, and many lodges now have bikes to rent. Try the Maya Mountain Lodge near Santa Elena, Pine Ridge Lodge on the Chiquibul Road, or Red Rooster in San Ignacio. Most of the region's many attractions are easily reached from any of the Cayo's lodges or campgrounds, and there are many destinations worth visiting (see Chapter 6). The main routes are well-maintained dirt roads, and they are relatively uncrowded. This area's primary advantages are slightly cooler temperatures and lower humidity than the coast, with relatively few biting insects. Watch for rain, however, as these mostly dirt roads become mud in a hurry.

Side trips from either the Cayo or Belize District include the Belize Zoo, Guanacaste National Park, Community Baboon Sanctuary, Blue Hole National Park, St. Herman's Cave, Five Blues National Park, Crooked Tree Nature Sanctuary, Gales Point Manatee Sanctuary, and the Mayan ruins of Altun Ha. Because Belize is a narrow country (about 70 miles wide), an ambitious cyclist can make it all the way from Belize City to Guatemala in a single day. A good midpoint is Monkey Bay Nature Reserve, which welcomes cyclists and provides food, drink, and lodging. Another popular one-day excursion is from Dangriga to the Cockscomb Basin Wildlife Sanctuary, with interesting rest stops en route at Hopkins and Maya Center.

Customs officials at the international airport and land border crossings are now accustomed to seeing tourists bring bicycles into Belize, but it is a good idea to carry proof of ownership or have your passport stamped with the bike specifically listed. This is a precaution against having to pay import duty on the item, since authorities may assume the bicycle will be sold in Belize, where they are quite expensive. In traveling to the cayes, remember that domestic airplanes are small, propeller-driven craft that may be unable to accommodate large bicycles unless they are disassembled. Most passenger boats, however, can easily store such cargo.

Inside Belize

Where to Stay

Note: Many hotels, lodges, and guest houses in Belize automatically add a 10 percent service charge and/or a 6 percent mandatory government room tax to all bills. A surtax of 3 percent on all credit card charges is also commonplace.

Rate schedule (double occupancy, all prices in U.S. dollars, subject to change):
HIGH: $66 and up
MODERATE: $36 to $65
LOW: $35 or less

Belize District

HIGH

Belize Best Western Plaza
Mile 3, Northern Highway
Belize City
Tel. 2-32302, fax 2-32301,
U.S.A. (800) 327-3573
(shops, swimming pool, restaurant, bar, airport shuttle, air conditioning, cable TV, near airport, tours)

Bellevue Hotel
5 Southern Foreshore
Belize City
Tel. 2-77051, fax 2-73253
(also rents cottages on St. George's Caye)

Château Caribbean
6 Marine Parade
Belize City
Tel. 2-30800, fax 2-30900
(restaurant and bar overlooking Caribbean)

Maruba Resort and Jungle Spa
Maskall Village
Tel. 3-22199
U.S.A. (800) 627-8227 or (713) 799-2031, fax (713) 795-8573
(10 miles north of Altun Ha ruins; offers boating, bird-watching, swimming, and complete spa)

Radisson Ft. George Hotel
Box 321, 2 Marine Parade
Belize City
Tel. 2-33333, fax 2-30276
U.S.A. (800)333-3333, Canada (402) 967-3442
(swimming pool, travel agency, gift shop)

Maya Landings Lodge
Moho Caye
Tel. 2-35350, fax 2-35466
(island lodge, restaurant, marina, diving and fishing service)

Ramada Royal Reef Hotel and Marina
Newton Barracks Road
Belize City
Tel. 2-32672, fax 2-31649
U.S.A. (800) 228-9898
(restaurant, gift shop, convention center, swimming pool, marina)

Villa Hotel
13 Cork Street
Belize City
Tel. 2-32800, fax 2-30276
U.S.A. (800) 421-0000,
fax (213) 487-5467

MODERATE

Belize Guest House and Restaurant
2 Hutson Street
Belize City
Tel. 2-77569

Bird's Eye View Lodge
Crooked Tree Village
Tel. 2-72304
(bird-watching, boating, nature treks)

Chan Hiix Lodge
(Robert Brooks)
Spanish River
Tel. 2-73787, fax 2-77891
(bird-watching specialist near Crooked Tree; access by boat)

Colton House
9 Cork St.
Belize City
Tel. 23-4466
(remodeled colonial home in historic neighborhood, full of antiques)

Crooked Tree Resort
(Sam Tillett)
Crooked Tree Village
Tel. 2-77745, fax 2-31734
(lagoon, nature, and Mayan ruin tours; meals, horseback rides)

Dibasei Guest House
26 Hydes Lane
Belize City
Tel. 2-33981, fax 2-32136
(Garifuna owned and operated with gift shop and restaurant on premises; cultural tours to Dangriga and surrounding Garifuna villages)

Fort Street Guest House
(Hugh and Teresa Parkey)
Box 3, 4 Fort Street
Belize City
Tel. 2-30116, fax 2-78808
(assist in trips to interior, cayes, atolls; popular among adventure outfitters and conservation groups; room rates include breakfast; American owned)

Glenthorne Manor
(Winil Grant Borg)
27 Barracks Road
Belize City
Tel. 2-44212
(Belizean-style bed and breakfast; homey atmosphere)

Hotel El Centro
Box 122, 4 Bishop Street
Belize City
Tel. 2-72413, fax 2-74553

Kahlua Guest House & Bar
(James and Delia Wang)
120 Eve Street
Belize City
Tel. 2-31130, fax 2-31185
(air-conditioning; cable TV; oceanfront; occasional entertainment at night)

Kiss Hotel
8 Freetown Road/Mapp St.
Belize City
Tel. 2-33916, fax 2-31030
(boats for hire, large rooms, air conditioning; a bit out of town)

Hotel Mopan
(Tom and Jean Shaw)
55 Regent Street
Tel. 2-77351 or 2-77356
(bar and travel agency on premises; assists in conservation-oriented trips)

Paradise Inn
(formerly Crooked Tree Lodge)
(Rudy Crawford)
Crooked Tree Village
Tel. 24-4333
U.S.A. voice/fax (718) 498-1122
(bungalows on Crooked Tree Lagoon; restaurant, horseback riding, canoeing, boating, guided tours, fishing, Mayan ruins; bird-watching a specialty)

Royal Orchid Hotel
New Road & Douglas Jones Streets
Belize City
Tel. 2-32783, fax 2-32789

LOW

Community Baboon Sanctuary Bed and Breakfasts
Contact: Belize Audubon Society
Tel. 2-77369 or 2-78562
(stay with a Creole family; reservations preferred)

Eyre Street Guest House
7 Eyre Street
Tel. 2-77724
(basic rooms with communal shower and bath area)

Golden Dragon Hotel
29 Queen Street
Tel. 2-45271
(also operates Chinese restaurant)

Isabel's Guest House
Belize City
Tel. 2-73139
(three inexpensive rooms above a drug store)

Little Eden Bed and Breakfast
(Fred and Sally Cuckow)
Burrel Boom Cutoff, Northern Highway
Box 1317, Belize City
Tel. 2-8219
(budget accommodations near howler monkey sanctuary)

Monkey Bay Wildlife Sanctuary
(Matthew Miller)
Mile 31.5, Western Highway
Tel. 8-23180
(camping under thatch shelters at private nature reserve, basic rooms, caters to educational groups and backpackers)

North Front Street Guest House
124 N. Front Street
Tel. 2-77595
(basic rooms with communal bath and shower, breakfast available)

Seaside Guest House
3 Prince Street
Tel. 2-78339
(breakfast available; basic rooms; makes arrangements for Gales Point home-stays and Parrot's Perch Lodge in Cayo District)

Tillett's Hotel
Crooked Tree Village
Tel. 2-12026
(nature and birding tours)

Ambergris Caye and Caye Caulker

HIGH

Captain Morgan's Retreat
(Baldi Santos)
3.5 miles north of San Pedro,
Ambergris Caye
Box 38, San Pedro Town
Tel. 26-2567

U.S.A. (800) 447-2931
(beachfront casitas, freshwater pool, bar, restaurant, tours)

Caribbean Villas
(Wil and Susan Lala)
Ambergris Caye
Tel. 26-2715, fax. 26-2885
U.S.A. (913) 776-3738
(condo-style suites with ocean view, fully equipped kitchens, hot tubs; bicycles for rent; scuba, fishing, snorkeling and guided trips)

Journey's End Caribbean Club
(John and Jennie Rietz)
Box 12, San Pedro
Tel. 26-2173, fax 26-2028
U.S.A. (800) 447-0474
(waterfront cabañas, poolside villas; 4.5 miles north of San Pedro; windsurfing, snorkeling, sailing)

Mata Rocks Resort
(formerly House of the Rising Sun)
Ambergris Caye
Tel. 2-62336
U.S.A. (503) 645-7323
fax (503) 690-9308
(rooms with kitchens, 1.2 miles south of San Pedro)

Mayan Princess Resort Hotel
Box 1, San Pedro
Tel 2-62778, fax 2-6284
(suites with bathroom, living room, kitchen, and bedroom)

Paradise Resort Hotel and Villas
Box 25, Belize City (located near San Pedro)
Tel. 2-62083
(fishing, boating, restaurant and bar)

Ramon's Village Resort
(Ramon Nuñez)
San Pedro
Tel. 2-62071, fax 2-62214,
U.S.A. 800-MAGIC or (601) 649-1990
(diving instruction and services, sailing, fishing, snorkeling, boat charters)

Rock's Inn
San Pedro
Tel. 2-62326, fax 2-62358
(air-conditioned suites with kitchens, on beach north of San Pedro)

Spindrift Hotel
San Pedro
Tel. 26-2018, fax 2-62251
(Italian restaurant on premises)

Sun Breeze Beach Resort
San Pedro
Tel. 2-62191, fax 2-62346
(sailing, snorkeling, windsurfing, diving, scuba, volleyball; excellent fishing guide)

Victoria House
Box 22
San Pedro (2 miles south)
Tel. 2-62067, fax 2-62429
U.S.A. (800) 247-5159
(26 rooms on 16 beachfront acres, good restaurant, popular among adventure outfitters)

MODERATE

Barrier Reef Hotel
(Old Blake House)
San Pedro
Tel. 2-62075, fax 2-62719

Changes in Latitudes Bed & Breakfast Inn
San Pedro
Tel. 26-2986
(six room guest house with breakfast, air conditioning, and other amenities)

Coral Beach Hotel and Dive Club
San Pedro
Tel. 2-62013, fax 2-62864
(diving, snorkeling, fishing)

Green Parrot Resort
6 miles north of San Pedro
Tel. 26-2147
(beachfront cabanas, boating, fishing)

Out Island Beach Club
Caye Caulker
Tel. 2-22054,
U.S.A. (800) 771-1133
(beachfront cottage and tiki bar; diving, fishing, snorkeling, kayaking, birding, shopping, and dancing)

Royal Palm Inn
Box 18, San Pedro
Tel. 2-62148, fax 2-62329

San Pedro Holiday Hotel
(Celi McCorkle)
San Pedro
Tel. 26-2014, fax 2-62295
(rooms, bungalows, or apartments; complete dive shop; arranges snorkeling, fishing, and glass-bottom boat trips)

Thomas Hotel
San Pedro
Tel. 2-62061
(scuba services)

Tropical Paradise Hotel
Caye Caulker
Tel. 22-2124, fax. 22-2225

LOW

Ignacio Beach Cabins
Caye Caulker
Tel. 22-2212
(beach bungalows and camping; reef trips)

Marin's
(John Marin)
Caye Caulker
Tel. 2-22110
(reef trips)

Martha's Hotel
San Pedro
Tel. 2-62053, fax 2-62589

Milo's Hotel
Ambergris Caye
Tel. 26-2033, fax 26-2463
(good value)

Mira Mar
(Melvin Badillo)
Caye Caulker
Tel. 2-22110
(good value)

Rivas Guest House
Caye Caulker
Tel. 2-22127

Rubie's Hotel
San Pedro
Tel. 2-62063
(ask for Richie Woods, resident naturalist and reef expert)

San Pedrano Hotel
San Pedro
Tel. 2-62054

San Pedro Guest House
San Pedro
Tel. 26-3243
(good value)
Shirley's Guest House
Caye Caulker
Tel. 2-22145

Tom's Hotel
(Tom Young)
Caye Caulker
Tel. 2-22102
(snorkeling, reef trips, good value)

Vega's Far Inn
Caye Caulker
Tel. 2-22142, fax 2-31580
(camping, rooms)

Other Cayes

HIGH

Blackbird Caye Resort
(Al Dugan, Betty Taylor, Ray
Lightburn)
on Blackbird Caye, Turneffe Islands
Box 1315, Belize City
Tel. 2-30882, U.S.A. (800) 537-1431
or (713) 658-1142
*(conservation-oriented resort; diving,
swimming with dolphins, fishing)*

Blue Marlin Lodge
(Mike and Rosella Zabaneh)
Box 21, Dangriga
on South Water Caye, 27 miles east
of Dangriga
Tel. 5-22243, fax 5-22296
U.S.A. (800) 798-1558
*(diving and fishing lodge; offers dive boats,
tanks, snorkeling, trips to Glover's Reef;
complete dive shop)*

Cottage Colony
(on St. George's Caye)
Box 428, Belize City
Tel. 2-33571
*(colonial-style cottages on St. George's
Caye; restaurant, diving and fishing)*

Lighthouse Reef Resort
Northern Two Caye, Lighthouse Reef
Atoll
Box 26, Belize City
Tel. 2-31205, U.S.A. (941) 439-6600
*(fishing, diving, snorkeling, swimming;
private airstrip)*

Little Water Caye Resort
(off Placencia)
Box 1666, Belize City
Tel./fax 6-22267
(fishing, boating, snorkeling)

Manta Reef Resort
Glover's Reef Atoll
Box 215, Belize City
Tel. 2-31895, VHF channel 70
U.S.A. (800) 342-0053
(diving, fishing, snorkeling, swimming)

Pyramid Island Resort
(on Caye Chapel)
Box 192, Belize City
Tel. 2-44409, fax 2-32405
*(full-service diving and fishing lodge, air-
port)*

St. George's Caye Lodge & Cottages
(Fred Good)
Box 625, Belize City
Tel. 2-44190, fax 2-30461
U.S.A. (800) 678-6871
(full-service diving and fishing lodge)

Spanish Bay Resort
(on Spanish Lookout Caye)
Box 35, 71 N. Front Street
Belize City
Tel. 2-77288, fax 2-72797,
U.S.A. (800) 359-0747
*(diving, snorkeling, fishing, nature trips,
restaurant; dive shop and dive instruction)*

Turneffe Flats
Blackbird Caye, Turneffe Islands
Box 1676, Belize City
Tel. 2-30116, fax 2-78808
U.S.A. (800) 815-1304
*(fly-fishing specialists; snorkeling, beach
camping, diving)*

Turneffe Islands Lodge
Caye Bokel, Turneffe Islands
Tel. 2-2331
U.S.A. (800) 338-8149, fax (904) 641-
5285
(diving specialists)

Wippari Caye Lodge
(Hortense and George Cabral)
Wippari Caye
Tel. 6-23130
(fishing and snorkeling specialists)

MODERATE

Fairweather and Friends
(Elwood Fairweather)
on Tobacco Caye
Box 240, Belize City
Tel. 5-22201
(cabins; fishing, boating, reef tours)

Gaviota's Coral Reef Resort
Tobacco Caye
Tel. 5-22244
*(cottages; restaurant, bar; fishing, boating,
snorkeling)*

Island Camps
(Mark Bradley)
(campground and bungalows on
Tobacco Caye)
51 Regent Street
Belize City
Tel. 2-72109 or 5-22201
*(tents and bungalows, fishing and
snorkeling)*

Leslie Cottages
South Water Caye
Tel. 5-22004, fax 5-23152
U.S.A. (800) 548-5843
(cottages, dorm-style accommodations;
snorkeling, boating)

Ocean's Edge Lodge
Tobacco Caye
Tel. 5-22171

Ranguana Reef Resort
(Eddie Leslie)
Ranguana Caye
Tel. 6-23112
(four rustic cabañas with kitchens; fly-
fishing, snorkeling, boating, swimming)

Ricardo's Beach Huts &
Lobster Camp
Bluefield Range
Box 55 or 59 N. Front Street
(Mira Río Hotel)
Belize City
Tel. 2-44970 or marine VHF channel 68
(snorkeling, diving, fishing, camping, tours)

The Wave/Gallows Point Lodge
Gallows Point Caye
9 Regent Street, Belize City
Tel. 2-73054
(boating, scuba, fishing, reef tours)

LOW

Camp Mt. Zion
Punta Rocker's Island
Box 10, Dangriga
Tel. 5-22142
(cottages; fishing, boating, snorkeling)

Glover's Atoll Resort
(The Lomont-Cabral Family)
Long Caye, Glover's Reef
Box 563, Belize City
Tel. 5-23048
(beach bungalows; fishing, camping,
snorkeling, diving, kayaking, swimming;
facilities on Long and North East Caye)

Moonlight Shadows Lodge
(Rudolfo Avila)
Southern Long Caye
Tel. 8-22587
(snorkeling, diving, fishing; restaurant)

Reef End Lodge
(Roland Jackson)
Tobacco Caye
Box 10, Dangriga
Tel. 5-22171
(cabins, camping; boating, snorkeling,
fishing, reef trips)

Cayo District

HIGH

Belmopan Convention Hotel
Box 237, Bliss Parade and
Constitution Drive
Belmopan
Tel. 8-22340, fax 8-23066

Blancaneaux Lodge
(Colin and Ann Young)
Mountain Pine Ridge
Tel./fax. 92-3878
(cabaña-style accommodations, rooms in
main lodge; excellent Italian restaurant;
excursions arranged; private airstrip)

Chaa Creek Cottages
(Mick and Lucy Fleming)
P.O. Box 53
San Ignacio
Tel. 9-22037, fax 9-22501
(cabañas and camping; meals available;
butterfly farm; tours throughout Belize and
to Tikal; swimming, horseback riding,
canoeing, caving, overland expeditions;
arranges joint vacations with Placencia's
Rum Point Inn)

Cool Shade Resort
Barton Creek Farms
Tel. 9-22146
(swimming, horseback riding, Mennonite
visits, tours)

DuPlooy's Riverside Cottages &
Hotel
(Ken and Judy duPlooy)
Big Eddy, Chaa Creek Road
San Ignacio
Tel./fax 9-23301
U.S.A. (803) 722-1513
(on 20 acres, 9 miles southwest of San
Ignacio by Macal River; swimming, canoe-
ing, fishing, horseback riding, caving, pack
trips, nature treks, orchid garden, tours)

Ek'Tun
(Ken and Phyllis Dart)
701 George Price Boulevard
Benque Viejo
Tel. 9-32536, fax 93-2446
U.S.A. (303) 442-6150
(remote cottages on Macal River; nature,
archaeology, and cave tours; bird-watching;
hiking; canoe and boat trips)

The Grove Resort
Mile 62, Western Highway
Tel. 92-2421
(cottages, restaurant, swimming, pool, tours)

Hidden Valley Inn
(Bull or J. Christian Headley II)
Mountain Pine Ridge Forest Reserve
Box 170, Belmopan
Tel. 8-23320, fax 8-23334
U.S.A. (800) 334-7942
(meals included; tours available, advance reservations required; 18,000 acres includes Thousand-Foot Falls; 90 miles of trails for bird-watching, hiking, and camping; also owners of Manatee Lodge in Gales Point)

Mountain Equestrian Trails
(Jim and Marguerite Bevis)
Mile 8, Mountain Pine Ridge Road
Central Farm Post Office, Cayo
Tel. 2-44253/9-23310, fax 8-23235
(horseback trips throughout Mountain Pine Ridge, Maya Mountains, Vaca Plateau, Chiquibul Forest; swimming, horse-drawn wagons, nature treks, river rafting, guided wilderness camping trips)

Windy Hill Cottages
(Bob and Lourdes Hales)
Graceland Ranch
San Ignacio
Tel. 9-22017 or 9-22055, fax 92-3080
(Belizean-American ranch on outskirts of San Ignacio at confluence of Belize and Mopan rivers; horseback riding, canoeing, swimming, hiking, tours of interior; outdoor pool; 12-passenger pontoon boat for river trips)

MODERATE

Banana Bank Lodge
(John and Carolyn Carr)
Box 48, Mile 47, Western Highway
Belmopan
Tel. 8-22677
U.S.A. (800) 552-3419
(popular among adventure outfitters and groups; horseback riding, Tikal tours, canoeing, hiking, nature tours)

Black Rock Enterprises/Caesar's Place
Box 48
San Ignacio
Tel. 92-2341, fax 92-3449
(guest house at Mile 62, Western Highway; camping, cottages on Macal River, 8 miles southwest of San Ignacio)

Bullfrog Inn
25 Half Moon Avenue
Belmopan
Tel. 8-22111, fax 8-23155

Che Chem Ha Lodge
(William or Antonio Morales)
Vaca Plateau, south of Benque Viejo
Tel. 93-2109
(rustic lodge run by owners of Che Chem Ha Cave; meals, nature treks, cave tours, horseback riding; contact by VHF radio via Ek'Tun, Chaa Creek, or Eva's Restaurant)

Circle A Lodge
35-37 Half Moon Avenue
Belmopan
Tel. 8-22296

Crystal Paradise Resort
(Victor or Jeronie Tut)
Cristo Rey Village
Tel. 92-2823
(horseback riding, boating, birding, archaeology, nature treks, and tours; cabañas; restaurant; operated by Mayan-Creole family)

Las Casitas
22 Surrey Street
San Ignacio
Tel./fax 9-22475 or 9-22506
(horseback riding, fishing, boating; restaurant and bar)

Maya Mountain Lodge and Educational Field Station
(Bart and Suzi Mickler)
Box 46, San Ignacio
Tel. 9-22164, fax 9-22029
U.S.A. (800) 344-MAYA
(1 mile from San Ignacio in foothills of Mountain Pine Ridge; horseback riding, mountain biking, canoeing, hiking, tours; field station with classroom and reference library accommodates study groups)

Maya Ranch Guest House
Box 198, Belmopan
Tel. 92-2076
(two rooms in rural environment; horseback riding, buggy tours)

Mida's Eco-Resort and Eco-Tours
(Mike and Maria Preston)
Branch Mouth Road
San Ignacio
Tel. 9-23172/2101, fax 9-23172
(bungalows on river, nature-oriented tours, breakfasts)

Pine Ridge Lodge
General Delivery
San Ignacio
Tel. 9-23310, U.S.A. (216) 781-6888
*(American-owned cabin complex in pine
forest; swimming, hiking; equestrian, river,
archaeological, naturalist, bird, cave, and
jungle tours; excellent meals and trails)*

Plaza Hotel
4a Burns Avenue
San Ignacio
Tel. 92-3332

San Ignacio Hotel
(Escandar Bedran)
8 Buena Vista Street
San Ignacio
Tel. 9-22034 or 9-22125, fax 9-22134
*(on a hill overlooking Macal River within
San Ignacio town, restaurant, bar, pool,
basketball court)*

Snooty Fox Guest House
(Michael Waight)
64 George Price Avenue
Santa Elena
Tel. 92-3556 or 92-3193
*(cottages; private rooms with a shared
kitchen, canoe rentals)*

Warrie Head Lodge
(located in Teakettle Village)
P.O. Box 244
Belize City
Tel. 2-77185, fax 2-75213
*(6 miles from Belmopan; restaurant; swim-
ming, canoeing, horseback riding, hiking,
tours, birdwatching, art sales)*

LOW

Central Hotel
24 Burns Avenue
San Ignacio
Tel. 9-22253

Clarissa Falls Cabins
5.5 Mile, Benque Viejo Road
Tel. 93-2424 or 93-3916
*(boating, horseback riding, nature treks;
cottages located on riverbank)*

Cosmos Camping
(Chris Lowe)
Branch Mouth Road
San Ignacio
Tel. 92-2755
(riverside camping)

El-Rey Inn
Belmopan

Tel. 8-23438, fax 8-2262 *(lowest prices in
Belmopan; private baths, restaurant)*

**Five Blues Community Bed &
Breakfast**
(Leon "Lee" Wengrzyn)
St. Margaret's Village
Tel. 81-2005
*(cooperative bed and breakfast program
near Five Blues Lake National Park)*

Guacamallo Ruins Campground
(Dave and Eddie)
Macal River (8 miles southwest of San
Ignacio)
Tel. 92-2028
*(camping, boating, nature treks,
Mayan ruins)*

Hi-Et Hotel
12 West Street
San Ignacio
Tel. 92-2828
(breakfast available)

Martha's Guest House
San Ignacio
(bed & breakfast; arranges tours)

Maya Hotel and Restaurant
11 George Street
Benque Viejo
Tel. 9-32116

Nabintunich
San Lorenzo Farm
Tel. 9-32309, fax 9-32096
*(swimming, canoeing, horseback riding
near Mopan River)*

Parrot's Nest
(Fred Prost)
Bullet Tree Falls
Tel. 2-78339 or through Eva's Hotel,
San Ignacio
*(horseback riding, Mayan ruins, nature
treks, boat trips; stay in treehouses above
the Belize River next to bromeliad farm;
German spoken)*

Piache Hotel
18 Buena Vista Road
San Ignacio
Tel. 9-22032
(thatched cottages, tours available)

Rancho Los Amigos
(Ed and Virginia Jenkins)
San José de Succotz
Tel. 93-2261
*(built beneath Mayan pyramid;
swimming, hiking)*

Corozal District

HIGH

Santa Cruz Lodge
(Gervis Menzies)
1.5 miles from Libertad in Santa
Cruz Village
Tel. 4-22441, fax 4-22442
U.S.A. (800) 447-2931,
fax (218) 847-0334
(remodeled quarters of sugarcane executives; restaurant, bar, tours, colonial style bungalows)

Tony's Inn
(Tony and Dahlia Castillo)
Box 12, South End
Corozal Town
Tel. 4-23555, fax 4-22827
(arranges tours throughout Corozal District and Quintana Roo, Mexico)

MODERATE

Hotel Maya
Box 112, South End
Corozal Town
Tel. 4-22082, fax 4-22827
(oceanfront view, good restaurant)

Hotel Posada Mama
77 G Street So.
Corozal Town
Tel. 4-22107

LOW

Caribbean Village Resort
(Henry Menzies)
Barracks Road, South End
Corozal Town
Tel. 4-22045, or fax 4-23414
(waterfront rooms, camping; restaurant, travel information)

Diani's Hotel
Sarteneja Village
Tel. 4-32084
(fishing, boating; restaurant, bar)

Lagoon Camping
(Rosalie and William Dixon)
Santa Elena Highway
General Delivery
Corozal Town
(camping, meals, RV parking, sailboat and canoe rentals)

Nestor's Hotel
123 Fifth Ave. So.
Corozal Town
Tel. 4-22354
(Mexican restaurant on premises)

Orange Walk District

HIGH

Chan Chich Lodge
(near Gallon Jug, Río Bravo Conservation Area)
Box 37,
Belize City
Tel. 2-75634, fax 2-76961
U.S.A. (800) 343-8009
(located in plaza of ancient Mayan ruin within 250,000 acres of mostly pristine tropical forest wilderness; hiking, horseback riding, nature tours, canoeing, bird-watching)

Lamanai Outpost Lodge
(Colin and Ellen Howells)
Indian Church
Box 63, Orange Walk Town
Tel./fax 2-33578
(canoeing, windsurfing, tours of Mayan ruins, swimming, horseback riding, nature treks, boat trips, fishing)

MODERATE

D-Star Victoria Hotel (formerly Baron's)
40 Belize/Corozal Road
Orange Walk Town
Tel. 3-22518, fax 3-22847
(arranges jungle tours to Lamanai)

LOW

Chula Vista Hotel
Trial Farm
Tel. 3-22227

Jane's Hotels
2 Baker's Street and Market Lane
Orange Walk Town
Tel. 3-22473 or 3-22526
(Chinese restaurant on Baker's Street premises)

La Nueva Ola
73 Otro Benque Road
Orange Walk Town
Tel. 3-22104

Mi Amor Hotel
19 Belize/Corozal Road
Tel. 3-22031

Stann Creek District

HIGH

The Cove Resort/Mother Ocean's Tropic Hotel & Environmental Research Station
(Clint and Kelly Whitehead)
Box 007, Placencia
Tel. 6-22024, fax 6-22305
U.S.A. (800) 662-3091
(arranges fishing and reef trips; bungalows, restaurant)

Jaguar Reef Lodge
General Delivery
Hopkins Village
Tel 92-3452
U.S.A. (205) 428-1700,
fax (205) 428-1714
(thatched roof cabañas on the beach at Sittee Pt.; diving, dive instructions; trips to Cockscomb; sea kayaks and mountain bikes available; restaurant; snorkeling on cayes; supports conservation groups)

Manatee Lodge
(Bull and Christian Healey)
Box 170, Belmopan
(located in Gales Point)
Tel. 8-23321, fax 8-23334
(sportfishing, diving, manatee watching, birding, nature tours)

Rum Point Inn
(George and Corol Bevier)
Placencia
Tel. 6-23239, fax. 6-23240
U.S.A. (800) 747-1381,
fax (504) 464-0325
(Mayan-style lodge 3 miles north of Placencia Village; expedition outfitter; camping, fishing, diving, dive boat, river, nature tours; arranges joint vacations with Cayo's Chaa Creek Cottages; known for gourmet meals and excellent natural-history library)

MODERATE

Kitty's Place/Placencia Dive Shop
Placencia
Tel. 6-23227, fax. 6-23226
(camping, rooms, apartments; dive shop, snorkeling, sportfishing , windsurfing, canoeing, hiking, mountain biking, jungle trips; restaurant)

Nautical Inn
(Ben and Janie Ruoti)
Seine Bight Village
Tel. 6-22310
(scuba, snorkeling, fishing, tours, and many other activities)

Paradise Vacation Resorts
(Dalton Eiley)
Placencia
Tel. 6-23118 or 6-23179
(diving and fishing trips, nature tours, windsurfing)

Pelican Beach Resort
(Therese and Tony Rath)
Box 14, Dangriga
Tel. 5-22044 or 5-22541, fax 5-22570
(tours arranged to reef, Cockscomb Basin-Wildlife Sanctuary, Hopkins Village, Mayan ruins, Manatee Lagoon; also rents bungalows on South Water Caye)

Possum Point Biological Station/Bocatura Bank Campground
(Paul and Mary Shave)
Sittee River
Tel. 5-22006
(nature tours, reef trips, swimming, fishing, camping, snorkeling; also operates Wee Wee Caye accommodations)

Serenity Resort
south of Seine Bight
Tel. 6-22305
(cabañas on the beach; reef and inland tours)

Singing Sands Inn
(Sally and Bruce Steeds)
Maya Beach
Box 662, Belize City
Tel. 2-30014 or 6-22243
(cabañas, bar, restaurant on remote beach; fishing, snorkeling, diving, canoe trips; rents windsurfers, canoes, mountain bikes)

Sonny's Resort
Placencia
Tel. 6-23103
(on the beach in the village; restaurant, bar; arranges tours)

Billbird Inn
(located in Big Creek)
Box 1137, Belize City
Tel. 6-22092
(also pub-style bar, the Tipsy Toucan)

Turtle Inn
(Skip and Chris White)
Placencia
Tel. 6-22069, fax 6-23203
U.S.A. (303) 444-2555
(fishing and nature tours, dive shop with full certification)

LOW

Caribbean View Hotel
Hopkins Village
Tel. 5-22033

Catalina's Hotel
37 Cedar Street
Dangriga
Tel. 5-22390

Deb and Dave's Last Resort
Point Placencia
Tel. 6-23207
(airy, comfortable budget rooms; arranges tours and camping places)

Gales Point Bed & Breakfast
Gales Point
Tel. 2-78339
(community-operated guest house system; stay with a Creole family)

Hello Hotel
(Antonio Zabaneh)
Mango Creek, at Z-Line bus stop
Tel. 6-22011

Sittec River Guest House & Camping
(Min McKenzie)
Sittee River
Tel. 8-22149
(guest house and campground on river, co-owned with Glover's Atoll Resort)

Prospect Guest House
(Isaac Kelly)
Sittee River
Tel. 5-23389
(rooms and meals in Creole village; arranges local tours; same owner as Hub Hotel & Restaurant, Dangriga)

Ran's Travelodge Villas
Placencia
Tel. 6-22027
(furnished apartments, available long-term)

Riverside Hotel
135 Commerce Street
Dangriga
Tel. 5-22168, fax 5-22296
U.S.A. (800) 256-REEF

Sandy Beach Lodge
Hopkins
Tel. 5-22033
(community-operated bungalow lodge and restaurant)

Seaspray Hotel
Placencia
Tel. 6-23148
(beachfront rooms with ceiling fans)

Swinging Armadillos
Hopkins
Tel. 5-22033
(rooms, restaurant, bar, tours)

Toledo District

HIGH

Fallen Stones Butterfly Ranch
Box 23
Punta Gorda
Tel. 7-2126 or 7-2104
(cabins at butterfly breeding facility; meals and transportation available)

Mira Mar Hotel
Box 2, 95 Front Street
Punta Gorda
Tel. 7-22033
(arranges tours)

Slattery Field Station
Blue Creek
(field station and lodge operated by International Zoological Expeditions, tel. 800/548-5843 or 508/655-1461)

Traveller's Inn
Punta Gorda
Tel. 7-22568
(restaurant, bar; arranges tours, co-owned by Z-Line Bus Line)

MODERATE

G & G's Inn
49 Main Middle Street
Punta Gorda
Tel. 7-22086, fax 7-22469
(restaurant, bar; arranges tours)

Safe Haven Lodge
2 Prince Street
Punta Gorda
Tel./fax 7-22113
U.S.A. (800) 367-6823
(fishing, tours)

St. Charles Inn
23 King Street
Punta Gorda
Tel. 7-22149

LOW

Bol's Hilltop Hotel
(Dominicio Bol)
San Antonio Village
(no electricity; tours of Mayan villages and ruins)

Butterfly Ranch and Jungle Lodge
near Lubaantun ruins

Craig's Guest House
near Blue Creek

Dems Dats Doin/Toledo Visitors Information Center
(Alfredo and Yvonne Villoria)
Box 73, Punta Gorda
Tel. 7-22470
(arranges overnight trips to stay with Kekchi and Mopan Maya families; trips to caves and Mayan ruins)

Friends of Lu Ha Laguna Village Guest House
Box 75, Punta Gorda (located in Laguna Village)
Tel. 7-22119
(accommodations in a Kekchi Maya village, craft shop)

Maya Trekking Guest House
San José Village

Nature's Way Guest House/Belize Adventure Travel
(William "Chet" Schmidt)
Box 75, 65 Front Street
Punta Gorda
Tel. 7-22119
(arranges tours; trips by boat available; contact point for Mayan villages' guest house system and Garifuna model village)

Oh's Guest House
near Lubaantun ruins

Rav's Guest House
Big Falls Village

Roots & Herbs Jungle Lodge
near Blue Creek

Where to Eat

Belize City

Dit's
50 King Street
(great rice and beans)

Fort Street Restaurant
4 Fort Street
(Belizean and continental cuisine, famous desserts; reservations for dinner recommended)

G.G.'s Cafe and Patio
2-B King Street
(lunch and dinner in patio atmosphere)

Golden Dragon
Queen Street
(Chinese food)

Goofy's
6 Douglas Jones Street
(excellent Jamaican cuisine)

The Grill
164 Newtown Barracks Road
(lunch and dinner, specializes in seafood)

Lumba Yaad Bar and Grill
Mile One, Northern Highway
(Belizean barbecue, live music weekends)

Macy's Cafe
18 Bishop Street
(native Belizean and Creole cooking, wonderful patio)

New Chon Saan Palace
1 Kelly Street
(air-conditioned, more elegant atmosphere)

Mom's Triangle Inn & Restaurant
7145 Slaughter House Rd.
(early breakfast, box lunches, gift shop)

Searock
corner of Handyside and Queen Sts.
(best Indian food in Belize)

Belmopan

Bullfrog Inn
25 Halfmoon Avenue
(a favorite meeting place; restaurant and hotel)

Cayes

Elvi's Kitchen and Bar
Pescador Drive (Middle Street)
San Pedro, Ambergris Caye

The Hut
San Pedro, Ambergris Caye

Lily's Restaurant
San Pedro, Ambergris Caye
(seafood)

Little Italy Restaurant
San Pedro, Ambergris Caye
(Italian and Belizean cuisine, located in Spindrift Hotel)

The Pier
San Pedro, Ambergris Caye
(in Spindrift Hotel, known for chicken racing)

The Pizza Place
Barrier Reef Drive
San Pedro, Ambergris Caye
(pizza, sandwiches; eat in, take out, or have delivered)

Royal Palm
San Pedro, Ambergris Caye
(East Indian food)

Sand Box
Caye Caulker

San Pedro Grill
Fido's Courtyard
San Pedro, Ambergris Caye

Tropical Paradise
Caye Caulker
(seafood)

Cayo District

Belbrit Restaurant and Bar
30-A Burns Avenue
San Ignacio
(Belizean and British food and drink)

Blancaneaux Lodge Restaurant
Blancaneaux Road, Mountain Pine Ridge
(Francis Ford Coppola's wines, pasta recipes, and pizza oven; maybe the best place to eat in Belize—and one of the most expensive)

Eva's Restaurant
(Bob and Nestora Jones)
22 Burns Avenue
San Ignacio
(also gift shop and tourist information,

radio contact with many lodges and tour operators)

J.B.'s Place
Mile 33
Western Highway (near Belize Zoo and Monkey Bay)
(food, gift shop, gas station, bar)

Sandcastle Bar & Grill
Manza Plaza (next to bus station)
San Ignacio
Tel. 092-3213, U.S.A. (609) 751-5472
(full-service restaurant and bar owned by long-time American expatriate Dan "Remo" Montgomery, who also arranges Float Belize river trips; besides excellent food, travel information is cheerfully dispensed at the bar)

Serendib
27 Burns Avenue
San Ignacio
(Sri Lankan and Belizean food)

Corozal District

Crises Restaurant
Corozal Town
(Belizean cuisine, evening dancing)

Dubie's
44 Fifth Avenue
Corozal Town
(Belizean food)

Hailey's Restaurant
at Caribbean Village Resort
Corozal Town
(local food, seafood; breakfast, lunch, dinner)

Tony's Inn & Beach Resort
Corozal Town
(outdoor bar facing Corozal Bay; full-service restaurant inside)

Orange Walk District

HL's Burger
Orange Walk Town

Lamanai Outpost Lodge
Indian Church
(fresh fruit and fish a speciality)

New Restaurant
6 San Antonio Road

Stann Creek District

BJ's Restaurant
Placencia
(specializing in seafood and juices)

Burger King
St. Vincent's Street
Dangriga
(hamburgers and American-style food, not connected with the franchise of the same name)

Flamboyant Restaurant and Bar
Placencia

The Galley
Placencia
(seafood , hamburgers, full bar)

Hummingbird Cafe
Mile 25.5 Hummingbird Highway

Jene's Restaurant and Bar
Placencia
(fresh seafood on the beach)

Over the Waves
Hopkins
(seafood)

Stone Crab Restaurant
Placencia
(seafood; bar and hotel on premises)

Tentacles Restaurant and Bar
Placencia
(Italian food, seafood, chops, Sunday buffet)

Starlight Cafe
121 Commerce Street
Dangriga
(Chinese food)

Toledo District

Chiclero's Restuarant and Bar
Columbia Village
(Mayan cuisine)

Granny's Kitchen
Front Street
Punta Gorda
(American-style breakfasts)

Kowloon Restaurant
35 Middle Main Street
Punta Gorda
(Chinese food)

Man Man's Five Star Restaurant
Far West Street
Punta Gorda
(home-cooked Garifuna food)

Punta Caliente Hotel and Restaurant
108 José María Nuñez St.
Punta Gorda
(Garifuna specialties, seafood)

Tourist Information

Belize Tourism Industry Association
Box 62, 10 North Park St.
Belize City
Tel. 2-75717, fax 2-78710

Belize Tourist Board
Box 325, 83 N. Front Street
Belize City
Tel. 2-77213 or 2-73255,
fax 2-77490

New York Office:
421 Seventh Ave., Suite 701
New York, NY 10001
Tel. (800)624-0686 or (212) 563-6011,
fax (212) 563-6033

Belize Embassy
2535 Massachusetts Ave. NW
Washington, DC 20008
Tel. (202) 332-9636,
fax (202) 332-6741

Transportation

Air Travel

INTERNATIONAL AIRLINES

Aerovías
Tel. 2-75445
U.S.A. (305) 885-1775
(semiweekly flights to and from Flores and Guatemala City)

American Airlines
U.S.A. (800) 433-7300,
Canada (800) 433-7300
Belize 2-32522
(daily flights from Miami)

Aviateca
International Airport
Belize City
U.S.A. (800) 327-9832
(semi-weekly flights to and from Flores, Guatemala City, and Cancún)

Continental
32 Albert Street
Belize City
U.S.A. (800) 231-0856, Canada
(800) 525-0280, Belize 2-78309
(daily flights from Houston with connections to the rest of the U.S. and Central America; actively supports conservation work in Belize)

TACA
Belize Global Travel
44 Albert Street
Belize City 2-77185 or 2-77363,
U.S.A. (800) 831-6422,
Canada (800) 387-6209 (except Quebec, 800 263-4063, and Ontario, 800 263-4039)
(daily flights from Houston, Miami, and New Orleans, with connections to New York, Washington, San Francisco, and Los Angeles; also connections to the rest of Central America)

DOMESTIC AIRLINES

Island Air
General Delivery
San Pedro, Ambergris Caye
Tel. 2-62180 or 2-31140, fax 2-62192
(daily flights to and from San Pedro, Caye Caulker, Caye Chapel, Municipal airport, International airport, plus charters)

Maya Airways
Box 458, 6 Fort Street
Belize City
Tel. 2-45968 or 2-44032
U.S.A. (504) 522-2311
(daily flights to and from seven airports in Belize; charters available to other destinations; semi-weekly flights to Guatemala)

Sky Bird
Belize City
Tel. 2-32596 or 2-52045, ext. 515
(daily flights between Belize City and Caye Caulker)

Tropic Air
P.O. Box 20
San Pedro, Ambergris Caye
Tel. 2-62012, fax 2-630807; in Belize City 2-45671; in U.S.A. (800)447-2931, except Texas (713) 449-5230
(daily flights to and from seven airports in Belize, plus twice weekly to Flores/Santa Elena in Guatemala; charters available to Cancún, Mérida, Cozumel, Cayman Islands, Roatan)

Bus Companies

Batty Bus Service
15 Mosul Street
Belize City
Tel. 2-72025
(points north and west)

Novelo's Bus Service
West Collet Canal
Belize City
Tel. 2-77372
(points west)
Venus Bus Service
Magazine Road
Belize City
Tel. 2-73354 or 2-77390
(points north)

Z-Line Bus Service
Magazine Road
Belize City
Tel. 2-73937, or 6-22211
(points south)

Boats and Ferries

If you arrive in Belize by private vessel, you must report your arrival to police or immigration immediately. No permits are required, but you need the usual official documents, clearance from the last port, and manifests for crew, passengers, stores, and cargo. No permits are required. Allowable points of entry are Belize City, Corozal/Consejo, Dangriga, San Pedro, Barranco, and Punta Gorda.

Private boats can be arranged between Consejo, Sarteneja, and other northern villages to Mexico's Yucatán. They can also be hired from Belize City, Placencia, Punta Gorda, and other places for trips into Guatemala and Honduras. A planned crossing between La Unión, Mexico, and Blue Creek in the Orange Walk District may be operable by the time you read this.

A passenger ferry provides regular twice-weekly (Tuesday and Friday at noon) service from Punta Gorda to Puerto Barrios, Guatemala, with connections there to interior Guatemala and Honduras. The crossing takes about 3 hours, and you must have documents in order before embarking. Telephone: 7-22065. Tickets are about $7 one-way, and it is best to purchase them in advance at Godoy's Shop in Punta Gorda. The ferry no longer stops in Lívingston, Guatemala.

It arrives from Puerto Barrios around 10 a.m. Tuesdays and Fridays. A weekly ferry (actually, a large motor-powered canoe) also operates between Dangriga and Puerto Cortes, Honduras. It leaves Wednesday mornings from the north side of Stann Creek, by the bridge. The trip takes about 10 hours, and you can clear immigration at the office on Commerce Street. Ask at The Hub restaurant/hotel in Dangriga for further details.

Many boats ply the waters between Belize City, Caye Chapel, Caye Caulker, and Ambergris Caye. The Andrea I and II leave the Bellevue Hotel dock (5 Southern Foreshore) for San Pedro at 4:00 p.m. weekdays, 1:00 p.m. Saturdays. The return crossing is at 7:00 p.m. Trips take about 1 hour and 15 minutes. A boat for Ambergris called the Hustler leaves the A & R Texaco Service Station on North Front Street at 4:00 p.m. weekdays and 9:00 a.m. on Sundays, returning at 7:00 a.m. Another, the Thunderbolt, leaves at 11:00 a.m. daily (10:00 a.m. Sunday) from the Front Street side of the Swing Bridge. The Thunderbolt departs from San Pedro at 7:00 a.m. daily for Belize City. The Triple J leaves for San Pedro at 9:00 a.m. daily from the Swing Bridge (with stops at Caulker and Chapel by request), returning at 3:00 p.m. Both the Soledad and the Pegasus shuttle between Belize City (the Texaco station on N. Front Street) and Caye Caulker on an irregular daily schedule. Travel time is about 45 minutes. The one-way fare to Caulker is about $8 and to Ambergris about $10. Cruise ships visiting Belize include the American Canadian Caribbean Line (800-556-7450) and OdyssAmerica (800-221-3254). Check with your travel agent about other cruise ships that may stop in Belize.

Airplane Charters

ALL BASED IN BELIZE CITY

Cari-Bee Air Service, tel. 2-44253

Island Air Service, tel. 2-621880 or 2-31140, fax 2-62192

Javier's Flying Service, tel. 2-45332, fax 2-32731

Maya Airways, tel. 2-7215 or 2-62611; U.S.A. (800) 552-3419

Su-Bec Air Service, tel. 2-44027 or 2-62170, fax 2-30389

Tropic Air (see Domestic Airline)

Car Rental

Avis Rent-A-Car
International Airport or
Radisson Ft. George Hotel
Belize City
Tel. 2-31987

Budget Rent-A-Car
771 Bella Vista Rd.
Belize City
Tel. 2-32435, fax 2-30237

Crystal Auto Rental
1.5 Mile, Northern Highway
Belize City
Tel. 2-31600, fax 2-31900
(rents used cars and arranges driveaway trips from Houston; valid driver's license and damage deposit required; all major credit cards accepted)

ECO-Kar Rental
Northern Highway
Ladyville
Tel. 025-2797
(conservation oriented and low cost)

Hertz Rent-A-Car
Bella Vista Rd.
Belize City
Tel. 2-32710

Alistair King
Texaco Service Station
Box 67, Far West Street
Punta Gorda
Tel. 7-2126, fax 7-2104
(four-wheel-drive available; vaild driver's license required; offers tours)

Maxima Car Rental
Maxima Hotel
Hudson Street
San Ignacio
Tel. 92-2265

Melmish Mayan Rentals
Box 934
Belize City
(based at international airport)
Tel. 2-45221, fax 2-77681

National Car Rental
International Airport
126 Freetown Rd.
Belize City
Tel. 2-31586, fax 2-52272

Local Tour Guides and Travel Agencies

Belize City

Baboon River Canoe Rentals
Burrell Boom,Belize
Tel. 28-2101
(boat trips on Belize River and Mussel Creek)

Belize Global Travel Service
41 Albert Street
Tel. 2-77185, fax 2-75213
(full service: tickets, tours, hotels)

Belize Land Air and Sea Tours, Ltd.
(Capt. Nicolas Sanchez)
58 King Street
Tel./fax. 2-73897
(charter boat, land, and diving tours)

Caribbean Holidays Ltd.
81 Albert Street
Tel. 2-72593, fax. 2-78007
(full service, also works with students, senior citizens)

Ricardo Castillo Tours
(Ricardo Castillo)
Box 55, 59 N. Front Street
Tel. 2-44970 or VHF marine channel 68
(offshore and inland tours, cottages on Bluefield Range Caye)

Seven Candles Cab Service
(Winston Seawell)
Box 820
Belize City
Tel. 2-31979 or 25-2461
(air-conditioned van; archaeology tours, historical sites; bookings for other tours, air charter, and resorts)

Jal's Travel and Tours
(Lombardo Riverol)
Box 918, 148 N. Front Street
Tel. 2-45407, fax 2-78852
(full-service travel agency; specializes in trips to see manatees; caving; bird-watching and Mayan ruins)

Native Guide Systems
(Homer S. Leslie)
Box 1045, 6 Water Lane
Tel. 2-75819, fax 2-74007
(natural history tours, custom trips a specialty)

Mayaland Tours
64 Bella Vista
Tel. 2-30515, fax 2-32241

(tours throughout Belize and adjacent parts of Mexico and Guatemala)

MayaWorld Safaris
Box 997
Belize City
Tel. 2-31063, fax 2-30263
(boat trips on New River from Orange Walk Town to Lamanai, tours of Mayan ruins and other sights)

Mesoamerica Tours Ltd.
(John Llewelyn)
Ramada Royal Reef Hotel
Barracks Road
Tel. 2-30625, fax 2-30750
(custom and individual tours; destinations include Altun Ha, Crooked Tree Wildlife Sanctuary, Community Baboon Sanctuary, Xunantunich, Belize Zoo, Lamanai, Mountain Pine Ridge, Tikal)

Juan Moore Tour & Travel Services
(Doug and Lou Moore)
19A Cleghorn Street
Box 1910, Belize City
Tel. 2-32331, fax 2-31711
(fishing, diving, reef, and interior trips; salt-water fly-fishing and "Belizean hospitality" specialist)

Royal Palm Travel Services
Belize International Airport
Tel. 2-52534, fax 2-62329
(sightseeing, adventure, archaeology, and nature tours)

S & L Travel Services and Tours
(Lascelle and Sarita Tillett)
P.O. Box 700, 91 N. Front Street
Tel. 2-77593, fax 2-77594
(specializing in business trips and custom vacations, including adventure tours to the Cockscomb, Mountain Pine Ridge, Crooked Tree, Lamanai, and Baboon Sanctuary, plus archaeology expeditions and sportfishing trips)

Tubroos Tree Adventures
P.O. Box 1412, 146 Barrack Road
Belize City
Tel. 2-33398, fax. 2-30385

Belmopan
Tessa Fairweather
24 Santa María
Tel. 8-22412 or 8-23234
(nature tours, cave exploration; specializing in Mayan archaeology)

Vincent Gillett
Department of Archaeology
Tel. 8-22106
(archaeology tours)

Cayes

Amigo Travel
San Pedro, Ambergris Caye
Tel. 2-62180, fax 2-62192
(full-service agency, scooter and bike rental, snorkeling, reef and interior tours)

Travel and Tour Belize, Ltd.
San Pedro, Ambergris Caye
Tel. 26-2031, fax. 26-2185
(diving, snorkeling, fishing, archaeology)

Cayo District

Chaa Creek Inland Expeditions
(Mick and Lucy Fleming)
Box 53
San Ignacio
Tel. 9-22037, fax 9-22501
(guided expeditions to Mayan ruins, Mountain Pine Ridge, Vaca Plateau, Macal River, Tikal; horseback riding, nature trails, canoeing, trained mules for extended jungle trips)

The Divide Ltd.
(Neil Rogers, Jim Bevis)
Nord Farm, Mile 63 Western Highway
Central Farm, Cayo
Tel. 8-22149, fax 8-23235
(natural history tours, rafting, horseback trips, caving, waterfalls, Mayan ruins, wilderness camping)

Guacamallo Treks
(John and Beth Roberson)
c/o S& L Travel
Box 700, Belize City
Tel. 2-77593, fax 2-77594
(horseback trips throughout the Cayo)

Ian Anderson's Adventurous Belize
(Caves Branch)
Box 332, Belize City
Tel. 2-33903, fax 2-33966
(expeditions by inner-tube through flooded caves, rainforest treks)

Maya Mountain Lodge
(Bart and Suzi Mickler)
Box 46, San Ignacio
Tel. 9-2164, fax 92-2029
(similar to Chaa Creek services above, plus excursions to Caracol, Cockscomb Basin Wildlife Sanctuary, and barrier reef; specialists in educational seminars and family-oriented nature travel)

Pine Ridge Lodge
(Gary and Vicki Seewald)
Chiquibul Road, Mountain Pine Ridge
Tel. 92-3310, U.S.A. (216) 781-6888
(caving, nature treks, equestrian, birding, and archaeology tours)

Alwyn Smith
Bullet Tree Road
San Ignacio
Tel. 2155 or 3077
(taxi service and tour guide; Mayan ruins, Cayo, Tikal, Mexico)

Corozal District

Manuel Hoare
13 G Street South
Corozal Town
Tel. 4-22744, fax. 4-23375
(Belizean archaeology expert and boatman)

Jal's Travel and Tours
Corozal Town
Tel. 4-22163
(complete travel agency and tour services)

Menzies Travel and Tours, Ltd.
(Henry Menzies)
Ranchito Village
Corozal Town
Tel. 4-22725, fax 4-23414
(tours in northern Belize; archaeology tours; Mexico and Guatemala guided tours)

Orange Walk District

Godoy & Sons
(Luis and Carlos Godoy)
4 Trial Farm
Orange Walk Town
Tel. 3-22969
(specializes in orchids and bromeliads of Belize, boat trips up New River to Lamanai and beyond)

Jungle River Tours
(Antonio and Herminio Novelo)
Box 95, 20 Lovers Lane
Orange Walk Town
Tel. 3-22293, fax 3-22201
(river trips, jungle tours; Lamanai; strong Belizean archaeology expert)

Lamanai Outpost Lodge
(Colin and Ellen Howells)
Box 63, Orange Walk Town
Tel./fax 2-33578
(windsurfing, boat trips, canoeing on New River Lagoon in Orange Walk District)

Atilano Narvallez
Guinea Grass
Tel. 3-22081
(boat rental, jungle river tours of Lamanai)

Stann Creek District

Allen Andrewin
Gales Point
Tel. 5-22087
(jungle and boat tours, guide services)

Dalton Eiley
Paradise Vacation Hotel
Placencia
Tel. 6-2046, ext. 119
(natural history tours, guide to cayes, fishing, diving, boating)

Cagey Eiley
Placencia
Tel. 6-23161
(fishing guide, boat for hire)

Rosado Tours
(Jorge Rosado)
35 Lemon Street
Dangriga
Tel. 5-2020 or 5-22119
(nature trips, reef charters and accommodations, Mayan village and cave tours)

David Vernon
Placencia Inland Tours
Tel. 6-2046, ext. 116
(natural history, river trips, ruins, Cockscomb Basin Wildlife Sanctuary)

Toledo District

Dem Dats Doin
(Alfredo Villoria)
Box 73, Front Street at the Wharf
Punta Gorda
Tel. 7-22470
(nature tours, Mayan village trips and overnights, customized expeditions, permaculture farm, bed and breakfast)

Nature's Way Guest House/Belize Adventure Travel
(William "Chet" Schmidt)
Box 75, 65 Front Street
Punta Gorda
Tel. 7-22119
(Mayan villages guest house and Garifuna model village contact; boat trips to cayes)

Requena's Charter Service
(Julio Requena)
P.O. Box 18, 12 Front Street
Punta Gorda
(boat trips to cayes, rivers; scheduled trips to Puerto Barrios, Guatemala; tours to caves, ruins, indigenous villages)

Foreign Travel Agencies and "Adventure Travel" Outfitters Specializing in Belize

Above The Clouds Trekking
Box 398
Worcester, MA 01062
U.S.A. (800) 233-4499
(nature treks)

Adventure Source International
5353 Manhattan Circle, #103
Boulder, CO 80303
U.S. (800) 346-8666 or (303) 499-2296

Adventures and Delights
300 West 36th Ave., #1B
Anchorage, AK 99503
U.S.A. (907) 276-8282

Barefoot Vacations
7114 Moores Lane
Brentwood, TN 37027
Tel. (800) 251-1000,
fax (615) 371-8891
(Mayan ruins, scuba, deep-sea fishing, reef trips)

Belize Services
(Charles and Patrick Colby)
5959 Westheimer, Suite 124
Houston, TX 77057
Tel. (800) 880-MAYA or (713) 781-8274, fax (713) 781-4629
(Belize travel specialists, including nature, reef, and Mayan ruin tours; hotel and airline bookings; car rental; special knowledge of Corozal and Orange Walk districts)

Belize Tradewinds
8715 W. North Avenue
Wauwatosa, WI 53226
U.S.A. (800) 451-7776 or (414) 258-6687, *(hotels; fishing and dive tours)*

Belize Travel Representatives
5 Grogans Park, Suite 102
The Woodlands, TX 77380
Tel. (800) 451-8017,
fax (713) 298-2335
(owner Tommy Thomson is an old Belize hand who can arrange any kind of trip you want)

Best of Belize
(Jacqueline Tipton)
672 Las Gallinas Road
San Rafael, CA 94903
U.S.A. (800) 735-9520,
fax (415) 479-2380
(hotel and airline booking; nature,
diving, fishing, and snorkeling; also books
Honduras, Guatemala, and Costa Rica)

Big Five Expeditions Ltd.
2151 E. Dublin-Granville Road
Columbus, OH 43229
U.S.A. (800) 541-2790
(nature and photography tours)

Bill Dvorak's Kayak &
Rafting Expeditions
17921 US Hwy 285
Nathrop, CO 81236
U.S.A. (800) 824-3795
(white-water expeditions; supports river
conservation)

Eco Adventures
632 Emerson Street
Palo Alto, CA 94301
U.S.A. (415) 321-1113
(customized itineraries for independent
travelers)

Ecosummer Expeditions & Tours
1516 Duranleau Street
Vancouver, B.C. V6H 3S4, Canada
Tel. (604) 669-7741,
fax (604) 669-3244
U.S.A. (800) 688-8605
(sea kayaking, river running, caving,
Mayan ruins, horseback riding, nature
tours)

Environmental Journeys/Earth
Island Institute
300 Broadway, Suite 28
San Francisco, CA 94133-3312
U.S.A. (510) 655-4526,
fax (510) 547-2881
(dolphin research, snorkeling, diving on
Blackbird Caye through Oceanic Society
Expeditions)

Great Trips
P.O. Box 1320
Detroit Lakes, MN 56501
U.S.A (800) 552-3419 or (218) 847-
4441, fax (218) 847-4442
(interior, reef, and sportfishing trips; "tropi-
cal paradise" specialists)

Imagine Travel Alternatives
(Dyanne Kruger)
Box 27023
Seattle, WA 98125

U.S.A. (206) 624-7112
("soft adventure" tours of Belize, with
extensions to Costa Rica and Guatemala;
hiking, canoeing, Mayan village tours)

International Expeditions
(Steve Cox, Tom Grasse)
One Environs Park
Helena, AL 35080
U.S.A. (800) 633-4734 or
(205) 428-1700,
fax (205) 428-1714
(archaeological, barrier reef, and natural
history tours; family trips; ecology work-
shops; rain forest pharmacology work-
shops; extensions to Tikal; co-sponsor of
Crooked Tree Cashew Festival)

International Zoological
Expeditions
210 Washington St.
Sherborn, MA 01770
Tel. (800) 548-5843 or (508) 655-
1461, fax (508) 655-4445
(marine and rainforest ecology seminars
and excursions in Toledo District, and on
barrier reef and Glover's Reef)

Journeys
3516 NE 155th, Suite B-2
Seattle, WA 98155
U.S.A. (800) 345-4453
(conservation-oriented tours)

Laughing Heart Adventures
P.O. Box 669
Willow Creek, CA 95573
U.S.A. (800) 541-1256
or (916) 629-3516
(nature-oriented river and reef trips)

Magnum Belize
Box 1560
Detroit Lakes, MN 56502
Tel. (800) 447-2931,
fax (218) 847-0334
(travel planners for Belize visitors at every
budget and interest level)

Massachusetts Audubon Society
5 S. Great Road
Lincoln, MA 01773
U.S.A. (617) 259-9500
(natural history tours guided by staff n
aturalists)

Monkey River Expeditions
1731 44th Avenue, S.W., Suite 100
Seattle, WA 98116
Tel. (206) 660-7777,
fax. (206) 938-0978
(Monkey River tour by sea kayak, Mayan
ruins, visit to cayes)

Mountain/Sobek Travel
6420 Fairmount Avenue
El Cerrito, CA 94530
U.S.A. (510) 527-8100
(conservation-oriented expeditions)

Ocean Connection
16734 El Camino Real
Houston, TX 77062
Tel. (800) 365-6232,
fax (713) 486-8362
(diving, fishing, snorkeling, sailing, tours, hotels, airfare)

Oceanic Society Expeditions
Ft. Mason Center, Bldg. E
San Francisco, CA 94123
Tel. (800) 326-7491,
fax (415) 474-3395
(dolphin research trips to Blackbird Caye, with extensions to Half Moon Caye, Tikal, and interior Belize; manatee and turtle research trips to Gales Point; bird and howler monkey research trips to Lamanai)

Preferred Adventures
(Karen Johnson)
One West Water Street, Suite 300
St. Paul, MN 55107
Tel. (612) 222-8131,
fax (612) 222-4221
(conservation-oriented nature trips, bird-watching tours)

Remarkable Journeys
(Nancy Landau, Mark Scholl)
Box 31855
Houston, TX 77231-1855
Tel. (800) 800-1939,
fax (713) 728-8334
(interior, reef, and sailing trips with Tikal extension)

River Travel Center
P.O. Box 6-B
Pt. Arena, CA 95468
U.S.A. (800) 882-7238
(emphasis on natural history)

Slickrock Adventures
P.O. Box 1400
Moab, UT 84532
U.S.A. (801) 259-6996
(ecology-minded kayaking, camping, fishing, snorkeling)

Special Expeditions
(Sven-Olaf Lindblad)
720 Fifth Ave.
New York, NY 10019
U.S.A.(800) 762-0003
or (212) 765-7740

(conservation-oriented snorkeling, photography, and nature tours; reef and atoll trips, Tikal and Bay Islands extensions; based aboard shallow-draft 238-foot, 80-passenger ship Polaris*)*

Steppingstone Environmental Education Tours
(Margie Scanlon)
P.O. Box 373
Narberth, PA 19072
U.S.A. (800) 874-8784,
fax. (610) 649-3428
(vacation and educational tours for school groups, nature and archaeology enthusiasts, birdwatchers, snorkeling, diving, botanical artists workshops; supports conservation)

Travel Belize, Ltd.
Boulder, CO
U.S.A. (800) 626-3483
(dive packages, tours, air connections)

Tread Lightly
One Titus Road
Washington Depot, CT 06794
U.S.A. (800) 627-8227
(rain forest ecology, conservation; contributes to local environmental projects)

University Research Expeditions Program
University of California at Berkeley
Berkeley, CA 94720
U.S.A. (510) 642-6586
(research in environmental studies, archaeology, humanities, paleontology)

Voyagers International
Box 915
Ithaca, NY 14851
U.S.A. (607) 257-3091
(natural history, ornithology, photography)

Wildland Adventures
3516 NE 155th Street
Seattle, WA 98155
U.S.A. (800) 345-4453
(tours specializing in Mayan archaeology, cultural diversity, tropical nature, and the barrier reef; hires local guides and contributes to conservation and community projects through the Earth Preservation Fund)

Winter Escapes
(Daniel Weedon)
P.O. Box 429
Erickson, MB R0J 0P0, Canada
Tel. (204) 636-2968,
fax (204) 636-2202
(bird-watching, nature tours)

Fishing and Diving Services

Amigos del Mar Dive Shop
Box 53
San Pedro, Ambe0rgris Caye
Tel. 26-2706, fax 26-2648
(complete dive shop)

Melvin Bandillo Jr.
Caye Caulker
Tel. 022-2111
(fishing guide)

Barbachano Tours
9500 S. Dadeland Blvd., #71
Miami, FL 33156
U.S.A. (800) 327-2254
(dive packages from the U.S.)

Belize Dive Center
San Pedro, Ambergris Caye
Tel. 26-2797, U.S.A. (305) 938-0860
*(dive packages, instruction; located at
Belize Yacht Club)*

Belize Diving Services
Caye Caulker
Tel. 22-2143, or marine VHF
channel 68
(complete dive shop)

**Belize River Lodge/Maya Landings
Yacht Club**
Box 459
Belize City
Tel. 025-2002, fax 025-2298
*(complete dive shop and diving resort on
Moho Caye)*

Blackline Marine Service
Box 332, Mile 2 Northern Highway
Belize City
Tel. 2-44155, fax 2-31975, marine
VHF channel 70
*(complete dive shop, hull and engine repairs,
fishing/diving and sightseeing charters,
marina with fuel, water, and ice)*

Blue Marlin Lodge
South Water Caye
P.O. Box 21
Dangriga
Tel. 05-22296, fax 5-22296
(full-service diving and fishing resort)

**Blue Planet Divers and Diving
School**
(Klaus Eiberle and Mark Van Thillo)
based on *Heraclitus* off Blackbird Caye,
Turneffe Islands
Box 1795
Belize City

Tel. 2-76770, fax 2-76203
U.S.A. (602) 825-5075
*(NAUI scuba certification; dive trips; dive
master and rescue diver courses; specialty in
reef ecology and open water; group rates)*

Blue Runner Guiding
(Kenny Villanueva)
Placencia Village
Tel. 6-23153 or 6-23130
*(heavy and light tackle or trolling sportfish-
ing trips; snorkeling; reef, river, and coast)*

Bottom Time Dive Shop
San Pedro, Ambergris Caye
Tel. 26-2348, fax 26-2821
*(dive shop, scuba instruction, night diving,
sailing charters, equipment rental; located in
Sun Breeze Hotel)*

Roberto Bradley, Jr.
Ambergris Caye
Tel. 026-2116
(fishing guide)

Pow Cabral Flyfishing
Placencia
Tel. 022-2234, U.S.A. (800) 333-5691
(sport- and fly-fishing)

Caribbean Charter Services
Box 752, Mile 5 Northern Highway
Belize City
Tel. 2-45814
*(boat charters, car rental, diving and
fishing tours)*

Coral Beach Hotel and Dive Club
San Pedro, Ambergris Caye
Tel. 2-62013 or 2-62001
*(packages for snorkelers, divers, fishermen,
beachcombers)*

Frenchie's Services
Caye Caulker
Tel. 022-2111
(fishing and diving guides)

Romel Gomez/Luz Guerrero
Ambergris Caye
Tel. 026-2034
(fishing guides)

Nolan Jackson
Tobacco Caye
Box 10, Dangriga
(fishing guide)

Kingfisher Belize Adventures
(Stanley Winborne and Charles Leslie)
Placencia
Tel. 6-23104, U.S.A. (800) 403-9995,
fax (919) 676-9910
(camping, bungalows, bar, restaurant, fly-cast/spincast, inshore, offshore)

Kitty's Placencia Dive Shop
(Kitty Fox and Ran Villanueva)
Placencia
Tel. 6-22027
(complete dive shop, transportation to reef and atolls; also bicycle rentals, river trips, kayaking, beachfront lodging)

Francis "Billy" Leslie
Ambergris Caye
Tel. 026-2128
(fishing guide)

Lighthouse Reef Resort
Northern Two Caye, Lighthouse Reef
Box 26, Belize City
(complete fishing and diving services)

Manatee Lodge
Gales Point
Box 170, Belmopan
Tel. 8-23321, fax 8-23334
(sportfishing specialists)

Manta Resort
Glover's Reef
Box 215, 3 Eyre Street
Belize City
Tel. 2-31895 or (800) 342-0053,
marine VHF channel 70
(dive and fishing resort on 12-acre island)

One Moore Tour
(Doug and Lou Moore)
Box 1910, 19A Cleghorn Street
Belize City
Tel. 2-32331, fax 2-31711
(fishing specialist, guided inland and reef tours with emphasis on traditional hospitality)

Out Island Divers
Box 7, San Pedro, Ambergris Caye
Tel. 2-62151,
U.S.A. (800) BLUE-HOLE
(dive boat specialists)

Melanie Paz
Ambergris Caye
Tel. 026-2437
(fishing guide)

Pegasus Boat Services
Caye Caulker
Tel. 022-223
(fishing guides, boat charters)

Pisces Dive Service
(Mike and Beverly McCarty)
Placencia
Tel. 6-23183
(certified NAUI and NASDS scuba instruction, photography services)

Reef Divers Ltd.
Ramon's Reef Resort
San Pedro, Ambergris Caye
Tel. 2-62371, fax 26-2028
(complete dive shop)

Ricardo's Adventure Tours
Caye Caulker
Tel. 2-22138
(river trips, island hopping, fishing, diving)

Rothschild Travel Consultants
900 West End Ave., Suite 1B
New York, NY 10025
U.S.A. (800) 359-0747
(diving and fishing packages, adventure trips)

Scuba Tours
5 Paterson Avenue
Little Falls, NJ 07424
U.S.A. (800) 526-1394,
fax (201) 256-0591
(dive trips, live-aboard packages)

Sea & Explore
1809 Carol Sue Ave., Suite E
Gretna, LA 70056
(800) 345-9786, fax (504) 366-9986
(diving and fishing trips; represents several live-aboard dive boats)

Sea Masters Company, Ltd.
Ambergris Caye
Box 59, Belize City
Tel. 026-2173, fax 026-2028
(fishing and diving services)

Sea Safaris
3770 Highland Ave, Suite 102
Manhattan Beach, CA 90266
U.S.A. (800) 821-6670
or (213) 546-2464
(dive trips, live-aboard diving packages)

Sun Breeze Beach Hotel
San Pedro, Ambergris Caye
Tel. 2-62347, fax 2-62346
(dive shop, fishing trips, windsurfing, hotel, restaurant)

Travel Belize Ltd.
637-B S. Broadway
Boulder, CO 80303
U.S.A. (800) 626-3483
(dive trips)

Tropical Adventures Travel
11 Second Avenue
Seattle, WA 98109
U.S.A. (800) 247-3483
or (206) 441-3483
(scuba specialists)

Turneffe Flats
Blackbird Caye, Turneffe Islands
Tel. 2-45634, U.S.A. (605) 578-1304,
fax (605) 578-7540
(sportfishing and diving specialists)

Turneffe Islands Lodge
Caye Bokel, Turneffe Islands
Box 480, Belize City
(800) 338-8149, fax 3-0276
(diving and fishing specialists)

James Westby Fishing Guide
Placencia Village
Tel. 6-23283
(fishing guide specializing in fly-fishing)

Wippari Caye Guiding
(George and Breeze Cabral)
Wippari Caye
Tel. 6-23130
*(fly-fishing guides, specialing in bonefish,
permit and tarpon; lodging)*

Richard Young, Jr.
Belize City
Tel. 2-74385
*(light tackle fishing guide specializing in
tarpon, snook, and bonefish on flats or
rivers)*

Live-Aboard Dive Boats

Belize *Aggressor I* , *II,* and *III*
(100-foot dive boats)
based at Ft. George Pier, Belize City
Drawer K, Morgan City, LA 70381
U.S.A. (800) 348-2628

Coral Bay (62-foot dive boat) **and**
Offshore Express
Coral Beach Hotel
San Pedro, Ambergris Caye
Tel. 26-2001
U.S.A. (800) 433-7262
or (305) 563-1711

La Strega (85-foot dive boat)
Box 673
Belize City
Tel. 2-3108, U.S.A. (800) 433-DIVE

M.V. *Greet Reef* (65-foot dive boat)
Box 214A
Corpus Christi, TX 78415
U.S.A. (800) 255-8503
or (512) 854-0247

Out Island Divers
(operators of *Reef Roamer I, II,* and *III)*
Box 7
San Pedro, Ambergris Caye
Tel. 2-62151,
U.S.A. (800) BLUE-HOLE

M.V. *Manta IV*
Box 13
San Pedro, Ambergris Caye
Tel. 2-62371, fax 2-62028
U.S.A. (800) 473-1956
*(overnight dive trips to Turneffe and Light-
house atolls; interior tours)*

M.Y. *Gallic*
Tel. 2-31351
U S.A. (800) 468-0123
*(52-foot dive boat, specializing in Glover's
and Lighthouse Reefs)*

Ramada Royal Reef Hotel
Barracks Road
Belize City
U.S.A. (800) 228-9898
(berth for various dive boats)

Wave Dancer
based at Ft. George Pier, Belize City
Peter Hughes Diving
6851 Yumuri St., Suite 10
Coral Gables, FL 33146
U.S.A. (800) 932-6237

Mountain Biking, River Trips, Sea Kayaking, Sailing

Adios Charters
(Mike and Bonnie Cline)
Placencia
Tel. 6-23154
(36-foot trimaran for day charters to area cayes for snorkeling)

Amigo Travel
San Pedro, Ambergris Caye
Tel. 26-2180
(scooter and bicycle rental, sailing, other services)

B&M Mountain Bike Hire
(Eric or Mel Barber)
26 Burns Ave.
San Ignacio
Tel./fax 092-2382
(mountain bikes for rent; also sales, service and repair; maps and route information)

Bike Belize
104 New Road
Belize City
Tel. 2-33855
(moped, minibike, scooter, and bicycle rental; camping, guided tours throughout Belize)

Caye Caulker Sailboats
The Reef Hotel
Caye Caulker
Tel. 22-2196
(sailboat rentals)

Fanta-Sea Charters
(Michael and Donna Hill)
Box 768
Belize City
Tel. 2-33033, fax 2-3712
U.S.A. (303) 226-1193
(day and overnight snorkel trips on 45-foot catamaran Stingray, *based in Belize City at Ramada Reef Hotel marina)*

Heritage Navigation
Paradise Hotel Dock
San Pedro, Ambergris Caye
Tel. 26-2394
(island and reef cruises on 66-foot sailboat Winnie Estelle*)*

Hinterland Tours
3 Eve Street
San Ignacio
Tel. 92-2475
(river, ruin, and jungle trips)

Island Expeditions
4585 Commercial Street
Vancouver, BC V5N 4G8, Canada
(800) 667-1630 or (604) 879-9800, fax
(604) 684-3255
(sea kayaking)

Journeys of Discovery
1516 Duranleau St.
Vancouver, BC V6H 354 Canada
U.S.A. (800) 688-8605
Canada (800) 465-8884
(sea kayaking and rain forest expeditions)

Kayak & Rafting Expeditions
17921 S. Highway 285
Nathrop, CO 81236
(sea kayaking, river trips)

Oceanwide Sail Expeditions
Westfalenstrasse 92
D-58636 Iserlohn, Germany
U.S.A. (800) 732-6725
(eight-day sailing tours aboard the Rembrandt van Rijn*)*

Paradise Bicycle Tours
(Tom Hoskins)
P.O. Box 1726
Evergreen, CO 80439
Tel. (800) 626-8271
(bicycle tours)

Pegasus Boat Charter
Box 743
Tel. 2-31138
(boat charter for reef, river, and caye trips)

Red Rooster Peddle & Paddle Tours
(Tom, Jeanette, and Shaw Ellis)
Red Rooster Bar & Grill
2 Far West Street
San Ignacio
Tel. 9-23016, fax 92-2057
(mountain biking trips, raft trips, bicycle rental)

Reef-Link Kayaking
(Eddie Leslie and Kirk Barrett)
Ranguana Lodge and Reef Resort
Plancencia and Ranguana Caye
Tel. 6-22027, U.S.A. (515) 279-6699
(sea kayak rentals and tours; manages bungalows and campground for kayakers on Ranguana Caye)

Sailing Fantasy
Ramon's Reef Resort
San Pedro, Ambergris Caye
Tel. 2-62439
(catamaran trips and rental, operators of El
Tigre*)*

Slickrock Adventures
Box 1400
Moab, UT 84532
(801) 259-6996
(sea kayaking, windsurfing)

Sunrise Boat Tours and Charters
(Jim Novelo)
Caye Caulker
Tel. 2-22195
*(trips to cayes near and far, including
weekly excursion to Half Moon Caye)*

Timeless Tours
2304 Massachusetts Avenue
Cambridge, MA 02140
Tel. 7-2119, U.S.A. (800) 370-0142
*(7- to 12-day sailing/camping excursions
with 38-foot schooner based in Punta Gorda,
overnight on cayes and jungle rivers)*

Toni Canoes
22 Burns Avenue
San Ignacio
Tel. 92-2267
(river and canoe trips)

Wilderness Alaska/Mexico
(Ron Yarnell)
1231 Sundance Loop
Fairbanks, AK 99709
Tel. (907) 479-8203
(sea kayaking)

Archaeological Expeditions

Earthwatch
Box 403, 680 Mt. Auburn Street
Watertown, MA 02272
(work-study archaeological tours)

**Far Horizons Archaeological and
Discovery Trips**
(Mary Dell Lucas)
P.O. Box 91900
Albuquerque, NM 87199-1900
U.S.A. Tel. (800) 552-4575 or
(505) 822-9100, fax (505) 828-1500
*("cultural discovery" trips to Mayan vil-
lages and ruins, led by archaeologists
trained in Belize; can arrange canoeing,
horseback riding, fishing and boat trips)*

Institute of Mayan Antiquities
(Ron Whipple)
6828 Wofford Drive
Dallas, TX 75227

U.S.A. (214) 381-2311
*(remote-sensing research trips to Mayan
ruins in Belize and Guatemala)*

**Smithsonian Odyssey Tours
& Research Expeditions**
1100 Jefferson Dr. S.W.
Washington, DC 20560
U.S.A. (800) 524-4125 or (202) 357-
4700 *(study tours and research expeditions)*

**University Research Expeditions
Program**
University of California at Berkeley
Berkeley, CA 94720
U.S.A. (510) 642-6586
*(research expeditions in archaeology; devel-
ops cooperative projects with scientists from
developing nations)*

Birding Expeditions

International Expeditions
One Environs Park
Helena, AL 35080
U.S.A. (800) 633-4734
*(bird-watching and other nature-oriented
tours)*

Manomet Bird Observatory
Box 1770
Manomet, MA 02345
U.S.A. (508) 224-6521
(bird-watching tours)

Massachusetts Audubon Society
South Great Road
Lincoln, MA 01773
U.S.A. (800) 289-9504
(bird-watching and natural history tours)

Victor Emanuel Nature Tours
Box 33008
Austin, TX 78764
U.S.A. (512) 328-5221
*(bird-watching and other nature-oriented
tours)*

Appendix

Government-Protected Areas

Aguas Turbias Nature Reserve
Bladen Nature Reserve
Blue Hole National Park
Burdon Canal Nature Reserve
Chiquibul National Park
Cockscomb Basin Wildlife Sanctuary
Crooked Tree Wildlife Sanctuary
Crown Reserve Bird Sanctuaries (6)
Five Blues Lake National Park
Glover's Reef Marine Reserve
Guanacaste National Park
Half Moon Caye Natural Monument
Hol Chan Marine Reserve
Laughingbird Caye National Park
Manatee Special Development Area
Monkey Bay Nature Reserve
Paynes Creek/Monkey River Wildlife Sanctuary
Río Blanco Falls Nature Reserve
Río Grande Reserve
Temash and Sarstoon Delta Wildlife Sanctuary
Terra Nova Medicinal Plant Reserve
Turneffe Islands Marine Reserve
(*The above does not include government-protected Mayan "archaeological monument"
sites, such as Caracol, Xunantunich, Lamanai, and Altun Ha.*)

Privately Protected Areas

Belize Agroforestry Research Center
Belize Zoo and Tropical Education Center
Black Cat/Sapodilla Lagoon Nature Reserve
Blue Creek Nature Reserve
Carrie Bow Caye and Twin Cayes Research Station
Community Baboon Sanctuary
Gales Point Manatee Community Sanctuary
Hidden Valley Nature Reserve
Ix Chel Farm and Tropical Research Center

Man O' War Caye
Monkey Bay Wildlife Sanctuary and National Park
Possum Point Biological Station
Río Bravo Conservation and Management Area
Shawfields Nature Reserve
Shipstern Nature Reserve
Slate Creek Preserve
Tapir Mountain Nature Reserve
Wee Wee Caye Research Station

Conservation Groups

Belize Audubon Society
Box 1001, 12 Fort Street
Belize City
Tel. 2-35004

Belize Center for Environmental Studies
(Lou Nicolait)
Box 666, 55 Eve Street
Belize City
Tel. 2-45739

Belize Natural History Society
(Bruce Miller)
Gallon Jug, Orange Walk District

Belize Zoo & Tropical Education Center
(Sharon Matola)
Mile 30, Western Highway
Box 1787, Belize City

Belize Youth Conservation Corps
27 Regent Street
Belize City
Tel. 2-75972

Community Conservation Consultants
Howlers Forever, Inc.
(Rob Horwich)
RD 1, Box 96
Gays Mills, WI 54631
(608) 735-4717

Ix Chel Tropical Research Foundation
(Rosita Arvigo, Greg Shropshire)
Chaa Creek Rd.
San Ignacio, Cayo District

Indian Law Resource Center
(Curtis Berkey, Armstrong Wiggins)
601 E. Street, S.E.
Washington, D.C. 20003
(202) 547-2800

LightHawk
P.O. Box 8163
Santa Fe, NM 87504
(505) 982-9656

Manomet Bird Observatory
P.O. Box 936
Manomet, MA 02345
(508) 224-6521

New York Botanical Garden
(Michael J. Balick)
Dept. of Economic Botany
New York Botanical Garden
Bronx, NY 10458
(718) 817-8763

Programme for Belize
(Joy Grant)
Belize City
Tel. 2-75616, fax 2-75635

Slate Creek Reserve
(Jim and Marguerite Bevis)
Central Farm P.O., Cayo District
Tel. 92-3452

Tropical Conservation Foundation
P.O. Box 31
CH-2074
Marin-Ne, Switzerland
(038) 334344

Wildlife Conservation Society
New York Zoological Society
185th St. and So. Blvd., Bldg. A
Bronx, NY 10460
(212) 220-5155

World Wildlife Fund—U.S.
1250 24th St., NW
Washington, DC 20037
(202) 293-4800

Prohibitions

The following activities are prohibited by law in Belize: the removal, sale, and exportation of black or any other kind of coral without a license; hunting without a license; picking wild orchids in a forest reserve; removing, defacing, or destroying archaeological artifacts; spearfishing or collecting crustaceans while wearing scuba diving apparel without a special Fisheries Department permit; possessing or exporting turtles or materials made from turtles without a license; overnight camping in any public place, including a forest reserve, without permission from the proper authorities; collecting out of season any lobster (March 15-July 14), conch (July 1-September 30), or sea turtle (June 1-August 31).

The U.S. Customs Service and the Fish and Wildlife Service bar items made with crocodile, alligator, lizard, and snake skins as well as anything made of sea turtle shells or ostrich skins. Souvenirs made of feathers are also banned, as are dried butterflies or turtles and any jaguar or ocelot skin. A complete list of such items is available through most travel agents or federal offices.

Art Galleries and Museums

Arts & Crafts of Central America
Burns Ave.
San Ignacio
Tel. 9-32351
(arts and crafts from Belize, Guatemala, and their neighbors)

Baron Bliss Institute
1 Bliss Parade
Belize City
Tel. 2-77267
(Mayan artifacts, public library, art and culture exhibits)

Community Baboon Sanctuary Natural History Museum
Bermudian Landing, Belize District
(local artifacts, howler monkey displays, natural history)

El Caracol Gallery & Gift Shop
32 Macaw Avenue
Belmopan
Tel. 8-22394
(stone carvings, sculptures, ceramics, jewelry, basketry, prints, musical instruments)

Galería Hicaco
Caye Caulker
Tel. 2-22178
(photos, prints, arts and crafts)

García Sisters Museum & Gift Shop
Box 75
San Ignacio
(museum and gift shop on Cristo Rey Road in San Antonio Village; slate carvings on Mayan themes, handmade cards, medicinal herbs and teas)

Go Graphics and Gifts
23 Regent Street
Belize City
Tel. 2-74082
(T-shirts, handicrafts, books, carvings, souvenirs)

Itzamna' (Magaña) Gift Shop and Museum
San Antonio Village, Cayo District
(Mayan stone and wood carvings by the Magaña family, also tapestries)

Mayan Artifact Vault
Department of Archaeology
Belmopan
Tel. 8-22106, fax 8-23345
(vault contains Mayan artifacts; open by appointment two days in advance on Monday, Wednesday, and Friday only from 1:30 to 4:00 p.m.)

Melinda's Historical Museum
21 St. Vincent's Street
Dangriga
Tel. 5-22266
(Garifuna handicrafts and artifacts; open daily except Thursday and Sunday; $1 admission)

Mexican Cultural Center
Barracks Road
Belize City
(Mexican-funded museum and visitors' center emphasizing Mayan history and archaeology; located near Ramada Royal Reef Hotel)

National Handicraft Sales Center
Box 291, Fort Street
Belize City
Tel. 2-33833, fax 2-33636
(wide variety of native handicrafts at reasonable prices; wholesale and retail sales)

New Hope Trading Company
Buena Vista Road
San Ignacio
Tel. 9-22188
(exotic wood crafts)

Rachael's Art Gallery
39 West Albert Street
Belize City
Tel. 2-77488
(contemporary Belizean art, novelties, art supplies)

Stone Maiden Arts & Crafts Shop
Western Highway at Xunantunich Ferry
San José Succotz, Cayo District
(contemporary Mayan arts and crafts)

Embassies and Consulates

Note: The following is a partial list.

Canadian Consulate
85 North Front St.
Belize City
Tel. 2-31060

Costa Rican Embassy
2 Sapodilla Street
Belmopan
Tel. 8-22725

Honduran Embassy
91 North Front Street
Belize City
Tel. 2-45889

Mexican Embassy
20 North Park Street
Belize City
Tel. 2-30193

United States Embassy
Hutson Street and Gabrouel Lane
Belize City
Tel. 2-77161

Scientific Names of Flora and Fauna Mentioned

Note: This is *not* a comprehensive list of Belize's flora and fauna. Those species listed below, with the exception of insects and crustaceans, are only those mentioned in the text.

Birds

Agami heron *(Agamia agami)*
American coot *(Fulica americana)*
American redstart *(Setophaca ruticilla)*
Aztec parakeet *(Aratinga astec)*
barred forest falcon *(Micrastur ruficollis)*
barred antshrike *(Thamnophilus doliatus)*
belted kingfisher *(Ceryle alcyon)*
black-chinned hummingbird *(Archilochus alexandri)*
black-headed trogon *(Trogon melanocephalus)*
black rail *(Laterallus jamaicensis)*
blue grosbeak *(Guiraca caerulea)*
brown-hooded parrot *(Pionopsitta haemotosis)*
brown jay *(Psilorhinus morio)*
brown pelican *(Pelicanus occidentalis)*
citreoline trogon *(Trogon citreolus)*
collared aracari *(Pteroglossus torquatus)*
collared forest falcon *(Micrastur semitorquatus)*
common wood nymph *(Thalurania furcata)*
crested guan *(Penelope purpurascens)*
emerald toucanet *(Avlacorhynchus prosinus)*
eye-ringed flatbill *(Rhynchocyclus brevirostris)*
gray-breasted crake *(Laterallus exilis)*
great curassow *(Crax rubra)*
great blue heron *(Ardea herodias)*
green-backed heron *(Butorides striatus)*
green-winged teal *(Anas crecca)*
harpy eagle *(Harpia harpyja)*
jabiru stork *(Jabiru mycteria)*
keel-billed motmot *(Electron carinatum)*
keel-billed toucan *(Ramphastos sulfuratus)*
king vulture *(Sarcoramphus papa)*
least grebe *(Tachybaptus dominicus)*
limpkin *(Aramus guarauna)*
magnificent frigatebird *(Fregata magnificens)*
mangrove warbler *(Dendroica erithacorides)*
mealy parrot *(Amazona farinosa)*
Montezuma oropendola *(Psarocolius montezuma)*
northern jacana *(Jacana spinosa)*
ocellated turkey *(Agriocharis ocellata)*
olivaceous cormorant *(Phalacrocorax olivaceus)*
orange-breasted falcon *(Falco deiroleucus)*
ornate hawk eagle *(Spizaetus ornatus)*
Philadelphia vireo *(Vireo philadelphicus)*
prothonotary warbler *(Protonotaria citrea)*

pygmy kingfisher *(Chloroceryle aenea)*
red-footed booby *(Sula sula)*
red-lored parrot *(Amazona antumnalis)*
ringed kingfisher *(Ceryle torquata)*
roadside hawk *(Buteo nitidus)*
rose-throated becard *(Pachyramphus major)*
roseate spoonbill *(Ajaia ajaja)*
roseate tern *(Sterna dougalli)*
rough-winged swallow *(Stelgidopteryx ruficollis)*
rufous-capped warbler *(Basileuterus belli)*
scaly-throated foliage gleaner *(Anabacerthia variegaticeps)*
scarlet macaw *(Ara macao)*
slaty-breasted tinamou *(Crypturellus boucardi)*
smoky brown woodpecker *(Venilious fumigatus)*
snail kite *(Rostrhamus sociabilis)*
sooty tern *(Sterna fuscata)*
squirrel cuckoo *(Piaya cayana)*
tropical mockingbird *(Mimus gilvus)*
vermiculated screech-owl *(Otus guatemalae)*
vermillion flycatcher *(Pyrocephalus rubinus)*
white ibis *(Eudocimus albus)*
white hawk *(Leucopternis albicollis)*
white-crowned parrot *(Pronis senilis)*
white-crowned pigeon *(Columba leucocephala)*
white-fronted parrot *(Amazona albifrons)*
white-necked jacobin *(Florisuga mellivora)*
wood stork *(Mycteria americana)*
yellow-billed cacique *(Amblycercus holosericeus)*
yellow-headed parrot *(Amazona ochrocephala)*
yellow-lored parrot *(Amazona xantholora)*
yellow-throated euphonia *(Euphonia hirundinacea)*
Yucatan jay *(Cyanocorax yucatanicus)*

Mammals
agouti *(Dasyprocta punctata)*
armadillo *(Dasypus novemcinctus)*
Atlantic bottlenose dolphin *(Tursiops truncatus)*
Baird's tapir *(Tapirus bairdii)*
black howler monkey *(Alouatta pigra)*
brocket deer *(Mazama americana)*
Central American river otter *(Lutra longicaudus)*
Central American spider monkey *(Ateles geoffroyi)*
coati *(Nasua nasua)*
gray fox *(Urocyon cinereoargenteus)*
greater bulldog bat *(Noctilio leporinus)*
jaguar *(Panthera onca)*
jaguarundi *(Felis yagouaroundi)*
kinkajou *(Potos flavus)*
margay *(Felis wiedii)*
ocelot *(Felis paradalis)*
paca *(Agouti paca)*

puma *(Felis concolor)*
spinner dolphin *(Stenella longirosrus)*
tayra *(Eira barbara)*
Virginia opossum *(Didelphis virginiana)*
West Indian manatee *(Trichechus manatus)*
white-lipped peccary *(Tapirus pecari)*
white-tailed deer *(Odocoileus virginiana)*

Reptiles
boa constrcitor *(Constrictor constrictor)*
fer-de-lance *(Bothrops atrox)*
hawksbill turtle *(Eretmochelys imbricata)*
hickatee *(Dermatemys mawii)*
iguana *(Iguana iguana)*
loggerhead turtle *(Staurotypus triporcatus)*
Morelet's crocodile *(Crocodylus moreleti)*

Fishes
Atlantic sailfish *(Istiophorus albicans)*
blue marlin *(Makaira nigricans)*
blue-striped grunt *(Haemulon criurus)*
great barracuda *(Sphyaena barracuda)*
horse-eye jack *(Caranx latus)*
king mackerel *(Scomberomorus cavalla)*
Spanish mackerel *(Scombermorus maculatus)*
tarpon *(Tarpon atlanticus)*
wahoo *(Acanthocybium solandi)*
white marlin *(Tetrapturus albidus)*
yellow-tail snapper *(Ocyurus chrysurus)*

Trees
banak *(Virola koschnyi)*
barba jolote *(Pithecellobium arboreum)*
black mangrove *(Avicennia)*
breadnut *(Brosimum alicastrum)*
bullhoof *(Drypetes brownii)*
ceiba *(Ceiba pentandra)*
coconut *(Cocos nucifera)*
cohune palm *(Orbignya cohune)*
copal *(Protium copal)*
guanacaste *(Enterolobium cyclocarpum)*
gumbo-limbo *(Bursera simaruba)*
ironwood *(Dialium guianense)*
logwood *(Haematoxylon campechianum)*
mahogany *(Swietenia macrophylla)*
mamee apple *(Pouteria mammosa)*
mapola *(Bernoullia flammea)*
mylady *(Aspidosperma cruenta)*
negrito *(Simarubra glauca)*
palmetto palm *(Acoellorhaphe wrightii)*
quamwood *(Schizolobium parahybum)*

red breadnut *(Trophis racemosa)*
red mangrove *(Rhizophora mangle)*
Santa María *(Calophyllum brasileinse var. rekoi)*
sapodilla *(Manilkara zapota)*
Spanish cedar *(Cedrela odorata)*
waika chewstick *(Symphonia globulifera)*
wild mammee *(Alseis yucatanensis)*
yemeri *(Vochysia hondurensis)*
ziricote *(Cordia sebestena)*

Glossary of Belizean English

The Creole English dialect spoken by most Belizeans of African-European descent is sometimes difficult for outsiders to understand. It has not only a lilting Caribbean cadence but also a grammatical structure that borrows heavily from the African languages used by slaves originally brought to Belize from West Africa to work in the logging and sugarcane industries. When talking among themselves, the Creole can be almost completely unintelligible to foreigners; however, they are used to quizzical looks and are gracious about answering questions in more standardized English. All public school instruction, by the way, is in standard English. Here is a brief translation of some Creole words and phrases:

Baboon ya de fu we	We're for the baboons
Bacra (also spelled backra)	White man
Bad ting nebah gat owner	An unfortunate event never has an owner
Bettah belly bus den bikkle waste	Better to eat too much than to waste good food
Boil up	Fish stew
Bush (or Belize breeze)	Local marijuana
Cow no bidness eena hoss glop	A cow has no business in a horse race
Coward man kep soun bone	The cautious fellow lives longer
Dat boy done mek she fat	That boy made her pregnant
Dis de fu we chicken	This is our chicken (slogan of Quality Poultry Products, a Mennonite-owned poultry firm)
Fishaman nevah say he fish tink	A fisherman never says his fish stinks (Self-criticism never happens)
He a two-eye mon in a one-eye town	He is smart
He kin skin a dog wid he tongue	(Refers to a popular but erroneous Creole myth that the docile tapir will kill dogs and other domestic animals)
High bush	Dense jungle
If you drink de Belize watta, you mus com bak	One visit to Belize is not enough
I study B-Town and I don' mess around	I know Belize City; therefore, I am careful
Jimba	Cane fishing pole

Jump up	A festive dance
Nak yo own tang	Do your own thing
Nebba caal de crocodile bit mout til you done cross de ribba	Don't make trouble until you are safely out of danger
No put puss fo mind butter	Don't leave known thieves in positions of trust
Only daag bahk an chase	Only dogs bark and chase (Do one thing at a time)
Sleeping policeman	An asphalt speed-bump placed across a road-way
Tea	The evening meal (as in England and Australia)
Teef neva prospa	Thieves never prosper
Tell me ears now	Talk to me
Wah fu happen haffu happen.	What is to happen has to happen.
Wah way a goin?	What way are you going?
Wah way a won?	What do you want?
Yah mon!	Yes!
Yu pahk up a go?	Are you leaving?

Suggested Reading

Travel Guides

Adventure Guide to Belize, Harry S. Pariser. Edison, N.J.: Hunter Publishing, 1995.

Adventuring in Belize, Eric Hoffman. San Francisco: Sierra Club Books, 1993.

Belize by Kayak, Kirk Barrett. Des Moines, IA: Reef-Link Kayaking, 1994.

Belize Guide, Paul Glassman. Champlain, N.Y.: Open Road Publishing/Passport Press, 1994.

Belize Handbook, Chicki Mallan. Chico, Calif.: Moon Publications, 1993.

Bicycling in Latin America, Walter Sienko. Seattle: Mountaineers Publishing, 1993.

Fodor's Costa Rica, Belize, Guatemala: The Complete Guide with the Best Beaches, Parks, and Ruins, Carolyn Price, ed. New York: Fodor's/Random House, 1993.

Frommer's Costa Rica, Guatemala & Belize on $35 a Day, Karl Samson with Jane Aukshunas. New York: MacMillan, 1995.

La Ruta Maya: Guatemala, Belize & Yucatán, Tom Brosnahan, ed. Oakland: Lonely Planet Publications, 1994.

The Maya Route: La Ruta Maya, Richard Harris and Stacy Ritz. Berkeley: Ulysses Press, 1993.

The New Key to Belize, Stacy Ritz. Berkeley: Ulysses Books, 1994.

The Rough Guide to Guatemala and Belize, Mark Whatmore and Peter Eltringham. New York/London: Penguin/Rough Guides Ltd.,1993.

World of the Maya

The Ancient Maya, S. Morley and G. W. Brainerd. 3d ed. Stanford: Stanford University Press, 1956.

The Blood of Kings: Dynasty and Ritual in Maya Art, Linda Schele and Mary Ellen Miller. Ft. Worth: Kimbell Art Museum, 1986.

The Complete Visitor's Guide to Mesoamerican Ruins, Joyce Kelly. Norman: University of Oklahoma Press, 1982.

Guide to Ancient Maya Ruins, C. Bruce Hunter. Norman: University of Oklahoma Press, 1986.

Maya Land Rights in Belize and the History of Indian Reservations, Curtis Berkey, Indian Law Resource Center, 1994.

Time Among the Maya, Ronald Wright. New York: Weidenfeld & Nicholson, 1989.

Warlords and Maize Men: A Guide to the Maya Sites of Belize, Byron Foster, ed. Belize City: Cubola Publications, 1989.

Flora and Fauna

A Belizean Rain Forest: The Community Baboon Sanctuary, Robert Horwich and Jon Lyon. Gay Mills, Wisc.: Orangutan Press, 1990.

Belize: A Country Environmental Profile and Field Study, Robert Nicolait and Associates. San José, Costa Rica: Hnos Sucs, S.A., 1984.

Birds of Mexico and Central America, Steve Howell and Sophie Webb. New York: Oxford Press, 1993.

The Bladen Branch Wilderness: A Special Report, Nicholas Brokaw and Trevor Lloyd-Evans. Manomet Bird Observatory, 1987.

"Checklist of the Birds of Belize," Wood, Leberman, and Weyer. Pittsburgh: Carnegie Museum of Natural History Special Publication No. 12.

The Diversity of Life, Edward O. Wilson. Cambridge: Belknap Press of Harvard University Press, 1992.

Field Guide to Mexican Birds, Roger Tory Peterson and Edward L. Chalif. Boston: Houghton Mifflin, 1973.

Guide to Corals and Fishes, Jerry Greenberg. Miami: Seahawk Press, 1972.

Jaguar, Alan Rabinowitz. New York: Arbor House, 1986.

Jungle Walk: Birds and Beasts of Belize, Katie Stevens. Belize City: Angelus Press, 1989.

A Neotropical Companion: An Introduction to the Animals, Plants, and Ecosystems of New World Tropics, John C. Kricher. Princeton: Princeton University Press.

Neotropical Rainforest Mammals: A Field Guide, Louise H. Emmons. Chicago and London: University of Chicago Press.

One Hundred Birds of Belize, Carolyn M. Miller. Washington: International Council for Bird Preservation.

Orchids of Guatemala and Belize, Oakes Ames and Donovan Stewart Correll. New York: Dover, 1985.

Rainforest Remedies: One Hundred Healing Herbs of Belize, Rosita Arvigo and Michael Balick, Twin Lakes: Lotus Press, 1993.

Reef Fish and Reef Creatures, Paul Humann. Jacksonville: New World Publications.

Sastun: My Apprenticeship with a Maya Healer, Rosita Arvigo with Nadine Epstein. San Francisco: Harper Collins, 1994.

History and Culture

Creole Proverbs of Belize, Colville N. Young. Belize City: National Printers Ltd., 1988.

Hey Dad, This Is Belize, Emory King. Belize City: Tropical Books, 1984.

Inside Belize: A Country Guide, Tom Barry. Albuquerque: Inter-Hemispheric Education Research Center, 1992.

I Spent It All in Belize, Emory King. Belize City: Tropical Books, 1986.

On Heroes, Lizards and Passion, Zoila Ellis. Benque Viejo, Belize: Cubola Publications, 1989.

Profile of Belize, Society for the Promotion of Education and Research. Belize City: Cubola Publications/SPEAR Press, 1990.

Spirit Possession in the Garifuna Community of Belize, Byron Foster. Benque Viejo, Belize: Cubola Publications.

Publications Available in Belize

Belize Business & Travel Directory, Henson & Associates. Belize City: Angelus Press, 1988.

Emory King's Driver's Guide to Beautiful Belize, Emory King. Belize City: Tropical Books, 1990.

Magazines and Newspapers About Belize

Amandala
(weekly; independent newspaper)
3304 Partridge Street
Belize City

Belize Currents
(semi-annual; general interest magazine)
2159 Summer Avenue
Memphis, TN 38112

Belize First
(quarterly; general interest magazine with travel orientation)
280 Beaverdam Road
Candler, NC 28715

Belize Magazine
(quarterly; general interest and conser-
vation magazine)
P.O. Box 74
San Pedro, Belize
or
Box 803283
Dallas, TX 75380

**Belize Natural History Society
Papers**
c/o Bruce Miller
Gallon Jug, Orange Walk District

Belize Review
(monthly environmental education,
conservation, and ecotourism magazine)
P.O. Box 1234
Belize City

Belize Times
(weekly; PUP newspaper)
Box 506, 3 Queen St.
Belize City

Belize Today
(bimonthly; free; business-oriented
magazine)
Belize Information Service
Box 60
Belmopan

Cayo Trader
(weekly newspaper for Cayo District)
3 Ress Drive A
San Ignacio

Center Forum
(conservation magazine)
Belize Center for Environmental
Studies
Box 666, 55 Eve Street
Belize City

Chamber Update
(monthly; business magazine)
Belize Chamber of Commerce
& Industry
Box 291, 63 Regent Street
Belize City

San Pedro Sun
(weekly; independent newspaper)
Box 35
San Pedro, Ambergris Caye

People's Pulse & Beacon
(weekly; UDP newspaper)
7 Church Street
Belize City

Reporter
(weekly; independent)
Box 1217
Belize City

Index

Other Books from John Muir Publications

Rick Steves' Books

Asia Through the Back Door, $17.95
Europe 101: History, Art, and Culture for the Traveler, $17.95
Mona Winks: Self-Guided Tours of Europe's Top Museums, $18.95
Rick Steves' Baltics & Russia, $9.95
Rick Steves' Europe, $17.95
Rick Steves' France, Belgium & the Netherlands, $13.95
Rick Steves' Germany, Austria & Switzerland, $13.95
Rick Steves' Great Britain, $13.95
Rick Steves' Italy, $13.95
Rick Steves' Scandinavia, $13.95
Rick Steves' Spain & Portugal, $13.95
Rick Steves' Europe Through the Back Door, $18.95
Rick Steves' French Phrase Book, $4.95
Rick Steves' German Phrase Book, $4.95
Rick Steves' Italian Phrase Book, $4.95
Rick Steves' Spanish and Portuguese Phrase Book, $5.95
Rick Steves' French/German/Italian Phrase Book, $6.95

Natural Destinations

Belize: A Natural Destination, $16.95
Costa Rica: A Natural Destination, $17.95
Guatemala: A Natural Destination, $16.95

For Birding Enthusiasts

The Birder's Guide to Bed and Breakfasts: U.S. and Canada, $17.95
The Visitor's Guide to the Birds of the Central National Parks: U.S. and Canada, $15.95
The Visitor's Guide to the Birds of the Eastern National Parks: U.S. and Canada, $15.95
The Visitor's Guide to the

Birds of the Rocky Mountain National Parks: U.S. and Canada, $15.95

Unique Travel Series

Each is 112 pages and $10.95 paper, except Georgia.
Unique Arizona
Unique California
Unique Colorado
Unique Florida
Unique Georgia ($11.95)
Unique New England
Unique New Mexico
Unique Texas
Unique Washington

2 to 22 Days Itinerary Planners

2 to 22 Days in the American Southwest, $11.95
2 to 22 Days in Asia, $10.95
2 to 22 Days in Australia, $11.95
2 to 22 Days in California, $11.95
2 to 22 Days in Eastern Canada, $11.95
2 to 22 Days in Florida, $11.95
2 to 22 Days Around the Great Lakes, $11.95
2 to 22 Days in Hawaii, $11.95
2 to 22 Days in New England, $11.95
2 to 22 Days in New Zealand, $11.95
2 to 22 Days in the Pacific Northwest, $11.95
2 to 22 Days in the Rockies, $11.95
2 to 22 Days in Texas, $11.95
2 to 22 Days in Thailand, $10.95

Other Travel Titles

The 100 Best Small Art Towns in America, $12.95
The Big Book of Adventure Travel, $17.95
California Public Gardens, $16.95
Indian America: A Traveler's Companion, $18.95
The People's Guide to Mexico, $19.95
Ranch Vacations: The Complete Guide to Guest and Resort, Fly-Fishing, and Cross-Country Skiing Ranches, $19.95

Understanding Europeans, $14.95
Undiscovered Islands of the Caribbean, $16.95
Watch It Made in the U.S.A.: A Visitor's Guide to the Companies that Make Your Favorite Products, $16.95

Automotive Titles

The Greaseless Guide to Car Care, $19.95
How to Keep Your Subaru Alive, $21.95
How to Keep Your Toyota Pickup Alive, $21.95
How to Keep Your VW Alive, $25

Kidding Around Travel Series

All are $9.95 paperback, except for Kidding Around Spain, which is $12.95 paperback.
Kidding Around Atlanta
Kidding Around Boston
Kidding Around Chicago
Kidding Around the Hawaiian Islands
Kidding Around London
Kidding Around Los Angeles
Kidding Around New York City
Kidding Around Paris
Kidding Around Philadelphia
Kidding Around San Diego
Kidding Around San Francisco
Kidding Around Santa Fe
Kidding Around Seattle
Kidding Around Spain
Kidding Around Washington, D.C.